RUBENS
PAINTER AND DIPLOMAT

1. RUBENS

From an engraving

RUBENS

PAINTER AND DIPLOMAT

BY

EMILE CAMMAERTS

PROFESSOR OF BELGIAN STUDIES
IN THE UNIVERSITY OF LONDON

LONDON
FABER AND FABER LIMITED
24 RUSSELL SQUARE

FIRST PUBLISHED IN MCMXXXII
BY FABER AND FABER LIMITED
24 RUSSELL SQUARE LONDON W.C. I
PRINTED IN GREAT BRITAIN BY
R. MACLEHOSE AND COMPANY LIMITED
THE UNIVERSITY PRESS GLASGOW
ALL RIGHTS RESERVED

FOREWORD

So MANY learned and comprehensive books have been written on Rubens that any addition to their number requires an apology. It seems an impertinence to add a few hours' work to the arduous labour of the Rubens student, who has already waded through large volumes of correspondence and struggled in a maze of doubtful attributions. The author of this modest book seeks comfort in the thought that it will never be considered as a 'standard work', for it does not belong to any of the three categories into which the literature on Rubens is usually divided. It is neither a biography, dealing with the principal events which illustrate the master's life, nor a book of art criticism, completing or revising our knowledge of his works and methods of painting, nor a historical sketch of his political and diplomatic career. The harassed student will therefore find many excuses for ignoring a book which the author himself has some difficulty in classifying.

It is usually agreed that Rubens' outstanding characteristic was his many-sided activity. He was essentially a man of action, and found scope for his energy in various fields. A true description of his personality—if such a description were possible—should be compounded of all these activities, and would have to take into account the close relationship existing throughout his career, between the family man and the diplomatist, and between both of these and the artist. This relationship has not yet perhaps been given all the attention it deserves. Most writers on Rubens have very legitimately considered one aspect only of his life: they have studied either the man, the painter, or the diplomatist. Even those who have dealt with both his private and his public career have done so under separate headings, keeping in more or less watertight compartments a good many facts which appear in a truer perspective when allowed to intermingle. It is chiefly in order to bring these facts together and to emphasise their action and reaction that the present book has been written.

Had Rubens' life been more introspective, and had he been more conscious of his artistic ideals and of the part he was called upon to play in the development of European painting, this effort towards a more comprehensive view of his career might have appeared superfluous. It would have been enough to define the task he set himself to fulfil, and then to compare his ideals with his achievements. But, as far as can be gathered from the correspondence and from the works themselves, Rubens gave little attention to preconceived theories, devoting all his energy to the work in hand, and allowing himself to be led by circumstances towards any goal worthy of his efforts. He was essentially adaptable, and it is this adaptability which must be realised if we are to obtain a comprehensive view of his character and an accurate estimate of his genius.

The author lays no claim to originality in his survey of

Rubens' paintings and of the events which crowded his life. He has been content to make use of the material which has been so carefully brought together by a number of modern art historians better equipped than himself for solving technical problems. He hopes, nevertheless, that this book may help to dispel certain misunderstandings which still prevent a number of art lovers from giving to the master's work the appreciation it deserves. His main purpose has been to bring them into closer contact with one of the most vivid personalities which have ever graced the world.

EM. CAMMAERTS.

LONDON, *September* 1931.

CONTENTS

ILLUSTRATIONS

*All the pictures reproduced in this book are by Rubens,
except when otherwise indicated*

13

ILLUSTRATIONS

14

CHAPTER I

EARLY YEARS: 1577-1600

ONE SUNDAY afternoon, in the Year of Our Lord 1587, while the good citizens of Antwerp and their families were walking gravely in the Place de Meir, it was rumoured that Maria Pypelinckx, widow of Jan Rubens, had returned to her native town, with her daughter Blandine and her two sons Philip and Peter-Paul. The men in their high felt hats and ample breeches, the women in their tight-fitting caps and spreading skirts, looked every now and again towards the house which was known to belong to Maria and her sister Susanna, and in which the Rubens family had recently settled.

When asked by the young folk who this Maria Pypelinckx was, the elder men and women shook their heads solemnly. It was a sad story. Twenty years earlier, Jan Rubens, an alderman and one of the most prominent citizens of the town, lived in Antwerp with his wife and children, enjoying the respect of all. He had the reputation of being a learned man, having studied the law in Italy, but, like many others of his time, he had leanings towards the reformed faith and, a few months after the Iconoclast riots, was obliged to flee from the merciless retribution with which the Duke of Alva threatened him. Few people dared to correspond with him, but it was known that he had sought refuge in Cologne, where he earned a scanty living as a lawyer. He had died there recently, and it was only natural that his widow should come back to Antwerp, where she could be near her own family.

Had not Jan Rubens been 'bitten' by heresy? He had certainly been suspected of Lutheranism, but had died reconciled to the Church, and his widow and children had been seen that very morning attending High Mass at Notre-Dame. The good dame evidently intended to start afresh and to give her boys a proper education. She must have found the town greatly changed,—and the gossip drifted to other matters, such as the loss of trade, the war with the United Provinces, and the latest edict of the Government.

Meanwhile, behind her curtained windows, Madame Rubens was making her own plans and nursing her own memories. Popular feeling was right. Indeed she wished to start afresh, and to obliterate every trace of that long twenty years' trial, during which the life of her husband and the safety of her children had been so often threatened. She remembered only too well the early struggle in Cologne, and the danger of expulsion on account of Jan Rubens' suspected heresy; the material relief which followed when he became legal adviser and, later, confidential agent to Princess Anna of Saxony, who led a somewhat gay life in the city, while her husband, William the Silent, was endeavouring to recruit forces in Germany; the ominous estrangement between Jan and herself, when the Princess left Cologne for the little town of Siegen; and, finally, after

weeks without news of him, the sudden blow of learning at
the same time the betrayal of the man she loved and the
peril of imminent death in which he found himself. She had
forgiven him whole-heartedly after his first expression of
remorse; she had stood by him, writing repeatedly to Prince
William and to his mother, going herself to the Castle of
Dillenburg, where her husband was kept a prisoner; she had
begged and entreated, and finally threatened the Nassau
family with the exposure of the whole shameful scandal; she
had left in their hands as bail the larger part of the little
capital which she still possessed and, after two years of cease-
less struggle, she had finally obtained Jan Rubens' condi-
tional release within the boundaries of the town of Siegen.
He had come back to her an older and a wiser man, and they
had lived five more years in that small German town, under
the watchful eyes of their enemies. Philip was born there, in
1574, and Peter-Paul on June 28, 1577, on the eve of the
feast of the two apostles. Her baby was only a year old
when they had at last been allowed to return to Cologne.
There they had had to face further difficulties. Their small
fortune had been absorbed by the ransoms exacted by the
Nassaus and Jan Rubens had lost his business connections.
The last Cologne years were further darkened by the loss of
her second son Henry and of her last-born child Barthélemy.

After the tragedy of Dillenburg and the constant anxiety
which followed, her husband had not been strong enough to
overcome these fresh sorrows and difficulties. He had died in
her arms, and she had erected a stone over his tomb, on which
it was stated that they had lived together in Cologne 'for
nineteen years' and that, during the whole of their married
life, they had never had 'the slightest disagreement'. This

pious lie troubled her not at all. They had not left Cologne—she had taken care that the certificate given her by the municipality, on the eve of her departure, should confirm this misstatement. The Siegen episode should never have occurred, therefore it had not occurred. She had succeeded in wiping it out utterly. Her children should revere the memory of their 'debonair' and virtuous father. They should preserve a 'deep affection'[1] for the town of Cologne, where in fact their mother had been so miserable. They should receive a proper education and restore the good name and prosperity of the family. Their future should not be hampered by their father's errors and grievances. She would keep her secret and see that the few friends who shared it with her showed the same discretion. As long as her husband lived, she had done her duty towards him, shared his troubles and cherished him for better and for worse, through happy and evil days. She must now devote herself to her daughter and her three sons.

The eldest, Jean-Baptiste, had already left home for Italy. Philip had distinguished himself at school and might go to Louvain University, where most Belgian scholars went at the time. Peter-Paul would attend Master Verdonck's classes, learn Latin and Greek and become an accomplished gentleman. Maria's thoughts dwelt on that Benjamin of hers, so affectionate, impulsive, always eager to play and to work, above all to see new things and explore the world. She knew in her heart that she would not be able to keep him for long; she hardly dared to dream how far he might go, and, thinking of him, she would completely forget the skeleton in the family cupboard.

[1] These are the very words used by Peter-Paul in a letter to Geldorp dated July 25, 1637.

To Rumoldus Verdonck's school, therefore, close to the Choir of Notre-Dame, little Peter-Paul went, and was soon immersed in the intricacies of Latin and Greek grammar, in Virgil's sweet harmonies and Cicero's polished periods. He read the first four books of the *Aeneid* and the *Bucolics*, the *Oratio pro Archia Poeta* and *De Amicitia*; he even began to decipher Plutarch.[1]

From the age of ten to the age of fourteen, the boy went daily from the Place de Meir to the Cathedral and from the Cathedral to the Place de Meir, and most likely played truant on occasion, watching the ships sailing on the Scheldt and the masons restoring the houses that had been destroyed during the recent wars.

There were few ships to be seen in the port, and the ringing of trowels was heard in many quarters of the city. Peter-Paul was far too inquisitive not to notice these signs of the times and too lovable not to succeed in worming the story out of some old sailor or worthy burgher. There had been a time —some twenty years since—when big ocean ships from the Indies, from Italy, Spain, England and Germany, had lain closely packed together along the right bank of the river from the Werfpoort to St. Michael's Church, and when you could not hear yourself speak for the din made by rolling waggons and shouting dockers. Grass did not grow in the streets then, and you could not find a single empty house in the whole city. People lived crowded together, over a hundred thousand of them, and walking in the Meir you

[1] The school was apparently of good standing. It was frequented, among other Antwerp boys, by Balthazar Moretus, grandson of the celebrated printer Christopher Plantin, who later became a close friend of the Rubens brothers. Even then, though he was three years older than Peter-Paul, he liked him 'for his intelligence and kindly nature'.

could hear almost every language in the world. The great square of the Exchange was thronged with Florentine and Lombard bankers, English merchant adventurers, German Hanseatic merchants, Spanish and Portuguese traders. Nowhere else had there been so much buying and selling, nowhere else so much luxury, gaiety, movement and colour. Antwerp was the first port and the first market-place of Europe. But wars had destroyed everything. Now the Dutch held the mouth of the stream and allowed not a single ship to reach the town. Most of the foreigners had left, and the builders had not yet repaired the damage done by the recent siege and by the Spanish Fury of 1576.

The story of the sack and burning of Antwerp which took place in that year must have made the boy's flesh creep and have haunted his dreams. It was but little older than himself and the last wounds were scarcely healed: Those thousands of soldiers, rushing from the new Citadel, shouting 'Sant Iago! España! A sangre, a carne, a fuego, a sacca!' breaking into the houses, throwing their contents out of the windows, killing and torturing old men, women and children who had not escaped in time or were trapped in their hiding-places. He was shown the spot in the Meir where the armed citizens had made their last heroic stand, and the houses round the Grand' Place which had been burned down because their inhabitants had fired through the windows. He could see plainly the traces of restoration on the front of the Town Hall—the masterpiece of Cornelius de Vriendt—and the statue of the Blessed Virgin, patroness of the town, which had been placed in the centre, only a few months earlier.

There were other scars to be seen in the Cathedral, where Peter-Paul heard Mass with his family every Sunday, and in other churches; and when the boy asked why so many statues had disappeared from their niches and why the sunlight streamed through so many windows without taking on the hues of multicoloured glass, there were eye-witnesses of the Iconoclast rising of 1566 who were only too ready to give him a graphic and gruesome description of the blasphemous horrors they had seen.

He was obviously too young to understand the whys and wherefores of such wanton waste, but his whole nature must have rebelled against it. From his earliest years, he was a builder, a preserver of life. Man and his creations were so absorbingly interesting and sometimes so fine and great, that destruction in all its forms appeared the meanest sin, the most ghastly sacrilege. A hidden instinct must have told him that, if war had caused these disasters, he would fight war with all his might; that if temporal and spiritual pride were at the root of war, he would endeavour to soften pride in the hearts of men. He was moved no doubt by a secret ambition to contribute his share to the work of restoration which was going forward around him. Could he not raise up new churches and new palaces, and fill these blank walls with the brightest pictures Flanders had ever seen? In his Cologne days he had treasured a large Bible, illustrated by Tobias Stimmer. What greater dream could man have than to do for these churches what the Swiss artist had done for the Book of books?

In 1590, a crisis occurred in the Rubens family. It coincided with the marriage of the elder sister Blandine, to whom her mother gave a yearly allowance of 200 florins. Whether this restricted her resources, or whether some other mishap occurred, Maria Pypelinckx was obliged to sell the house

which she owned jointly with her sister Susanna, and to leave
the Meir for the more modest Kloosterstraat. The two boys
were naturally anxious to save their mother any further expense. Philip, who was sixteen years old, went to Brussels,
where he became secretary to Jean Richardot, who was soon
to be appointed President of the Privy Council; and Peter-
Paul, who was not yet fourteen, left Antwerp for Ouden-
arde, where he served as a page in the household of Marguerite de Ligne, widow of the same Comte de Lalaing who,
ten years previously, had played an important part as the
head of the 'Malcontents', a party which resented the fanati-
cism of the northern Calvinists and broke away from the
Union which had been sealed in Ghent and Brussels between
Protestant and Catholic Belgian nobles.

Marguerite de Ligne belonged to the Catholic faction of the
Belgian aristocracy, which had first made its peace with Spain.
She was proud of her name, and exacted from her little court
a punctilious observance of the strict etiquette of the time.
Peter-Paul, who had left Antwerp against his natural inclinations, could only stand this mode of life for a few months. As
soon as he had mastered the golden rules of courtesy and had
been initiated into the secrets of court life, he appealed to his
mother for release and urged her to place him as an apprentice in some artist's studio.

The fond Maria, who had perhaps for a moment been
dazzled by dreams of grandeur, was far too sensible to stand
in her son's way. She recognised that it was better to be happy
in one's trade than to remain dissatisfied in the palaces of the
great. It happened that the painter Tobias Verhaecht had
recently married into the Rubens family, and, bravely mas-
tering her disappointment, she allowed Peter-Paul to come

22

back to Antwerp and enter his studio. She little knew that, by becoming a skilled artisan, her son was in reality taking a short-cut towards the worldly honours of which she had dreamt.

*　　*　　*

When Peter-Paul started his artistic training, Antwerp had already regained, as a centre of art, a great deal of the reputation which it had enjoyed before the outbreak of the revolution. Shortly after the submission of the town to Farnese, artists and artisans had set to work again, and a lengthy list could be drawn up of religious and portrait painters, such as Martin De Vos, Frans Pourbus and Ambroise Francken, and of landscape-painters, such as Gilles van Coninxloo, the Brothers Bril and Jan Breughel, who had acquired a wide reputation. The engravers were equally active, and the well-known firm of Plantin, which had played so important a part in the story of the northern Renaissance, began once more to flourish. Looked at in the perspective of centuries, the artistic position of Antwerp and the rest of Belgium, on the eve of the seventeenth century, certainly seems inferior to what it had been in previous years, and Rubens appears as the magician who, with one wave of his wand, transforms decadence into power and defeat into victory. But, at the time, the young apprentice must have felt somewhat insignificant before the masters who were pointed out to him by their admirers, or with whom he himself came into contact.

It is impossible to gauge the influence which the contemporary art of Antwerp exerted on Rubens' development. The only signed and dated picture undoubtedly painted before his departure for Italy in 1600, is a small portrait in the style of a miniature, now in the Kunsthandel in Berlin. The rest is pure conjecture. It seems evident that his genius did not develop before the time when he came into contact with the masterpieces of the Italian Renaissance. Nevertheless, his eight years of training in Antwerp cannot lightly be dismissed. At this early stage, he was faced with the problem of finding his way among the tortuous artistic paths which threaded his native country. His highly sensitive temperament must have received certain strong impressions, and there is no doubt whatever that these were stored in the right place and retained for future use. The many changes which occurred twenty or thirty years later cannot be accounted for if we lose sight of what Peter-Paul saw and thought while he wandered through the Antwerp studios in the days of his apprenticeship. In the total absence of documentary evidence, the only means we have of understanding these early workings of his mind is to consider the various tendencies which had divided Flemish art during the two previous generations.

Since the beginning of the sixteenth century, Antwerp had become the chief artistic centre of the Netherlands. The great Quentin Massys, who died there in 1530, may be considered at the same time as 'the last of the Primitives' and as the forerunner of the Renaissance. His main work, the 'Entombment', in the Antwerp Museum, plainly shows the combination of mediaeval and modern characteristics. The central panel is strongly reminiscent of Van der Weyden, one of the outstanding masters of the fifteenth century school, while one of the wings, which represents Salome receiving the Baptist's head before Herod, is filled with a dramatic atmosphere which might almost be called Shakespearean. Although he continued the traditions and, to a certain extent, the technique of the mediaeval miniaturists of the previous century, Massys indulged in strongly-flavoured genre scenes, revealing the new spirit introduced into Flanders by Erasmus and the Humanists with whom he was closely associated.

Had this tendency been followed by disciples more worthy of such a master, the Flemish School might have proved to be if not as great, at least as original in the sixteenth century as it had been in the fifteenth. But the attraction of Italy had become so strong that the greatest ambition of the foremost painters of the period was to be worthy imitators of Raphael and Michaelangelo.

In Antwerp, Frans Floris was the principal exponent of this new 'Italianist' school. He sacrificed colour, which had been and was destined again to be the most important feature of Flemish painting, to perspective and anatomy, and set himself to solve new technical problems which had left his predecessors undisturbed. Floris and his elder Brussels rival Van Orley, in their pathetic efforts to emulate Italy, showed great talent and undoubtedly helped to pave the way for further developments. Their portraits preserved the solid and sincere qualities characteristic of the school, but the composite style of their religious and mythological pictures in the grand manner shows that they were not able to assimilate the influences to which they were so strongly subjected. Compared with their Italian models, they remain awkward and clumsy; compared with Flemish painters of earlier or later date, they appear stilted and affected. The vogue for Italianism was however so general that the reputation of these artists was unchallenged at the time, and that the new style was accepted as being far superior to the mediaeval style of the previous century. To quote the artist-writer Van Mander: 'When at last Rome began to blossom out again under the wise government of the Popes, some fine marble and bronze statues were found in her ancient soil. These were like a luminous dawn for our painting, and opened the eyes of those who practised the art, teaching them to distinguish beauty from ugliness and to discern in life and in nature the sovereign beauty of the bodies of man and beast'.[1]

Such an interpretation of the aims of art was directly opposed to the mystic and realistic conceptions of the Primitives, so deeply rooted in the Flemish temperament. It substituted for the life of the senses and imagination, intellectual values which had hitherto been foreign to the art of the country.

A few painters, however, had not been drawn into the general current. The most superficial comparison between the humorous and realistic pictures of Peter Breughel and the artists who followed in his wake, on the one hand, and the academic compositions of Mabuse, Floris and Van Orley, on the other, shows the depth of the gulf which separated the artists who worked for the bourgeoisie and the merchants, and those who sought the patronage of the Spanish governors and the aristocracy.

Breughel, who did most of his painting between 1560 and 1569, has too long been considered as a freak whose startling visions had a purely individualistic meaning. He is, in reality, the outcome of a national movement based on a long-standing tradition. Entirely free from Italian influences, he developed the satirical and fanciful imaginings of Jerome

[1] *Schilderboek,* 1604.

26

Bosch and applied to popular scenes and landscapes the realistic methods of Massys' early followers. But, in spite of his genius and originality, the sphere of his influence remained limited and, towards the end of the century, when the Southern Netherlands fell once more under the sway of Spain, it had become still more restricted.

The same could not be said of the school of landscape-painters founded at the beginning of the century by Patinir and Henri Bles. These artists and their followers combined, it is true, a deep feeling for colour and distance with fanciful features entirely foreign to our modern conception of landscape. But the shaky rockeries which they introduced into their pictures were not borrowed from Italian masters; they were merely the survival of the mediaeval miniaturists' method of raising the skyline by the introduction of abrupt hills and precipitous cliffs. During the whole century, landscape remained as impervious to Italian influences as portraiture, and the artists who settled in Rome, like the Brothers Bril, went there much more as teachers than as students. If their conception of nature was partly conventional, and if most of them failed to break away from the tradition of brownish foregrounds and bluish backgrounds, this must not be attributed to a desire to emulate a foreign style. Peter Breughel is perhaps the only landscape-painter of the period who achieved in certain cases, if not a truer, at least a more modern interpretation of nature; but his eldest son Jan, who was to become one of Rubens' most faithful collaborators, far from following in his father's footsteps, moved back towards the methods of an earlier period.

Whatever effect the teaching of any one of Rubens'

masters may have had upon the development of his genius, the young apprentice must have come into contact with the works of the following three groups of artists: the Italianists, the landscape-painters, and the Realists who specialised in genre scenes and still-life. He must thus have had many opportunities of seeing good portraits, semi-artificial land-scapes, and perhaps, even at that time, some masterpieces by Breughel the Elder. The importance of the latter was certainly not realised by the painters under whom he worked, and very likely not even by himself.

From the course of study followed by Peter-Paul, we may gather that he felt no special vocation for landscape, in the sense in which the word was understood at the time; por-traiture he adopted as a matter of course; but he was chiefly drawn to the study of large religious or mythological com-positions and to the worship of the Italian Renaissance which prevailed around him. He must have shared the ideas so well expressed a few years later by Van Mander, and have combined an ardent enthusiasm for modern Italy with a sincere love for Latin literature and Roman antiquities.

It was long since Joachim du Bellay, Ronsard's disciple, had sung the *Antiquitez de Rome*, but the feeling expressed in these sonnets was still shared by scholars and artists. After praising Ancient Rome's palaces, triumphal arches and temples, the poet goes on to emphasise the power of the proud Roman art which, after so many centuries, rises like the Phoenix from its ashes, and builds new monuments according to old designs:

> Regarde apres, comme de jour en jour
> Rome, fouillant son antique sejour,
> Se rebastit de tant d'œuvres divines;

Tu jugeras, que le daemon Romain
S'efforce encor d'une fatale main
Ressusciter ces poudreuses ruines.

Peter-Paul had not forgotten the pages of Cicero and
Virgil, painfully construed under Verdonck's guidance.
Latin had not been for him, as it is unfortunately for so many
schoolboys to-day, a dead language lightly learnt and more
lightly cast aside. Like most educated men of his time, he
continued to read the classics all through his life, and could,
without difficulty, carry on a correspondence with those who
preferred to address him in the learned rather than in the
vulgar tongue. In a letter written in December 1628, to his
friend Gaspard Gevaerts, or Gevartius, he begins: 'My
answer, couched in Flemish, will shew you that I do not deserve the honour you do me in addressing me in Latin . . .'
and goes on in fluent prose which, without rivalling that of
Tacitus, one of his favourite authors, is yet sufficient proof
that the practice of his art had not led him to neglect his
letters.

As a worshipper of Italy and of Ancient and Modern
Rome, the young Peter-Paul cannot have been specially
attracted by the art of Tobias Verhaecht, and it is to be
assumed that he entered his studio merely because Verhaecht happened to be the only artist who was acquainted
with the Rubens family. From what we know of Peter-
Paul's first master, he was a minor light in the group of
Antwerp landscape-painters who, like the brothers De
Momper and Van Coninxloo, followed at that time the
tradition of Patinir and Bles. His little picture, now in the
Brussels Museum, 'Hunting Scene with Maximilian I', does
not reveal any striking originality, and a drawing in the

Albertina merely shows that he had inherited from his predecessors a curious delight in the description of picturesque
rocks and caves. But he certainly enjoyed some reputation,
since he collaborated in the decorations prepared by the town
of Antwerp for the solemn entry of Archduke Ernest in 1594,
and we know that he had several pupils. If Peter-Paul benefited from his teaching—and no doubt he did, being far too
eager to learn his trade to lose any opportunity that offered
—he was certainly not deeply impressed by his example, and
it would be difficult to find any picture by Rubens which be-
trays Verhaecht's influence. Besides, the fact that he hastened
to change masters as early as 1592 is sufficient proof that he
felt drawn towards a more ambitious style of painting and
wished to learn from the Italianists what they themselves had
learned from Raphael and Michaelangelo.

His second master, Van Noort, remains to this day an
enigma to the art-historian. If we choose to ascribe to him
'The Calling of St. Peter' in the Church of St. Jacques at
Antwerp, and some other works displaying the same qualities of power and energy, and if we presume that Jordaens,
who shared with Rubens and about thirty others the benefit
of his teaching, derived from him his main characteristic of
healthy robustness, we may raise him on an artificial pedestal
and even trace to him the origin of the seventeenth-century
school of painting in Flanders. We may contrast his strong
features, as they appear in an etching by Van Dyck, with the
softer and graver face of Otto Vaenius, the third and last of
Peter-Paul's masters, and declare that it was in his studio and
under his influence that Rubens was brought into contact
with pure national traditions and began to realise his own
originality.

Unfortunately, such suppositions, however tempting they may appear, do not tally with hard facts. We know of no early picture by Rubens closely related to Van Noort's style, and the only works which can reasonably be ascribed to the latter, such as 'Christ blessing the Children', in the Brussels Museum, and some drawings at Antwerp and Vienna, do not reveal those qualities of strength and power which are typical of Rubens and Jordaens in their maturity. We must therefore be content to explain Peter-Paul's relations with Van Noort by the fact that the latter had a large following and that in his studio a young artist could at least learn the anatomy of the human figure and the rudiments of religious or mythological composition.

As soon, however, as he had mastered the first principles which his second teacher was able to impart to him, Peter-Paul must have been attracted towards a man of higher accomplishments and greater learning, who was considered at the time to be the leading artist of the Antwerp School. I mean Otto Van Veen, usually known as Otto Vaenius. If it is rash to oppose Vaenius to Van Noort, as representing the Italian fashions in contrast to national traditions, it may be safe to say that, compared with Rubens' second master, who seems to have been merely a conscientious craftsman, Vaenius shines as a scholar and somewhat of an aristocrat. He was said to descend from a bastard son of Duke John III of Brabant, and his father belonged to the small number of bourgeois, in the northern Netherlands, who had remained loyal to the King of Spain in spite of the revolution. Rather than submit to the Calvinists, he had left Leyden, of which he was burgomaster, to seek refuge in Liége. His son Otto, after spending eight years in Italy, where he had worked in Rome under Zuccaro, had followed Farnese's army into Antwerp and had soon established his reputation in the Guild of St. Luke, which he entered in 1594 and of which he became 'doyen' in 1598. When Peter-Paul entered his studio, Vaenius had held for over ten years the title of Painter to the Court of Spain, had taken a prominent part in the decoration of the town for the triumphal entry of Archduke Ernest, and was to take a still more prominent one in the preparations made for the reception of Archduke Albert and Archduchess Isabella, in 1599.

We know that, on this last occasion, Peter-Paul, who had been received into the Guild in the previous year, worked by his master's side. His position in Vaenius' studio must have been a peculiar one. He was over nineteen years old when he entered it, and, had he so wished, could have left it two years earlier than he did. The study of painting alone could scarcely account for this long apprenticeship, for a comparison between the earliest works of the pupil and the best work of the master, such as the 'Marriage of St. Catherine', now in Brussels, is all in favour of the former. But Vaenius, from all accounts, was more than a mere craftsman and must have represented to a high degree in the eyes of Rubens that ideal of the gentleman-painter which he himself so much wished to realise. Vaenius was a scholar, a personal friend of the great Humanist Justus Lipsius. He was a man of culture and discrimination, with a sound knowledge of the classics and of Roman archaeology, and with a taste for allegory and symbolism. His influence on Rubens is unquestionable, but strangely enough it seems to have been the influence of the man of the world and the connoisseur rather than that of the painter. We are told that, before leaving for Italy, Rubens' style was very much akin to that of Vaenius,[1] but we must not lose sight of the fact that that style was not peculiar to the elderly Vaenius and the young Rubens. It was the style adopted by the decadent school of Italianists, who imitated the decadent school of the Italian Renaissance, who themselves imitated the series of great masters ranging from Raphael to Correggio. Though experts may delight in discovering individual characteristics in the Flemish painters of the late sixteenth century, to the layman they all appear very similar and their methods seem to be inspired by the artistic fashion of the period far more than by true originality. If Rubens painted in this manner, it was not so much owing to Vaenius' influence as to the fact that there was practically nothing else for him to do.

* * *

The most powerful geniuses in art and literature are generally slow-moving. They amaze us far more by their faculty for assimilation than by the boldness of their challenge to the accepted tastes and opinions of their time. They succeed, not by striking a high and lonely path leading away from the common herd, but by bestriding the trodden pastures of the valleys and making the herd follow them. A lyrical poet, such as Shelley, may burst upon the world like a bolt from the blue or Ariel from a cloud, but a Prospero, a painter of men and women, who must know their bodies and their souls before interpreting them, cannot merely draw on his feelings and imagination. He must take the world as he finds

---

[1]See Roger de Piles: *Vita Petri Pauli Rubenii*. Interesting comparisons might be made between some Rubens battle scenes and Vaenius' drawings for Tacitus' history of the wars between the Romans and the Batavians (*Batavorum cum Romanis Bellum*, 1612).

it, with its qualities and its errors, melt it in the furnace of his own enthusiasm, and thus create a new world, a new art, a new literature, apparently in outline very much the same as the old one, but in values and character so transformed and magnified that it seems scarcely credible that such beginnings should lead to such ends, that Shakespeare, for instance, should grow out of Shakespeare, or Rubens out of Rubens.

Before choosing his own road, among the various ways which opened out before him, Peter-Paul had to survey the ground on which he stood. He was in no hurry to assert himself. He passed from Verdonck to Van Noort and from Van Noort to Van Veen, increasing in knowledge and experience, not only of the painter's craft but also of nature and man, always in search of some greater master whom he could not successfully rival as he did Vaenius, and whose teaching would so stimulate his own creative power that he would at last discover his own independence and originality. From the days of his apprenticeship, there must have been in Rubens a strong, boyish spirit always ready to answer a challenge and to take for a challenge any work which provoked his admiration. It is as if a voice had called to him, on every occasion: 'Can you do this?' and as if he had answered eagerly: 'Let me try!' This can be safely assumed from all we know of his methods of 'copying' Italian masterpieces, long after he had established a universal reputation, and of imitating certain Dutch and German painters, at a time when his name ranked far above their own. It is part of the greatness of the man that he never ceased trying, that he always delighted in new experiments, that he never for one moment rested on his laurels. His artistic career is one long exploration, and in a certain sense it may be said that Rubens only discovered Rubens in the very last years of his life.

The first stage of this career was in Antwerp, but Antwerp, artistically speaking, had become at that time a northern outpost of Rome. As soon as the town was surveyed —at least that part of the town which an Italianist could admire—Peter-Paul was compelled to leave for Italy. He was drawn thither by the combined forces of modern Renaissance and ancient Classicism, by the great masters who had inspired his masters, and by the glorious monuments which represented the enthusiasm of his schooldays, by Raphael and Virgil, Michaelangelo and Tacitus, the Vatican and the Coliseum. Vaenius was for him the finest painter in Antwerp; he had become his friend and felt that he had absorbed the best of his teaching. He must therefore leave him and travel south, as Vaenius and almost all Flemish painters of the century had done before him.

He left Antwerp on May 9, 1600, full of hope and ambition: the hope of finding in that Holy Land of art the antique statues and modern paintings of which he had heard so much, the ambition to become a better artist by studying and copying them. He was nearly twenty-three and had been for two years past a member of his Guild. But the first in Antwerp might be the last in Rome. Before such a large and resplendent world, Rubens, from all we know of him, must have felt a very humble man. As he passed under the southern gate with his faithful companion del Monte, he must have thought far more of the old mother he had left behind and of his brother Philip and the chances of meeting him one day in Italy, than of his fine horse and gallant accoutrement; and, as he turned for a last look towards the spire of Notre-Dame, he must have had, like the wise man he already was, a foretaste of the difficulties which were awaiting him, and of the efforts he would have to make in order to come through this new ordeal, with honour if not with glory. Rubens has given us several self-portraits. When he left Antwerp, he must have looked far more like the dreamy artist in the Uffizi than like the dashing cavalier at Windsor.

2B. RUBENS: THE ENTOMBMENT

2A. CARAVAGGIO: THE ENTOMBMENT

CHAPTER II

ITALY: 1600-1608

THE JOURNEY from Flanders to Italy, by the shortest route, took at that time over five weeks. Rubens must have taken much longer, revisiting, as he may have done, Cologne, the town of his youthful memories, and reaching by slow stages, through Germany, the Tyrol and the Brenner Pass, the great metropolis of Venice.

It would be vain to attempt to reconstitute his impressions of the woody scenes of the Rhineland, the wild heights of the Alps and the dazzling brilliancy of Venetian marbles. Let us remember, however, that, in contrast to his predecessor Breughel the Elder, he was then more interested in the works of men than in the wonders of nature and that the eagerness with which he looked forward to the goal of his journey was not propitious to long contemplation.

He probably travelled along the historic road which had been followed, over and over again, by Northern invaders, and experienced to the full the wild delight which fills all Northerners who descend from the Alpine snows into the radiant Venetian Plain. It is the most dramatic approach to Italy's wonders, for the transition between southern France

37

and the Genoese coast is almost imperceptible, and neither Milan nor Turin can be said to belong to the Mediterranean world in the same way as does Venice.

Whatever circumstances led Rubens first to Venice, they may be considered as almost providential, for they brought him immediately into contact with the works of Titian, Veronese and Tintoretto, which had not hitherto exerted a strong influence on the development of the Flemish School. Relatively speaking, Venetian art flourished somewhat later than Florentine and Umbrian painting. It was therefore towards Florence and Rome and not towards Venice that the Flemish Italianists turned their steps, and, although Titian had already produced masterpieces eighty years before Rubens left Antwerp, it was not Titian but Michaelangelo and Raphael who indirectly inspired Vaenius at the end of the century, as they had directly inspired Mabuse and Floris at its beginning. This strange neglect of Venetian art considerably increased the difficulties which beset the path of these Italianists. In their anxiety to imitate the great masters of central Italy, they were not only obliged to relinquish the tradition of familiar realism established by the Flemish Primitives, but they also felt compelled to sacrifice the brilliant colouring which had made their school famous in the past, to strength of relief and draughtsmanship, one of the most admired features of Renaissance art. Venice might have provided the connecting link, for she was, in a way, the northern outpost of Italy. For climatic and other reasons, her painters found the same delight in glowing hues and warm light as the Flemings, and Titian, for one, had succeeded in combining richness of colour with strength of outline; but somehow, until that fateful year 1600, Titian's lesson had been lost on Flanders, and the fact that Rubens was from the first placed in a position to learn it, as soon as he reached the promised land of art, is strangely significant.

We are told that he only made a short stay in the town.[1] Soon after his arrival, he met some gentleman of the Duke of Mantua's following, who introduced him to his master. The latter engaged Peter-Paul forthwith as one of his Court painters, so that he soon left Venice for Mantua. But, even supposing that he only spent a few weeks among the canals and islets of the Laguna, the young painter must have had time to acquaint himself with some of Titian's masterpieces and with the grand style of Veronese and Tintoretto, in their large decorative compositions. He must have spent many hours in the Scuola di San Rocco, before the series of religious pictures with which Tintoretto had decorated the building during the last period of his life, and which had only been completed six years previously, and he must have been strongly impressed by the naturalistic methods adopted by this master in his interpretation of the Gospel story. He must also have wandered again and again through the great halls of the Doges' Palace, and more particularly through the Sala del Maggior Consiglio, where twenty episodes of Venetian history, pompously told by Bassano, Veronese and Tintoretto, confront the latter's colossal vision of 'Paradise'.

Within a few days, he must have realised the enormous gulf which separated the best productions of contemporary Flemish art from these powerful series of religious, allegorical and historical pictures in which the masters of Venice had exalted the secular and spiritual glory of their city. Such a sight could not but stir his ambition to do for the city of

[1]See Vita.

39

Notre-Dame what these men had done for the city of San Marco. If only he could succeed as they had done! Such fine dreams, however, were sobered by reflection. If ever Peter-Paul had fondly imagined that he had mastered his trade when he left his home, he realised now, in the presence of these works, that he still had everything to learn if he was to achieve greatness. If ever he had thought that he had become, if not the first, at least one of the first Flemish masters, he understood now that he must still play for many years the obscure part of a student, before attempting to create masterpieces such as those among which he was placed. It was in this humble mood that he followed Duke Vincenzo to Mantua.

The Duke was a typical representative of these minor potentates among whom Italy was divided at the time. The independence of his duchy was constantly threatened by the greater powers, such as Venice, Spain and the Pope, which he had to conciliate with unwearying diplomacy. He could, to a certain extent, rely on the support of his grandfather the Emperor Ferdinand; and when his wife's sister Marie de Medici married Henry IV of France, his position was still further strengthened. Like other princes of the period, he taxed his subjects mercilessly in order to indulge his expensive tastes. He was a great patron of the arts and, strangely enough, had made a special hobby of Flemish painting. Before engaging Rubens, he had already at his Court a mysterious 'Fiamingo' of the name of Jan; he had also secured the services of Frans, the last representative of the Pourbus family. This remarkable man had moreover invited to Mantua the great Monteverde, who was at that time laying the foundations of opera, as well as Galileo, who was revolutionising astronomy. The same catholicity of taste prevailed in his collections, which included antique sculptures, Flemish tapestries, lions, tigers, and even crocodiles. If we remember that a company of actors, the 'Gelosi', was also attached to his suite, we shall form some idea of the picturesque and somewhat startling surroundings into which the young Fleming was abruptly launched.

The journey from Venice to Mantua is not impressive, and Peter-Paul must have felt at the time the disappointment which afflicts most travellers who expect to discover the great landscapes of Italy and only find themselves among the monotonous plains of the valley of the Po. His life was no doubt spent mostly in the town, which holds a forbidding position, surrounded as it is on three sides by widespread marshes, and more especially in the castles and palaces of the Gonzaga family. The mediaeval Castello di Corte, with Mantegna's frescoes, can hardly have appealed to him to the same extent as the Renaissance Corte Reale, and the still more modern Palazzo del Te, erected by Giulio Romano outside the walls of the town. The personality of Raphael's well-known pupil, who had settled in Mantua after his master's death, pervaded the whole place and must have eclipsed, in the eyes of Rubens, the far greater genius of Mantegna. He had many opportunities of appreciating the bold decorations of the Corte Reale, and particularly the Sala dello Zodiaco, the ceiling of which is filled with the constellations of heaven. He must have admired, in the Palazzo del Te, the great mythological stories of Psyche and of the Fall of the Titans. It is possible to exaggerate the debt which Rubens owes to Giulio Romano, but he seems nevertheless to have preserved, from these first months spent in Mantua, a special liking for effects of foreshortening and for gigantic figures, as well as for a style of decoration which tends to open out wide perspectives in the walls and to raise the roof to the sky.

During this period, Peter-Paul was mostly engaged in copying certain works in the Duke's collections, in order to provide his patron with suitable gifts which should presently be distributed to the great lords whose favour was desired. But he must also have done some original work, among which a portrait of Vincenzo himself.

In October 1600, the Duke went to Florence to take part in the celebration of the marriage of his sister-in-law to King Henry IV of France. He took with him his new Flemish painter, so that the latter had the opportunity of witnessing the scene which he was to portray, over twenty years later, on the walls of the Luxembourg Palace. The episode is no doubt faithfully described, and historians may recognise Marie herself, the Grand Duke of Tuscany, who represented Henry IV (the marriage took place by proxy), and Cardinal Aldobrandini, who officiated at the ceremony. The architecture of Santa-Maria-del-Fiore, however, seems to have undergone a complete transformation in the mind of the artist. It has become florid and ornate in the true baroque style. Alluding to the Medici series, Rubens wrote to his friend Peiresc that he remembered witnessing the ceremony, and that he was present at the ball and supper which followed. But Rubens' memory was peculiar: he possessed the art of remembering everything, up to the smallest detail, which served his purpose—and of ignoring the rest. The sober architecture of Santa-Maria-del-Fiore did not suit his purpose, but the dress of the bride, as well as her lap-dog and the flowers scattered at her feet, are in all probability authentic.

The following year, Vincenzo was obliged to go to Croatia, there to place his troops at the service of the Emperor during the war. He was evidently anxious that the time of his chief painter should be well occupied in his absence, and allowed him to leave for Rome bearing a recommendation to Cardinal Montalto. There is good reason to presume that this decision was inspired by Peter-Paul himself, who, after his exploration of the art treasures of Venice, Mantua and Florence, must have longed to complete his studies and to reach the very centre of classic and modern art.

If Rome was for Rubens the treasure-house of Italy, the Vatican, with Raphael's Stanze and Michaelangelo's Sistine Chapel, was without doubt the treasure-house of Rome. The impression made upon him by these impressive decorative works was both deep and lasting. It may be traced in pictures such as his 'Last Judgment' and 'Fall of the Rebel Angels', which, for this reason, have somewhat rashly been ascribed to his Italian period. But, if we wish to penetrate the inner workings of Rubens' mind, we must not lose sight of the fact that he was able to keep a great deal of his material in store, for a very long time, before finding a suitable opportunity of making use of it. He no doubt preserved a large number of sketches made on the spot, for this very purpose. In other cases, he trusted to his visual memory, which must have been one of the most perfect that have ever existed.[1] In any case, the Vatican visit set its seal on his calling. If he had already been stimulated to paint great decorative composi-

[1]During his stay in Rome in 1606, he had an opportunity of admiring the well-known Aldobrandini's 'Bridal Feast', which had just been discovered. In 1628, twenty years after his departure from Italy, he was able to give to Peiresc a full account of the picture, with a detailed description of the dresses, ornaments and furniture.

tions by the works of Tintoretto and Giulio Romano, his admiration of Michaelangelo's and Raphael's masterpieces finally banished all other possibilities.

There is a certain danger, however, in overestimating the extent of the Great Masters' action on Rubens' mind, and in supposing that he contemplated the Renaissance art of Italy from our present-day point of view. We must not forget that there was still an intense artistic activity in Rome at the time of his visit. Both the 'Eclectics' and the 'Realists' were re-acting against the affected style of Zuccaro and the 'Mannerists', who had been Vaenius' masters. Annibale Carracci was decorating the Farnese Palace; Caravaggio was also working in Rome at the time. Among the younger generation, Guido Reni and Domenichino had already made their mark. The efforts of these older and younger masters could not leave Rubens indifferent. As a matter of fact, their work seems to have had a far more immediate effect on his technique than that of the Great Masters of the Renaissance.

He had been asked by Jean Richardot (the son of Philip Rubens' employer and Archduke Albert's agent in Rome) to re-decorate the Chapel of St. Helen, in the Church of Santa Croce in Gerusalemme, which had been the Archduke's church in Rome at the time of his cardinalship; and, after permission had been duly obtained from the Duke of Mantua, he proceeded to paint three panels: the one in the centre representing 'St. Helen discovering the True Cross', and two smaller ones, the 'Crowning with Thorns' and the 'Erection of the Cross'. The 'St. Helen' is somewhat reminiscent of Raphael's well-known 'St. Cecilia', but the wings, with their strong chiaroscuro and realistic rendering of Christ's body, show that Rubens was, by this time, well

44

3. THE FOUR PHILOSOPHERS

Pitti Palace, Florence

Photo, Alinari

acquainted with Caravaggio's methods. There are other proofs that, in the fierce quarrel which raged between 'Eclectics' and 'Realists', Rubens sided with the latter, without, however, allowing himself to be carried away by the melodramatic tendencies of their art. His fine interpretation of Caravaggio's 'Entombment', which he saw in Rome in the Chiesa Nuova, is a good example of this well-tempered admiration. The general design of the 'copy', now in Vienna, follows the original, but, while Caravaggio allows his dominant line to be broken by the dramatic action of his Holy Women, whose arms are thrown above their heads with a kind of windmill effect, Rubens sternly eliminates these distracting features and welds the whole group into one solid block.[1] The same leaning towards Italian realism may be traced in several of his religious works, up to the time of the 'Descent from the Cross', and there is no reason to be surprised when we hear that, after his return to Antwerp, the young master joined with Jan Breughel and other painters in purchasing Caravaggio's picture of 'Our Lady presenting the Rosary to St. Dominic', to be placed in the Dominican church of St. Paul at Antwerp.

The Duke meanwhile had returned to Mantua from his military expedition, and was urgently requesting the presence of his painter. It was only owing to the pressing demands of Jean Richardot, that Rubens was able to finish his triptych for Santa Croce. He left again for Mantua in the early spring of 1602 and must have done so all the more readily as he hoped to arrange a meeting with his brother Philip.

[1] The copy may have been made from a sketch after Rubens' return to Antwerp. See pl. 2A and 2B, p. 37.

The latter had also made remarkable strides in life during recent years. After working as secretary to President Richardot in Brussels, he had become tutor to his sons, with whom he had studied at Louvain under the famous Humanist, Justus Lipsius. At the end of his Louvain studies, the elder son, Jean Richardot, had left for Rome, while Philip Rubens had returned to Brussels with the younger. Two years later, in 1601, the tutor took his pupil to Italy, and stayed with him for a few months at the University of Padua. It is possible that Peter-Paul visited him there soon after his return to Mantua, and it is almost certain that the two brothers met at Verona, in July, together with Justus Lipsius and Woverius, another disciple of this master and an intimate friend of Philip. This meeting was commemorated by Peter-Paul in a picture usually known as the 'Four Philosophers' (in the Pitti), in which he himself is represented standing apart from the learned trio, over which looms the bust of Seneca, whose works Justus Lipsius had recently edited.[1] The scene takes place on a terrace, behind which is seen a view of the Palatine Hill, which has been identified with one of the master's early landscapes (in the Louvre). The 'Four Philosophers', which appears to have suffered from restorations, has been highly praised by some critics and perhaps too severely disparaged by others. It is still somewhat formal, and, whether it was painted at this time or some years later, can scarcely be considered as an example of the master's mature period.

* * *

Rubens' career was again and again interrupted by what may be called diplomatic episodes. The Princes who employed him learned to appreciate his engaging manner, sound

[1]See pl. 3, p. 44.

common-sense and absolute loyalty, so that, when they found themselves in a difficulty or were contemplating a particularly delicate mission, they preferred to use him rather than employ a more obscure and less trustworthy agent or some powerful noble who might have his own ends to pursue and his own axe to grind. Rubens' journey to Spain, begun on the 5th of March, 1603, had no special political purpose, but the Duke of Mantua had for some time been anxious to conciliate Philip III of Spain and especially his powerful minister, the Duke of Lerma. For various reasons, he considered that the time had come for him to obtain tokens of favour in exchange for handsome presents, and he forthwith bade Rubens bring to the Spanish Court such cumbersome gifts as a coach and seven bay horses, eleven arquebuses and a rock-crystal vase for the King, and a number of paintings and silver and gold vases for the Duke of Lerma; nor were the minor powers, such as the Duke of Lerma's sister, the Count of Villalonga, his favourite, and the director of the Chapel Royal, entirely forgotten.

Whether he showed it or not, Peter-Paul must have felt some reluctance to accept this mission, which took him away from his dearest studies and could scarcely enhance his prestige even as an artist, since most of the pictures sent to Lerma were copies from the great Italian masters, and since even these copies had been executed not by him, but by Facchetti, a Mantuan artist in the Duke's employ. Still, he was not yet in a position to oppose his patron's wishes, and his reluctance was no doubt somewhat weakened by the prospect of being presented to a king who was considered to be a great patron of the arts.

His forebodings, if he had any, were amply fulfilled. Instead of going straight to Genoa, he was sent first, with his heavy baggage, across the Apennines to Florence, and thence to Pisa, where he was received by the Grand-Duke of Tuscany, Vincenzo's uncle. He finally succeeded, after some loss of time, in obtaining a passage in a ship sailing from Leghorn to Alicante, where he landed at the end of April. He took a further twenty days to reach Valladolid, across the arid plateau of central Spain, and arrived there only to learn that the King was away and that he must await his return.

Vincenzo's painter, as is clearly shown by his own correspondence with Annibale Chieppio, the Duke's secretary, had been constantly worried during the journey by unforeseen delays and lack of money. He had even been obliged to advance part of the expenses from his own pocket. At Valladolid, he had been coolly received by Iberti, the Duke's agent at the Spanish Court, who doubtless looked askance upon Rubens' pseudo-diplomatic activities. To make things worse, some of the pictures destined for the Duke of Lerma were found to be damaged, and Iberti insisted that the 'Fiamingo' should restore them with the help of some Spanish painters. This Peter-Paul refused to do, on the ground that the deception was sure to be discovered and that, in his own words, 'he had always made it a principle not to be confounded with another, however great a man he might be'. After a further letter of protest to Chieppio, the damage was found not to be so irreparable as had at first been supposed, and it was agreed that Rubens should replace two of the pictures which could not be presented by two of his own, the 'Democritus', or 'Laughing Philosopher', and the 'Heraclitus', or 'Weeping Philosopher' (now at Madrid).

After so much trouble, Peter-Paul fully expected to be introduced to Philip III, when the latter returned to Valladolid in July and when the presentation of Vincenzo's gifts was solemnly made. But Iberti was far too jealous of his prerogatives to allow the Fleming to share with him the honours of the day, and the latter was only allowed to witness the ceremony from a distance. He was, however, more successful with the Duke of Lerma, who grew so enthusiastic about the fine copies which had been sent to him that he took them all for originals and greatly marvelled at Vincenzo's lavish generosity. The Duke was evidently drawn to the young painter, for, after proposing that he should remain at the Court of Spain, he commissioned him to paint his own portrait on horseback. Even Iberti was compelled to admit that Rubens acquitted himself of this task with great success. The work, which for a long time was thought to be lost, was discovered fifteen years ago among the collection of the Lerma family, and marks a new development in equestrian portraiture, for both rider and horse are facing the spectator instead of appearing in profile. This portrait was no doubt seen by the young Velasquez when he settled in Madrid some twenty years later.

Lerma had also commissioned Rubens to paint a series of decorative half-length figures of 'Christ and the Twelve Apostles', all of which, excepting the 'Christ', have been preserved at Madrid. Some of these may be considered as the most powerful and original productions of this period of the master's life.[1]

In spite of these tokens of appreciation, Peter-Paul was evidently impatient to return to Italy. He had finished the

[1]See pl. 4A and 4B, p. 52.

portraits of several Spanish ladies, which the Duke of Mantua wished to add to his gallery, and, when the latter suggested that he should go to Paris, there to paint more of such portraits, he firmly replied that he had not the means to cut a proper figure at the French Court and that, moreover, he had no wish to become one of the crowd of artists which the French sovereigns were then gathering together from Flanders, Florence, and even Savoy and Spain. These objections were no doubt genuine, but they were prompted by the feeling that his previous sojourn in Italy had been too short, and that there was still a great deal of work to be done there, not so much in Mantua as in Rome.

★ ★ ★

Vincenzo not only allowed himself to be persuaded by his painter's arguments, but gave him for the first time, on his return, a commission worthy of him: the decoration of part of the Jesuit Church at Mantua, in memory of the Duke's mother, who was buried there.

Before starting on this important work, Rubens may have paid a second visit to Venice and refreshed his early impressions of Tintoretto, whose influence is evident in the central picture now preserved in the Library of Mantua. This painting, which stood over the high altar, depicts the 'Adoration of the Trinity', worshipped by the kneeling Duke and Duchess, their parents and family. On the left, behind Vincenzo, kneels his father Guglielmo; on the right, behind Eleonora de Medici, kneels his mother Eleonora of Austria. The perspective and the attitude of the worshippers, who stand in strong relief, are reminiscent of Tintoretto. The same can scarcely be said of the Trinity, which appears now as a separate fragment, owing to the fact that, when the French

Republican army invaded Mantua in 1797, the work was cut into pieces in order to facilitate its removal. The remaining fragments have been lost, with the exception of a remarkable head-and-shoulders of young Vincenzo, the Duke's third son (now in Vienna). There is every reason to believe that the family group was originally complete, and included, besides the young Vincenzo, the two eldest sons, Francesco and Fernando,[1] his daughter Marguerite, and a greyhound, the Duke's favourite dog.

In spite of these mutilations, the 'Adoration of the Trinity' remains the chief decorative work painted by Rubens in Italy, just as the 'Twelve Apostles', in Madrid, shows his finest work on a smaller scale. In both cases, the individuality of the master is still somewhat overshadowed by the works he so much admired, but it begins to assert itself and to assimilate the style and technique of the great masters of the Italian Renaissance.

This remark does not apply to the two other large pictures painted by Rubens for the choir of the same church, and which stood on the right and left-hand sides of the high altar: the 'Baptism of Christ', which is reminiscent of Raphael's treatment of the same subject in the Vatican, and, in some details, of Michaelangelo's cartoon for the Pisan war; and the 'Transfiguration', which is merely a bold interpretation of Raphael's famous picture. The sombre colouring of these two works (now respectively at Antwerp and Nancy) shows what a long way Rubens had yet to go before ridding his eyes of the film which still prevented him from seeing nature in the true light of his own Flemish temperament.

[1] Two sketches of their heads by Rubens are still preserved at Stockholm.

Towards the end of the year, Peter-Paul obtained permission to leave Mantua for Rome, where he settled with his brother Philip in the Strada della Croce. Philip had been given an important appointment as librarian to Cardinal Ascanio Colonna, while apart from occasional commissions, Peter-Paul could rely on a more or less regular pension of 400 ducats a year from the Duke; so that the two brothers lived in comfortable circumstances, attended by two servants.

This was a time of close collaboration between them. Philip was preparing his *Electorum libri II*, in which he endeavoured to elucidate certain obscure passages in the classics, and for which his younger brother prepared a series of illustrations. This work was published by their friend, Moretus, in Antwerp, two years later. Besides painting copies and purchasing pictures for the Duke, Peter-Paul pursued his archaeological studies and began a collection of antique marbles, which was to become one of the most absorbing interests of his life. No doubt Philip helped him with his advice and his wider knowledge and scholarship.

This happy period of Peter-Paul's intense activity was interrupted by a severe attack of pleurisy. Feeling that his life was in danger, he vowed that, if his German doctor, Johann Faber, succeeded in saving him, he would give him one of his works. After his recovery, he presented Faber with a small picture (now at Aix-la-Chapelle) illustrating Aesop's fable of *The Cock and the Pearl*. This learned jest—the cock being, of course, the bird of Aesculapius—is, with the 'Laughing Philosopher' (now in Madrid), an early example of Rubenian humour. It is characteristic of the man that he was inclined to take himself somewhat seriously when life ran smoothly,

4B. ST. JOHN THE EVANGELIST
[1603–1604]
Prado, Madrid. *Photo, Anderson*

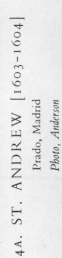

4A. ST. ANDREW [1603–1604]
Prado, Madrid
Photo, Anderson

while humour visited him in times of stress and on his sick-
bed. In one of his letters, Faber transcribed the legend which
accompanied the gift as follows: 'To the celebrated Johann
Faber, doctor of medicine, my Aesculapius, I dedicate this
picture in fulfilment of a vow made for the restoring of my
health when I was doomed.'

Rubens' tastes and interests were nothing if not catholic.
Not only did he add the study of Roman archaeology to
that of Italian painting, but he also felt drawn towards the
Flemish and German artists who were settled in Rome at the
time. From some of his early landscapes it has been inferred
that he must have come into close contact with his compatriot, Paul Bril, and among his later works may be found
several pictures strongly influenced by his friend Adam
Elsheimer, the German landscape-painter. Elsheimer, at that
time, was leading a somewhat Bohemian life in Rome, and
suffered constantly from the persecutions of his creditors.
When Rubens heard of his miserable death in a debtors'
prison, two years after his own departure from Rome, he
wrote:

'Such a loss should plunge all our profession into deep
mourning. It will not be easy to replace him, and, in my
opinion, he can never be equalled in small figures, landscapes and many other things. He has died in the full course
of his studies, and his harvest was still growing, so that one
could hope from him things which now will never be; destiny only showed him to the world'.

Here again, several years must elapse before the result of
this early influence can be seen. At the time, Rubens was
still striving to express himself in large decorative productions, and had accepted an important commission for the

Oratorian Church known as the Chiesa Nuova. Such a commission was highly flattering to the young Flemish painter, since many Italian artists of greater reputation might have been chosen in preference to himself. When, therefore, Duke Vincenzo recalled him to Mantua in November 1606, he insisted, in a letter to Chieppio, on obtaining an extension of leave, arguing that he owed it to his honour and reputation not to throw over this offer, which he had been compelled to accept because of the irregular payment of his pension. So sensible a request could not well be refused, and for a time Peter-Paul was entirely absorbed in the completion of this altar-piece, which represented 'St. Gregory and Other Saints adoring the Virgin'.

The work was not completed when he received, in May 1607, a further summons from Mantua, ordering him to follow the Duke to Spa, where the latter intended to take the waters. Peter-Paul was compelled to submit, but begged to be allowed to return to Rome in time to finish the picture before its unveiling, which had already been fixed for September. Cardinal Scipio Borghese—whose recommendation had doubtless secured the commission—having obtained a promise from the Duke to this effect, Rubens left Rome on June 12th.

Meanwhile, however, Vincenzo had given up the idea of going to the Netherlands, and proceeded to San Pietro d'Arena, a health-resort close to Genoa, where he remained until the end of August. It is probable that Rubens accompanied him on this occasion, and the pictures he painted at Genoa—such as the 'Circumcision' in the Church of Sant' Ambrogio—are usually ascribed to this year. It was also doubtless during these months that he made a series of drawings of Genoese Renaissance palaces, which were published fifteen years later, in a book in which he urged his compatriots to discard the 'barbarous' Gothic in favour of the 'magnificent' architecture of the Renaissance.[1]

On his return to Rome, Rubens completed his altar-piece for the Chiesa Nuova according to plan, but, when it was placed in position, he experienced a bitter disappointment. The light was so bad that practically nothing of the picture could be seen: 'One can hardly distinguish the figures', he writes to Chieppio, 'or appreciate the beauty of colour or the delicacy of the heads and draperies, which I worked at with great care and always from nature'. Rather than see his labour wasted in this way, he suggested to the Fathers of the Oratory that the work should be removed altogether and that he should paint instead three pictures on stone (in order to avoid reflected light), the central one representing the 'Angels adoring the Virgin' and the two others the 'Worshipping Saints' headed by St. Gregory and St. Domitilla. The first version was publicly exhibited for several days and, in his letter to Chieppio, Rubens lays emphasis on the admiration it aroused.

We can scarcely share these feelings to-day. Neither the Genoese 'Circumcision', nor the 'St. Gregory' altar-piece now preserved at Grenoble, nor the triptych in the Chiesa Nuova, shows any advance on the 1604-5 period. There seems even to be a certain loss of vigour and originality since

[1] It is somewhat puzzling that almost the only signed work of this period— the portrait of the Genoese *Marchesa Grimaldi* (Brigitte Spinola)—should be dated 1606, and it is argued from this that the painter may have spent some time in Genoa before going to Rome, at the beginning of that year. Supposing this to be the case, he might still have paid a second visit there with the Duke in 1607.

the time of the Mantuan 'Trinity'. This appears to be due to the influence of Correggio, whose methods were too foreign to Rubens' temperament to be properly assimilated by him. As a matter of fact, the atmosphere of Rome did not suit him nearly so well as that of northern Italy. His eager attention was drawn in too many directions at once, and a certain vagueness ensued.[1]

The main feature of Rubens' second sojourn in Rome is not so much his original work as his collection of important material from a close study of antique sculpture. Though he was in the habit of making use of anything that came to hand, he does not seem consciously to have borrowed entire figures and designs from contemporary art or from that of the Italian Renaissance, with the exception of acknowledged copies and obvious imitations, such as the 'Baptism of Christ' and the 'Transfiguration' painted for the Jesuit Church at Mantua. But when it comes to antique sculpture, he appears to feel that such borrowing is perfectly legitimate. This is made evident not only in work executed at Rome, but also in pictures painted many years later, after his return to Antwerp. Both the St. Maurus and the St. Achilles in the Chiesa Nuova triptych are reproductions of statues which Rubens must have seen in Rome at the time. He retained from his archaeological studies a liking for introducing actual statues into some of his compositions—such as, for instance, the bust of Seneca in the early picture known as the 'Four Philosophers' and the full-sized statue of 'Ceres' (Hermitage),

[1] If we are to add to the later Italian period the 'Entombment' of the Borghese Gallery, so long ascribed to Van Dyck, confusion becomes even worse confounded, for we find in this picture a revival of the Raphaelesque influence already noticeable in the Santa Croce picture.

5B. VENUS FRIGIDA [1614]

Museum, Antwerp

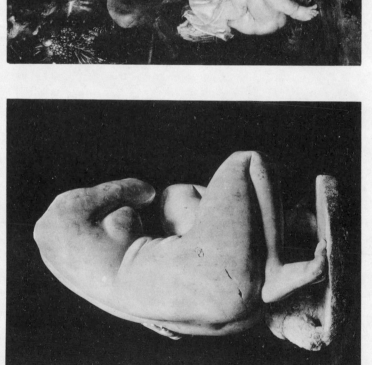

5A. CROUCHING VENUS

ANTIQUE MARBLE

Museo delle Terme, Rome.   *Photo, Anderson*

which was painted some years after Rubens' departure from Italy.[1] There is reason to believe that the crouching 'Venus Frigida' at Antwerp was taken from a headless statue of the goddess seen in Rome,[2] that the celebrated 'Battle of the Amazons' was inspired by an antique sarcophagus, and the gigantic 'St. Christopher', painted outside the 'Descent from the Cross', by the famous Farnese 'Hercules'.

But the most striking example of classical borrowing is to be found in a picture from the Medici Series, painted between 1621 and 1625, representing the 'Birth of Louis XIII at Fontainebleau'.[3] The allegorical figure of Cybele which dominates the picture can be identified with an antique statue of the goddess; the same applies to the figure of Hygeia, standing on the left, while the male genii carrying the child, on the right, is an exact reproduction of an image of Alexander the Great. Strangest of all, the queen herself, with her frills and laces, her brocades and gorgeous satin cloak, is reclining on a couch in exactly the same position as that of a female figure in austere draperies which Rubens must have seen during his stay in Rome. This extraordinary combination suggests that the master, in want of inspiration for the treatment of a subject not in itself particularly inspiring, had recourse to his collection of sketches and extracted

[1] The Seneca statue, in black marble, was at the time in the Villa Borghese; the 'Ceres' is based on a sketch of the figure of 'Pudicitia', now at Vienna. Seneca also appears in the 'Death of Seneca' (Munich).

[2] See pl. 5A and 5B, p. 56. According to Haberditzl (*Jahrb. der Kunsthist. Samml. des Kaiserhauses*, XXXIV, 3) Rubens must have seen the ' Kneeling Venus' now in the Vatican and reproduced in Episcopius' *Signorum Veterum Icones* (1673). There are, however, several replicas of this subject (Reinach: *Répertoire de la Statuaire*, I, 338).

[3] See pl. 6, p. 61.

therefrom the four figures he required. All that then remained to be done was to clothe them appropriately, to add two extra figures to link the group together, to introduce Marie's lap-dog as a touch of intimacy, and to cover the ground with a gorgeous carpet. Other scenes from the Medici Series—such as the 'Government of the Queen', in which Apollo strikes the same attitude as that of the 'Apollo Belvedere', while a demon opposes him with the same movement as that of the 'Fighting Gaul', in the Villa Ludovisi—are also impregnated with classicism. Rubens seems to have felt that his usual real-istic methods could not be successfully applied to the descrip-tion of Marie de Medici's life, and that all the resources of allegory and classical design were required to endow his decorative scheme with the necessary pomp and dignity.

*   *   *

In order to summarise the artistic development which Rubens had reached in October 1608, when he was suddenly recalled to Antwerp by the news of his mother's serious ill-ness, emphasis must be laid on the benefits he derived from his eight years' sojourn in Italy, rather than on his actual achievements in that country. True, several remarkable pic-tures, in which the artist's individuality reveals itself, have been ascribed to the Italian period on the strength of the fact that they have been in Italian collections for a very long time. But, as the painter retained his former connections after his return to the Netherlands, and carried out several commis-sions for Italian patrons up to the last years of his life, such ascriptions do not seem entirely justified. If, therefore, we base our judgment exclusively on the works which Rubens is known to have painted between May 1600, and October 1608, we must recognise that what we consider to-day as

Rubenian originality—that is to say, the interpretation of religion and history in realistic values, boldness of movement and vividness of colouring—had not yet been achieved. At the age of thirty-one, Rubens was still a student and an imitator, the finest art student the world has ever known and an imitator who, in many cases, succeeded in improving on his models; but nevertheless, as far as his own genius was concerned, still hesitant and making tentative efforts to strike the right path. The setback of 1606-1607, after the achievements of 1604-1605, is significant from this point of view. The fact that, after progressing rapidly under Venetian influences, Rubens should have been dazzled by Correggio's effects of light, and waylaid into a new kind of sentimentalism, shows the dangers to which he was exposed by his catholic tastes and perhaps, to a certain extent, by his artistic modesty. Though he was beginning to be conscious of his own worth and eager to uphold his reputation, he was so ready to admire others, and so anxious to emulate the latest object of his admiration, that he almost forgot that the part of an artist is not merely to copy and interpret, but to create. Contrary to some modern aesthetes, his own originality was the last of his preoccupations.

He seems to have had a premonition that he would soon leave Italy. His relations with Vincenzo had become strained during the last years, and he had done very little work for him. He was dissatisfied with the irregular payment of an insufficient salary, and was doubtless longing to see his mother, who was growing old, and his brother Philip, who had left him two years before to prepare for his nomination as Secretary to the Town of Antwerp. Only the fondness for his studies kept him in Rome: there were more pictures to admire, more sketches to make, more marbles to collect. Then came the abrupt summons, followed by a hasty note to Chieppio, dated October 8, 1608:

'I think it is my duty, since His Highness is not at Mantua, to render you an account of the necessity which compels me to what may seem impertinence—namely that to my already long absence I must add another in a country farther away, although I hope it may not be for too long. The reason is that yesterday I received very bad news of my mother's health. She is seriously ill with asthma which, added to the weight of her seventy years, leaves little hope for her but that end which is common to all humanity. It is a hard thing for me to hurry to such a spectacle; it is hard also for me to forego the permission of my serene patron. . . .'[1]

On the same day, Rubens left Rome, thinking no doubt that he would soon come back to pursue his studies and collect still more material for his inexhaustible store. But the gods decreed otherwise, and their decision was a wise one. Peter-Paul had left the Eternal City never to return there again.

When he arrived at Antwerp, on December 11th, with his faithful del Monte, having ridden hard all the way, and when he dismounted at the little house in the Kloosterstraat, he learned that Maria Pypelinckx had died as long ago as October 19th. The only thing he could still do for her was to raise a monument to her memory in the Abbey of St. Michael, where she was buried, and to place above it the

[1]This quotation is taken from *Sir Peter-Paul Rubens* by Anthony Bertram. I take this opportunity of thanking Mr. Bertram for allowing me to reproduce some of his excellent translations of the *Correspondence*.

6. BIRTH OF LOUIS XIII [1621-1625]

Louvre, Paris. *Photo, Bulloz*

picture of 'St. Gregory' which he had designed so carefully
for the Chiesa Nuova, thus dedicating to her the work
which he considered to be his finest achievement.

No mother ever better deserved such filial gratitude. She
had succeeded in rescuing the family from imminent ruin;
she had sacrificed her fortune to give her children a good
education and a fair start in life; she had allowed Peter-Paul
to follow his own vocation despite her personal ambitions;
she had neither delayed his departure for Italy nor hastened
his return. Her death was nevertheless the turning-point
in his artistic career. It occurred almost providentially at a
moment when Italian art, instead of fortifying his genius,
was beginning to weaken it. Had he remained in Rome indefinitely, following the example of some of his compatriots,
he might have become the greatest of the Italianists, a second
Moro, only with more vigour and imagination. What he
needed most in 1608 was to see the fresh, damp Flemish light
again, the clouds rolling across the Flemish sky, and Flemish
rivers, filled with the tide, flowing between low-lying pastures. He wanted a rest from what he himself fondly called
his 'studies', a direct intercourse with nature, the refreshing
influence of family life and old friends, after the worries of
artistic ambitions and the caprices of his Mantuan master.
He had been learning long enough, it was high time that he
should begin to teach. He had been long enough considered
as a promising young foreigner gracing with his presence the
sanctuary of art; it was now urgent that he should realise his
true value and find that, at least in his own country, there
was no living artist to rival him. He had gone to Italy in
search of tools, as the heroes of old went on mysterious
journeys in quest of the weapons which would help them to

do their glorious deeds. He was now fully equipped as a decorative and portrait painter, an ambassador and a scholar, a passionate collector with a taste for architecture, a patient student of Renaissance painting and antique sculpture, with portfolios bulging with sketches and a memory stocked with thousands of designs and subjects.

He was prepared to deal with almost everything: religion, mythology, allegory and portrait. If we except the pictures inspired by the joys and passion of family life and by the love of nature, there is practically no subject treated by him in later years which he had not already approached. The only thing still required for his full development was some sudden change or powerful emotion which would prompt him to make fuller use of his means of expression and to rely on himself rather than on others. His return to Flanders and Maria Pypelinckx' death gave him both.

That Rubens' mother had admired his work and taken pride in it appears from the wording of her will, in which she left to her sons all she possessed, except the pictures Peter-Paul had left with her and which she considered belonged to him:

'I give to my two sons the cooking utensils and everything else as they are at present, as well as all the books, papers and writings belonging to me, with the pictures in my possession which are only portraits; the other pictures, which are beautiful, belong to Peter-Paul, who painted them.'

She little realised how much more beautiful his pictures were to be in the near future, or the decisive part she had played in his career from the day of his birth to the day of her death. By bringing him back to Antwerp, she had made for him her last and greatest sacrifice.

CHAPTER III

ANTWERP AND THE NEW HOME

IN CROSSING the Southern Netherlands on his homeward journey, Rubens must have noticed some striking changes. When he had left, eight years before, the roads had been infested with robbers, villages depopulated and in ruins, and nearly ninety per cent. of the land left fallow. In Flanders, the streams and the sea had overflowed the dykes and great stretches of the countryside had been converted into marsh land. Now, the roads were once more comparatively safe; peasants could be seen ploughing their fields, and herds of cattle were scattered over the meadows. Although the large towns still bore the marks of the late crisis, and Antwerp, in particular, suffered much from the paralysis of her trade, there was a general air of prosperity in both the Walloon and the Flemish parts of the country. All along the Meuse, in the districts of Namur and Liége, the anvils were ringing again under the smiths' hammers and the beating of the tapestry-looms was heard in Brussels and Malines. Practically all traces of division between Calvinists and Catholics, Republicans and Monarchists, seemed to have disappeared and nearly everyone attended the services in the churches.

These changes did not astonish the traveller, for he had
had several opportunities of learning, from Philip and other
fellow-countrymen whom he had met in Italy, of the efforts
made by Archduke Albert and Archduchess Isabella to re-
trieve the country from the slough of despond into which it
had fallen at the end of the previous century. True, the enthusiastic hopes raised by their Joyous Entries into Brussels
and Antwerp, in 1599, had not all been fulfilled. The war
with the United Provinces had yielded no definite success,
and the mouth of the Scheldt was still in the hands of the
Dutch. In spite of their good intentions, the new sovereigns
had been unable to govern with the States-General, which
would not allow them the grants that Spain insisted they
should obtain. People were beginning to realise that, despite
their apparent independence, both Albert and Isabella were
really treated as governors by Philip III, and that their failure
to reconquer the Northern Provinces and the check received
at the battle of Nieuport, where Albert had been severely
wounded, had placed them in a subordinate position. But,
on the other hand, the military situation had considerably
improved of late. The Spanish forces, under Spinola, had
finally succeeded in taking Ostend, thus ridding the Flemish
countryside of the raids of the enemy. After an unsuccessful
attack launched against Antwerp by Maurice of Nassau, in
1605, the Dutch themselves had begun to tire of the war, and,
thanks to Albert's pacific efforts, an armistice had been concluded two years later. In the negotiations which followed,
it seemed clear that the new sovereigns of the Netherlands
had the interests of their subjects sincerely at heart, as they
used all the credit they still possessed to counteract Spanish
ambition and arrogance and to bring about an understand-

ing. They had, besides, taken energetic measures to stimulate industry and encourage a revival of agriculture, and charitable institutions for the relief of distress flourished under their patronage. The people looked upon Isabella as the direct heir of their lawful sovereigns, the only descendant of Mary of Burgundy, and the pomp which she displayed in public ceremonies and the strict etiquette observed at her Court at Brussels, far from provoking criticism, flattered the national pride.

The sovereigns were known to be devoted to each other and to lead an austere religious life, giving all their time and activity to the affairs of the State. They enjoyed, besides, the unrestricted support of the clergy and of a great number of worthy bourgeois whom they had recently ennobled, and who now formed a new class similar to the English gentry. According to a contemporary writer, 'more nobles were made in one year at that time than used formerly to be made in a hundred'.

Another quality which endeared Albert and Isabella to a number of people was their great love of art. They had followed with special interest the progress of Rubens' career in Italy. His first important decorative work—the triptych in Santa Croce—had been commissioned by the Archduke through Jean Richardot, and, soon after his return from Genoa in 1607, Vincenzo had received a letter from Albert asking him to allow his painter to return to Flanders to visit his family and settle personal affairs, to which the Duke had replied somewhat abruptly that the wish of Peter-Paul was to remain in Italy, 'as it was his own wish to keep him there'. The fact that the sovereign of the Netherlands exposed himself to this rebuff is sufficient proof of his eagerness to bring

Rubens back to his mother-country in order to secure his services. Now that the death of Maria had forced a decision and brought the wanderer home, it was a foregone conclusion that the Archduke would also do his best 'to keep him there'.

In August 1609, he presented him with a gold chain and a medal bearing his own likeness and that of Isabella. The following month, Rubens received letters patent from his sovereigns, appointing him Painter to their Palace and 'giving him full power and special orders of the said office'. He must have felt gratified on reading that he had received this appointment 'for the good report that had been made of his person, of his good sense and great experience, as much in painting as in several other arts', and for the 'full confidence' which his new patrons had 'in his loyalty and diligence'.

★   ★   ★

Though Peter-Paul had obviously been sincere when he had declared to Chieppio, on leaving Rome, his firm intention of remaining in the employment of the Duke of Mantua, he allowed himself to be persuaded for personal as well as for artistic reasons.

On his arrival in Antwerp, he had taken up his quarters in the old home in the Kloosterstraat, where Philip was living at the time. After his long absence, he must have experienced, in spite of his sorrow, the delightful feeling which comes to one when every street-corner awakens youthful memories and familiar faces appear on every side: not only his old masters Verhaecht, Van Noort and Vaenius, and his old studio friends, but the learned company of painters and scholars who, under the name of Romanists, met regularly to discourse on art and letters. Only those who had visited Italy were admitted to this society. Peter-Paul, who already knew

a good many of its members, was of course made welcome by
all, and Jan Breughel, the president, greeted the new member,
at the annual banquet on the 29th of June, as 'Signor Pietro-
Paolo Rubens'. It was doubtless soothing, after so many
struggles and difficulties under foreign skies, to return to the
congenial atmosphere of Antwerp and to enjoy once more
Flemish good cheer and conviviality.

But deeper influences were no doubt already at work.
Rubens had reached the age when even the pursuit of Art
and Knowledge is not enough to fill a man's life and, though
he would have been the last to admit it himself, the kind of
comfortable relaxation which followed his return to homely
surroundings was secretly leading him towards marriage and
the foundation of a family. Brother Philip, who had become
Secretary to the Town of Antwerp in January 1609, had,
three months later, married Maria de Moy, sister-in-law of
Jan Brant, an Antwerp lawyer of repute. In announcing this
great news to Doctor Faber, Peter-Paul declares that he has
been unable to think of anything lately but 'the service of the
ladies, as president of the fêtes'. He adds: 'I shall not hurry to
imitate him (Philip), since he has made so good a choice that
truly he is inimitable, and I should not like him to think my
wife an ugly creature beside his.'

He had apparently not yet fully appreciated the charms of
the bride's niece, Isabella Brant, who was one of the ladies to
whose service he devoted himself, or perhaps his very reluctance to 'give himself to the cult of Cupid' was merely a weak
attempt on his part to try and avoid the shafts of the god. Be
that as it may, it took him only a few months to make up his
mind and to persuade the lady of his choice to make up hers,

which, considering his many qualities, both moral and physical, can scarcely have been so difficult as Professor Heinsius, who wrote an eloquent Latin poem on the occasion of Rubens' wedding, would have us believe. The learned philologist is no doubt nearer the mark when he exclaims:

'How often did he not try by his art to free himself from his poignant longings, only to declare himself vanquished? Oh, how often did he not try to draw the sweet face of his well-beloved, and how often had not his hand to cease from work?'

Indeed, such failure to paint Isabella must have been for Peter-Paul a sure sign of the depth of his feelings. Why was it that, after sketching with remarkable ease and swiftness so many pictures, statues and portraits, he found himself paralysed and dissatisfied before this one girl's smiling face?

The consent of the learned and jovial Jan Brant was finally obtained, and the marriage duly celebrated, not in the parish church of St. Andrew—where it was registered afterwards —but in the church of St. Michael, where Peter-Paul's mother had been buried, so that Maria's spirit should watch more closely over her son's wedding. Philip rejoiced over this event in a florid Epithalamium in which his brother was compared successively to Apelles, Adonis and Cupid; he concluded by expressing the wish that, 'before the star with the golden aureole had accomplished its annual course', Isabella might boast of a descendant resembling her husband.

But by far the finest memorial of the marriage is Rubens' well-known portrait of himself and his bride under a bower of honeysuckle, now at Munich. It is painted with the utmost care in quiet tones, and the old-fashioned gala clothes give it an intimate and picturesque character almost unique in the artist's works. On this occasion, he seems purposely to have avoided any display of brilliancy and originality. The attention to detail, in the treatment of flowers, laces and embroideries, gives it an archaic and intensely Flemish character; and in spite of this, or perhaps thanks to this, the picture is pervaded with an atmosphere of quiet tenderness, almost shyly expressed by the way in which the bride's hand rests on that of the bridegroom, and her dress partly covers his shoe.

A comparison between the 'Honeysuckle Bower' and the nude portrait of Helen Fourment, Rubens' second wife, commonly known as *Het Pelsken*, and which was painted some thirty years later, gives us an idea, if not of the difference in the love he bore these two women, at least of the difference in the way he expressed it. It also gives us the full range of his feelings, from protective tenderness to overwhelming passion.

It has been said that, while there were a thousand women in Rubens' art, there were only three in his life: 'his mother, who formed him; his first wife, who shared the triumph of his early maturity; his second wife, who saw his mellow glory and watched his eyes dim, and closed them'.[1] It may be added that these thousand women can be reduced to a few dominant types, and that Isabella appears most frequently in the early period, while Helen plays the most varied parts in the latter. There were, however, other models, such as Susanna Fourment and Lady Gerbier, who are easily recognisable, in some historical and allegorical pictures, from their portraits by the same hand. But in neither of these cases, and in no other case, do we find any evidence that the master allowed his artistic or friendly interest to degenerate into sexual intrigue.

[1]Anthony Bertram: *Sir Peter-Paul Rubens.*

However astonishing it may appear to those who are accustomed to consider Rubens as the protagonist of sensuality, everything we know concerning his private life points to the fact that, in this respect at least, he did not follow the Renaissance tradition. He knew that such subjects as 'Susanna and the Elders', 'Lot and his Daughters', 'Nymphs pursued by Satyrs', and wild bacchanals, were in great demand, and he was even careful to point out to some of his patrons who were fond of nude figures, that certain pictures he wished to sell them were: 'excellent compositions with many very beautiful young girls.' He endeavoured to please them, knowing full well that he could transform the most rollicking scene into a painted poem singing the praises of passion, life and beauty. But he never indulged, as did some other Renaissance masters, in innuendoes or subtle ambiguities. His sensuality is either blatantly gross or frankly innocent; it is essentially unintellectual. Examine one by one the facial expressions in his bacchanals: you will find hilarious peasants disguised as satyrs, jolly old topers posing as Silenus, and robust wenches playing the part of Bacchantes, but you will not discover one smile as suggestive as that of the 'Gioconda', one look as charged with meaning as that of Titian's 'Venus'. This may be one of the reasons why some critics are disappointed by Rubens' pagan stories, but the same reason should exempt him from moral censure. He may be reproached either for his want of subtlety or for letting himself be carried away by his powerful temperament, but it is somewhat illogical to use both arguments against him at the same time.

In his *Hyperbolimoeus*, Gaspard Scioppius, who had met Rubens in Rome, pays him the following tribute:

'My friend Peter-Paul Rubens, in whom I know not which

7A. [?] NICHOLAS RUBENS [ABOUT 1615]

7B. [?] CLARA-SERENA RUBENS

most to praise, his talent for painting, in which he holds the highest rank attained by any man in our century, or his knowledge of belles-lettres, or his enlightened taste, or the uncommon charm of his speech and converse. . . .'

He proceeds to tell us that he once went to Tivoli with the Rubens brothers and Daniel Lhermite, secretary to the Grand-Duke of Tuscany. On the way, Lhermite recounted some obscene stories from Petronius and Aretino, to which Peter-Paul listened patiently. But when it came to drawing indecent pictures on the walls of the inn in which the company had stopped to rest and drink, the painter could no longer refrain from protest. The story is significant. Rubens was not a prig—no prig could have made himself so popular in the society of his time, or have expressed himself in art with so much freedom—but when it came to a nasty story or, still worse, an obscene drawing, when sensuality, instead of remaining the servant of art, became its master, the soul of the man rebelled against such blasphemy. He was not squeamish, and was essentially a man of the world, but, as R. L. Stevenson puts it so excellently: 'There are certain things which a gentleman cannot do, and there are certain others which he will not stand.' The drawing of obscene pictures was exactly that kind of thing to Rubens, and nothing in the world, no doubt, would have angered him more than the suggestion that his own nude figures might possibly be included in the same category.

In spite of his broad-brimmed hat and curling moustache, Rubens was not essentially a dashing cavalier. He was above all a staunch Flemish bourgeois, brought up by a good and virtuous mother, who must have warned him against his father's sins (without, however, mentioning his name), and living in the days of the Counter-Reformation, when pure living was again the fashion both in Court and town. Albert and Isabella set an example to their people, and the Brussels Court was a model to Europe. Such virtuous education and surroundings might not have had so deep an influence on another man. But all through Rubens' life there runs a sense of well-ordered economy. He was one of the most hard-working artists the world has ever known, but he knew that, in order to maintain his rate of production, he must use every available moment and keep himself fit both mentally and physically. From his early days, he had learned the stern lesson that there is no self-expression without self-repression, that the same imaginative power which stimulates the senses creates the vision which can be fixed on canvas, and that the greatest creative genius is of little use unless it is sternly employed on creative work. He was a good horseman, and could be met at times galloping through the countryside round Antwerp either on his long-tailed dapple-grey or on his strong bay, both of which can be recognised in several of his pictures. It was almost the only relaxation he indulged in, for, besides providing him with wholesome exercise, it taught him the wisdom of the centaur Chiron, which is to master one's passions and keep oneself in hand.

No greater error could be made than to consider Rubens, even when praising him, as a scorner of conventions, ready to break any social rule which might stand in his way. Here again, the contrast with Shelley may serve. Ariel could indeed defy public opinion and try to refashion the world according to his own ideal—lyrical poetry can almost stand by itself—but a great playwright cannot work without a theatre, a great decorative painter must find some walls to decorate, a great novelist depends upon his readers. A Shakespeare, a Rubens or a Dickens are bound to express themselves not outside but inside the society in which they are living, and will instinctively and of necessity adopt some of its conventions without in the least renouncing their own dignity and independence. The problem with which Rubens was faced was not how to adapt his personality to the ideas and fashions prevailing in Europe at the beginning of the seventeenth century, but how to adapt such ideas and fashions, in their artistic aspect, to his own individual method of painting. He was no time-server, but he endeavoured to make use of any opportunity which offered. He did not attack the ideas of his age, not only because he shared them to a great extent, but also because it would have appeared to him a waste of time and energy to challenge them. No one has ever doubted his intelligence or his learning, but his mind was not introspective. His business was with painting, not with social reform, and he no doubt rightly considered that he could not develop the latter without impoverishing the former.

He possessed a wide range of vision and a vast and sympathetic understanding, and endeavoured to satisfy all tastes and aspirations, depicting with equal readiness and alacrity pagan bacchanals and Christian miracles, the most trifling incidents in a patron's life and the greatest events in profane and sacred history. He was a devout Catholic, a faithful husband and a good citizen, but sensuality belonged to the order of things and he dealt with it, in his masterly way, as he dealt with any other human passion and emotion. He himself lived a sober and orderly life, but he understood an orgy when he saw it and succeeded in painting it better than anyone ever did before or since. Fauns capered and nymphs danced, pipes sounded and cymbals clashed, amidst a mad riot of colour. He fixed these visions in his pictures and kept them there.

*   *   *

Rubens' house was of course to be a palatial residence, built according to his own plans and worthy to contain his wonderful collections and his still more wonderful family. The site was bought two years after his marriage, and five more years were needed to complete the great work, which was considered by the artist-architect to be one of his finest achievements. Meanwhile, the young couple settled in Jan Brant's house in the Kloosterstraat, a few doors away from the old home.

Heinsius's prophecy was only partly fulfilled, for the eldest child was a daughter, Clara-Serena. She was baptised on March 21, 1611, her grandmother, Clara de Moy, standing godmother, and her uncle Philip godfather. Albert followed, three years later. This time, the Archduke himself consented to be godfather, and was represented at the baptism. After a further interval of four years, the youngest child was born, and called Nicholas, after Nicholas Pallavicini, a Genoese nobleman for whom Rubens had painted the 'Circumcision' in the Church of Sant' Ambrogio.

There is no doubt that the master sketched and painted his children again and again. Of Clara-Serena, who died at the age of twelve, we only know to-day the doubtful portrait in the Liechtenstein Gallery.[1] Albert as an infant appears in a sketch now in the British Museum, in two drawings in the Hermitage, in the 'Madonna adored by Penitents' at Cassel (as St.

[1]See pl. 7B, p. 71.

8. RUBENS AND SNYDERS: THE CHILD CHRIST, ST. JOHN
AND TWO ANGELS [1615–1616]

Baron Coppée Coll., Brussels.   *Photo, l'Epi*

John), and in various 'Adorations of the Kings' dating from the first Antwerp period. Of Nicholas we have a sketch, the 'Child with a Bird', in Berlin,[1] and three drawings in the Albertina; he was also used as the Child Christ in the Cassel 'Madonna', as one of the children bestriding lions in the 'Marriage of Marie de Medici', and in a number of Madonna pictures. The two boys have been identified over and over again in sacred and profane paintings of the Antwerp period, and some of these works have even been dated by the apparent ages of the children.[2]

It may be that, in certain cases, we must give up the fond belief that the fair-haired Nicholas played the part of the Child Christ to the dark-haired Albert's St. John, for some of these pictures would seem to have been painted before his birth; but the fact remains that fatherhood deeply affected the master's art and enabled him to renew the outworn conception of the Italian 'putti'. The latter, whether used as angels or as cupids, always preserved a certain conscious grace and an affected charm; they were a kind of compromise between the human and the divine; they were childlike of course in their features and attitudes, but they did not possess the innocent clumsiness of the man-cub, its grotesque awkwardness of movement prompting it to strenuous efforts to achieve very meagre results; they did not show that kittenish curiosity and puppy-like avidity which identify childhood with all spontaneous and untarnished life. There had been a time when religious painters had been able to represent the Child God, and the Raphaelesque conception of the angelic child had also fulfilled its purpose, but the seventeenth-century 'putti' had lost both divine and human qualities,

[1]See pl. 7A, p. 71.   [2]See pl. 8, p. 74.

and had become merely the artificial creations of late Renaissance artistry. Rubens had painted some of them in Sant' Ambrogio in Genoa and in the Chiesa Nuova in Rome. When, however, he saw his own babies lying in their cradles, he realised how conventional those other babies had been. Following his realistic trend of mind, he decided that henceforth all the children who were to appear in his works— whether as angels, cupids, or sprites—should be human children, like his own.

There is no need to trouble about chronological details. Broadly speaking, from 1613, when Clara-Serena was two years old, up to 1620, when Nicholas was two, Rubens was under the spell of a paternity-complex. He already had important commissions to carry out during this period, but he seems to have spared all the time available for painting babies. Apart from the sketches already mentioned, their merry crowd fills the 'Charity' in the Schoenborn collection, the group of 'Jesus, St. John and Angels' in Vienna, the 'Assumptions of the Virgin' in Brussels and the Louvre, the 'Garland of Fruit' in Munich; children form a living frame for the 'Madonnas' in Munich and the Prado, and appear again and again as the Christ Child or St. John and the Angels in a number of Holy Families.

The Madonna is nearly always Isabella—not the girlish Isabella of the 'Honeysuckle Bower', but the riper woman of the Berlin portrait, with her oval face and pointed chin, and those curious almond-shaped eyes which give her an almost fawnlike expression.[1] As the Mother of God, her lids are usually lowered, and she is often surrounded by blooming

[1]See pl. 9A, p. 76.

9B. RUBENS AND BREUGHEL [1620–1624]
VIRGIN AND CHILD
Museum, Brussels

9A. PORTRAIT OF ISABELLA BRANT
[1622–1625]. Kaiser Friedrich Museum, Berlin
Photo, Franz Hanfstaengl, Munich

bowers or wreaths of flowers, carefully painted in the old miniature style by Jan Breughel, who had already become Rubens' collaborator. In this, as in the 'Honeysuckle Bower', there is a curious return to archaism, as if the quiet content of the married man had for a time appeased his restless spirit and led him to look more attentively on the early Madonnas of the Flemish school. His realistic interpretation is, nevertheless, evident. Just as his Italian 'putti' become human children after he had become a father, so his Italian Madonnas—which were a kind of compromise between the divine and the human in woman—lose all artificiality after he has become a husband. The likeness to Isabella is not always so apparent as in the 'Virgin with Forget-me-Nots', in Brussels,[1] and the 'Virgin bending over her Child's cot', in Sanssouci. Sometimes, as in the 'Madonna' of the Hermitage,[2] the 'Madonna surrounded with a Garland', in Munich, and the 'Holy Family' in the Pitti, the type appears darker; but the outlines of the face and the quiet, restful expression can be recognised over and over again during this period. As the father seems to have superseded the lover in Peter-Paul, Isabella is to him above all a mother, nursing her children, watching them play, or holding them proudly in her arms.

The master's devotion to his family not only influenced his mind and imagination, by prompting him to multiply such intimate pictures, but seems also to have affected his technique. One of the surest tests by which experts recognise nowadays a genuine Rubens, is the remarkably bright colouring of the flesh, giving the skin a kind of radiance which

[1]See pl. 9B, p. 76.

[2]In the absence of precise data, all mention of Rubens' pictures in the Hermitage must be taken as being made before the recent sales.

might be sought in vain among the works of Italian masters or among the painter's own works of the Italian period. It was only after his return to Flanders that he discovered the special quality of Flemish light, and, after his marriage with a Flemish woman, that he fully realised the beauty of the Flemish complexion. It is not only 'milk and roses', but satin and mother-of-pearl as well—in short, just what Rubens made it appear to be, when he used his wife and children for his sacred and profane pictures. Strangely enough, this very quality was to remain in future the hall-mark of his genius.

*   *   *

As has already been mentioned, the master was making preparations for settling into a new house. He had acquired at Mantua a certain taste for pomp and luxury, and could now easily afford to give his family a dwelling worthy of his own reputation. He was a generous man and, like most generous men of his day, was in the habit of spending lavishly, and there was no object on which he was more inclined to do so than the house over which Isabella was to rule and in which Clara-Serena and Albert (Nicholas was not yet born) were to work and play. There was, besides, a large collection of marbles and pictures to be housed, and accommodation had also to be found for the two vast studios in which the master and his pupils were to paint. Add to this Rubens' hobby for architecture, as shown by his book on the Genoese palaces and his countless sketches of ornamental decoration, and it will be seen that everything combined to induce him to lavish endless care on the building, and to devote many years to its completion. In fact, Peter-Paul was so eager to provide Isabella with a suitable house, that she had to wait for it nearly half her married life.

The painter-architect preserved the old house, which he had acquired with the grounds on the Wapper, more or less in its original state, but he built beside it a much larger three-storeyed mansion, richly decorated with pilasters, porches surmounted by pediments, niches containing statues, urns and other devices. The two buildings were separated by a large courtyard and linked together with a three-arched portico surmounted by a balustrade. This portico led into well-planned gardens, enriched with a pavilion (still standing) and an artificial grotto, from which came a spring of water; both pavilion and grotto were adorned with pagan statues.

Family life seems to have been kept separate from artistic activities: the former was spent in the old building, the rooms of which must have been very similar—with their low-beamed ceilings and latticed windows—to those which may still be visited to-day in the Plantin-Moretus Museum. The two houses, indeed, were compared at the time by friends who received the hospitality of both, and in a letter congratulating the descendant of the famous printer and Rubens' old schoolfellow on some embellishments which he had lately carried out, Woverius—whom we remember meeting at Verona as one of the Four Philosophers—writes as follows:

'Well done, my dear Moretus, go on restoring the glory of your race not only by your art and scholarship, but also by the magnificence of your dwelling. Happy our Antwerp which can boast of two such citizens as Rubens and Moretus! Their houses will be admired by foreigners and visited by travellers'.

The writer's prophecy has been fully realised with regard to the mansion occupied by Moretus, and may soon be realised again, in spite of the injuries of time, with regard to

Rubens' home, if the efforts made by the municipality of Antwerp to restore it meet with the success they so well deserve.

In the Stockholm Museum, there is a picture by an unknown hand representing the living-room of a large Antwerp house, with dark oak furniture, a monumental fireplace, and several pictures on the walls. It is quite possible that the lady of the house, who is holding a fan, is Isabella, and that the three children grouped round a chair are Clara-Serena, Albert and Nicholas. In any case, the picture hanging over the fireplace can be identified with the first version of Rubens' 'Lot and his Daughters'.

The fact that the master should have decorated such a room with such a picture is another proof that he did not experience before the latter the qualms which seem to trouble some people to-day, and that he shared the idea of the old Humanists that a beautiful thing can never do any harm. If his heroes behaved well, their example ought to stimulate the young to act in the same way; if, on the other hand, they became the prey of their senses, they would be a warning against a similar weakness. Rubens was apparently inclined to place the best possible construction on everything, for, in a dedication inscribed on an engraving of one of his versions of 'Susanna and the Elders', sent to the Dutch poetess Anna Roemers Visscher, he calls this picture: 'A rare example of Chastity'. He looked on it from the point of view of Susanna —not of the Elders.

The new house was not only to be a dwelling worthy of the Rubens family, but also an example of Renaissance architecture as opposed to Gothic, which had so long kept its hold on Flanders. No doubt the master was thinking of himself when he wrote in the Preface of his *Palazzi di Genova*, published in 1622:

'We note how men of taste are introducing, to the great honour and embellishment of their land, that architecture which has true symmetry and conforms to the rules established by the ancient Greeks and Romans.'

He favoured the new style, not only on account of its harmony, but also because 'the domestic convenience of a house is almost always in concord with the regularity and beauty of its form'.

This worship of the classic style appeared at every turn, in both house and garden. Peter-Paul could not live without being surrounded with the images of pagan gods and the busts of ancient heroes. We are told that, in the early days of Mantua, Duke Vincenzo coming upon him unexpectedly, was not a little surprised to hear him declaiming lines from Virgil while wielding the brush; it seems as if each stroke must have kept time with the rhythm of the verse. This is not a solitary instance. When the Danish doctor, Otto Sperling, visited the master in Antwerp in 1621, he also was surprised to notice that he worked to the accompaniment of a reading from Tacitus.

Obviously the house would not have been complete had it not displayed a number of inscriptions from its owner's favourite authors. Two of these at least have been preserved to us; they are both quotations from the Tenth Satire of Juvenal. The first of them runs as follows:

Orandum est, ut sit mens sana in corpore sano.
Fortem posce animum, et mortis terrore carentem,
Nesciat irasci, cupiat nihil.

The fact that two lines have been added to the well-known reference to 'a healthy mind in a healthy body' is significant. We must also pray for a brave heart 'that knows not the fear of death . . . and is innocent of fear and cupidity', otherwise the gifts of the gods may be wasted. To know neither fear nor anger was one of the pillars of Rubens' practical philosophy. He was not content to inscribe these principles on the portico of his house, he practised them in his life with a kind of fearless patience.

The second quotation from Juvenal, written on the portico, is the necessary complement of the former, for submission to an inevitable fate is another condition of all sound pagan or Christian philosophy:

> Permittes ipsis expendere numinibus, quid
> Conveniat nobis, rebusque sit utile nostris . . .
> Carior est illis homo, quam sibi.

The Romans, in the critical days of their Empire, when they lived in constant personal danger, left it to the gods to decide what was right and considered them to be better friends to man than man himself. The Christians of Rubens' time were perhaps not so submissive to their destiny, as long as they thought themselves capable of controlling it, but when the fatal blow struck them, the ancient wisdom stood them in good stead.

* * *

When, on the 20th of June, 1626, Isabella died suddenly—probably of the plague, which was devastating Antwerp at the time—Rubens went through a terrible spiritual crisis. Up to then, his life had run remarkably smoothly, and he had been able to realise all the wishes of his boyhood. He had had great adventures, made a rapid career, enjoyed the favours of the great and the admiration of his compeers. He had married the girl of his choice, rejoiced in the blooming wonder of his children, and built himself a fine house filled with treasures. Better, perhaps, than any man of his generation, he had been able to live his dream. Life, indeed, especially since his return to Antwerp, had been almost like a dream to him, and we see him walking on air, from success to success, and resting blissfully among his family after each fresh achievement. Almost every week brought with it a new masterpiece, a new discovery, a new cause for pride and excitement. There had been, it is true, in 1611, the great sorrow of Philip's death and, in 1623, the bitter loss of his first-born, Clara-Serena; but Isabella had been near him then, and had helped him to overcome his grief. These troubles had been only like the faint rumbling of the storm compared with the lightning which now struck the house, ruined all hope, wrecked all ambition, and brought dreamland abruptly down to earth.

Many friends were of course ready to offer Peter-Paul the sincere but somewhat tedious comfort of their religion and philosophy. He must have heard many times such arguments as those used by Peiresc after Clara-Serena's death: Human life is ephemeral; God favours us by taking away those we love and keeping them near Him, sheltered from illness and suffering; instead of mourning your loss, you should rejoice in the belief that God's purpose has been achieved for the mysterious ends which He pursues and which must necessarily be good for yourself as well as for the deceased. . . .

Rubens' answer to such offers of comfort is characteristic. It deserves to be quoted in full, not only because it is one of the rare utterances in which he unveils his inner soul, but also because it shows us the strength he derived, at one and the same time, from his Christian faith and his pagan wisdom. Both of these are curiously combined and almost inseparable. It seems as if Catholic religion were stiffened by Humanist scholarship. Classicism stands beside Christianity like a strong prop beside a flower; the prop bears no bloom, but it prevents the flower from breaking:

'You are right to remind me of the necessity of fate which does not bend to the caprices of our passions, and which, as an effect of the supreme will, owes us no explanation of its decrees. It is for fate to command as absolute master, it is for us to obey as slaves, and we have nothing else to do, in my opinion, but to make this servitude as easy and as honourable as possible by submitting willingly. And yet, at this moment, it is a duty which seems to me very heavy and well-nigh unbearable. Your wisdom tells me to rely upon time. Perhaps time will do for me what reason should have done, for I have no pretentions to stoical impassiveness, and I do not even believe that feelings so greatly in accordance with their object can be contrary to the nature of man, nor that he should regard with equal indifference all that happens in the world. I am convinced *aliqua esse quae potius sunt extra vitia quam cum virtutibus*, and that these objects bring with them in our soul a kind of emotion *citra reprehensionem*. Truly, I have lost a most excellent helpmate; one whom it was possible, nay even right, to cherish with reason, for she had none of the failings of her sex: no fretful temper, no womanly weakness, nothing but goodness and graciousness; her virtues made her beloved of all during her lifetime; since her death they have been the cause of universal regret. Such a loss seems to me very real, and, since the only remedy for all evils is the forgetfulness which comes with time, I must look to time alone for help. But it will be difficult for me to separate my grief for this loss from the memory which all my life long I must keep of my dear and honoured wife. A journey would perhaps best help to remove me from so many things which continually renew my sorrow, *ut illa sola domo moeret vacua stratisque relictis incubat*. The changing pictures which meet the eyes during a journey do much to fill the imagination and deaden the heart's pain. Moreover, it is true *quod mecum peregrinabor et me ipsum circumferam*, but believe, I pray you, that it would be a great comfort to me to see you and your brother, or to do something that might be pleasing to you. I am deeply touched by your friendly consolations in my trouble, and thank you sincerely for the correspondence you promise me in the absence of M. de Valavez'.

This letter was written from Antwerp on July 15, 1626, to Rubens' French friend, Dupuy. The writer cannot accept the dictates of ancient stoicism, for he is unwilling to remain indifferent to the tragedies of life. He submits with the greatest difficulty to the decisions of a supreme Power, and apparently only does so because it is the dignified and honourable attitude to adopt. Such submission is perhaps better expressed by the quotation from Juvenal than by any Christian precept, for it is easier to deliver one's fate into the hands of vague deities than smilingly to receive a wound from the Hand of all Wisdom and Goodness. The idea of considering the catastrophe as a blessing does not even occur to him. He records his suffering in moderate but none the less burning words: he has lost his companion, whose memory alone now fills his 'empty house' and his 'desolate couch'. Such separation is devastating for any ordinary man; how much more cruel it must have been for one of the most sensitive and imaginative artists of all time! He does not only miss an abstract presence, but thousands of concrete impressions. His widowerhood extends to every sense; he must have felt as if his eyes, his ears, his hands themselves were benumbed with pain, and he frankly refuses to admit that such grief can be sinful. He accepts the blow with something of the heroism of an old Roman, without revolt but also without fear:

Fortem posce animum, et mortis terrore carentem.

He acknowledges the wound, without trying to soften it, but also without insisting that it must forever poison his life. A journey will do some good, no doubt, and time is the great healer. . . . But it will be very difficult.

It is worth insisting on the attitude which Rubens assumes in this letter, for it is characteristic of the best men of his day. He is not a mystic, for, if the hope of some future reunion helps him through the crisis, he does not give it concrete expression. Neither is he a pagan, for spiritual pride cannot compensate him for the suffering he experiences. His rich and healthy humanity is as far removed from the Ascete as from the Stoic, and he is too sincere to call a defeat a triumph. At the same time, the letter is essentially unromantic: the grief is bad enough, scarcely bearable; there is no need to make it worse or to cure it by desperate methods; it must be accepted and endured, until its fire abates. . . . But it will be very difficult. Isabella's death does not transform her into a kind of all-pervading spirit which absorbs the soul of her lover, so that his life becomes meaningless. She remains now exactly what she was before: the painter's companion, who helped him in difficulties, and who was the mother of his children. She is no longer there, but he must pursue his journey and look after his family as best he can. This is the sober truth; its cruelty need not be emphasised by any exaggeration.

We may look on Peter-Paul, in these days of his grief, as on one of those heroes, such as Decius Mus, whose story he told so well, and who preserved, in the most fateful hours of their life, a healthy sense of proportion and that deep-seated conviction which keeps the world afloat: that though men may be born and men may die—yea, even women—there remains a certain amount of work to be done in this world, and that nothing must prevent us from doing it.

CHAPTER IV

RUBENS' RELIGIOUS STYLE

IT IS impossible to state the exact time when the many experiments made by the painter-student and the various influences to which he was subjected, assumed their proper place in his artistic development and allowed his individuality to assert itself. We may, nevertheless, consider the years 1609-1614 as marking a new departure in Rubens' career, for it was in 1609 that he painted the large 'Adoration of the Kings' (now in Madrid) for the Town Hall of Antwerp, and in 1614 that he completed the triptych of the 'Descent from the Cross' for the chapel of the Guild of Arquebusiers, in the Cathedral, where it still hangs to-day. These works, together with the 'Erection of the Cross' painted in 1610, definitely established his reputation as the greatest church decorator outside Italy. And when all is said, it is above all as a decorator that he must be appreciated.

There has been a tendency, of late years, to try to minimise the importance of the great pictures at Antwerp, in the Prado, the Louvre and elsewhere, in order to concentrate public attention on Rubens' portraits and, more particularly, on the wonderful landscapes he painted during the last years of his life. It is true that the master's religious, historical and allegorical paintings lend themselves to certain obvious criticisms, and quite naturally some of his admirers have found it easier to avoid these criticisms by dwelling on the works which hold an almost unassailable position; but this method must necessarily cause misapprehensions. Insistence on portraiture has led to invidious comparisons with Velasquez, on the one hand, and with Rembrandt, on the other; while the praise bestowed on the later landscapes to the exclusion of other works has fostered the idea that the master was merely a landscape-painter of supreme genius, who was unfortunately led astray by the Jesuits and the great princes of Europe and persuaded by them to squander his natural gifts on superficial and showy productions.

Nothing could, however, be farther from the truth. Apart from the sound principle according to which every artist, writer, or musician should be judged by the works to which he has devoted the greatest amount of time and care, we know from Peter-Paul's letters that he considered decorative art to be the most congenial field for his activity. His impatience at being ordered to Paris by the Duke of Mantua, there to paint a few more beautiful ladies, has already been mentioned, while his satisfaction at receiving commissions for large decorations occurs again and again in his correspondence. It can easily be shown that this satisfaction was not merely caused by a desire for material advantages, for, in some cases, the sketches for such works were undertaken before the order was definitely given, and, in others, the remuneration was not in proportion to the time and care devoted to them. As a matter of fact, it would have paid Rubens far better to confine himself to the painting of what he calls 'little curiosities'. This expression occurs in a letter to William Trumbull, dated the 13th of September, 1631, in which he expresses his gratification at the suggestion made by James I and the Prince of Wales that he should decorate 'the hall of the new palace'—that is to say, the Banqueting-House in Whitehall. The writer adds: 'I confess that my natural inclination is to execute large works rather than little curiosities. Each man has his gift; mine is such that no enterprise, however great or varied in subject, daunts my courage.'

There is no doubt that if Rubens had been asked by which of his works he wished to be judged, he would have chosen his decorative paintings; and, since the larger number of these deal with religious subjects, the appreciation of the master's religious art cannot possibly be evaded, in spite of the many difficulties which the question presents to the modern critic.

One of these difficulties is the curious confusion which so frequently occurs to-day between religion—that is to say, the historical conception of God and its expression in the domain of reality and imagination—and a special aspect of religion with which we have become more and more accustomed to connect poetical, musical and artistic interpretative works: mysticism.

Roughly speaking, the mystic may be defined as the religious man or woman who sees visions, hears voices or, in any other way, enters into direct individual contact with the divine world. Ruskin and other critics have very properly insisted on the paramount value of works of art which possess that special mystical quality. They have told us, for instance, how biased our forefathers were in disparaging Gothic cathedrals in comparison with Renaissance churches, and Fra Angelico's and Giotto's frescoes in comparison with Raphael's, Michaelangelo's and Titian's interpretations of Christian art. Their main argument implied that, if a work is intended to exalt our religious fervour, its value should to a certain extent be in proportion to the intensity of the religious feelings it translates. But they went farther. Having narrowed down the field of religion to pure mysticism, they frequently denied all artistic qualities to pictures and monuments dealing with religious subjects which did not show that mystic character, and reflected, for instance, classic or realistic influences. It is easy to understand why Rubens, in whom these classic and realistic tendencies are so strongly marked, should have suffered more than any other great master from such prejudices.

It would not be enough to answer that, according to modern views, the subject of a picture does not matter at all, and that its beauty merely derives from the suggestive harmony of lines and colours. A painter is, it is true, neither a theologian nor a philosopher, but the interpretation he gives to his personal conceptions or to the ideals of his time cannot entirely be separated from these conceptions and ideals. In such matters, the judgment of the general public differs from that of the expert, and it is with the former and not with the latter that we are here concerned.

*   *   *

The essential fact to grasp, if we wish to understand Rubens' thoughts when he painted his first great religious works, such as the 'Adoration of the Kings', the 'Erection of the Cross' and the 'Descent from the Cross', is that he, more than

any other artist in Europe, was the representative of the
Counter-Reformation in the Roman Catholic world, and
that the Counter-Reformation answered a definite purpose,
which any writer, architect or artist had to fulfil if he desired
to express the ideal for which the movement stood.

The Italian Renaissance of the fifteenth and sixteenth centuries had already revived Classicism and enlisted the old
pagan gods and ancient pagan philosophy in the service of the
Christian Church. In many cases, this bore fruit not only in
the domain of art but also in that of ethics and religion. The
Renaissance produced in the Humanist one of the finest types
of artist and scholar the world has ever known, who succeeded in combining the noblest qualities of both civilisa-
tions, as is exemplified by the letter quoted above, written by
Rubens to Dupuy after the death of Isabella. On the other
hand, the Renaissance was, if not responsible for, at least
associated with, serious abuses, and provoked violent reac-
tions towards a purer and more ascetic form of worship, such
as the movements led by Savonarola in Italy and by the Calvinists in the Netherlands. The Church could not ignore
these attacks and, as early as 1563—three years before the
Iconoclast outbreak—the Council of Trent had already
adopted a series of strong measures forbidding that 'any
image referring to a wrong dogma and which could mislead
the ignorant' be placed in a church. All kinds of impurity
were to be avoided and images must not be too suggestively
attractive. Bishops were enjoined to exert the strictest supervision in these matters, and the freedom enjoyed by painters,
carvers and illuminators in former days was severely curtailed.

Such ecclesiastical control was no new feature in the history of Christian art, for, since the early Middle Ages, the clergy had never ceased to supervise and had frequently inspired the work of the artist; but, in former days, the appearance of pagan subjects beside Christian ones, instead of causing scandal, seemed perfectly harmless. In the chancel of Limoges Cathedral, for example, carved as late as 1533, the Christian Virtues and the Fathers of the Church fraternise with the Great Deeds of Hercules; and, in the same way, the images of Ceres and Bacchus and the love-story of Pyramus and Thisbe may be found in a French Book of Hours dated 1524. Not only were such liberties thenceforth forbidden, but, in order to prevent further criticism from the Protestant side, all the apocryphal or doubtful incidents relating to the Gospel, which had provided the artists of previous centuries with so many moving and beautiful themes, were also excluded.

It is significant that the decisions of the Council of Trent were interpreted with far greater rigour in northern Catholic countries, in close contact with the Protestant world, than in the South. Two years after the Iconoclast rising, Jean Molanus, who taught at Louvain University, published a discourse entitled: *De Historia sanctarum imaginum et picturarum*, in which he endeavoured to interpret and apply to concrete cases the dictates of the Council. After protesting against the reproach of idolatry made against the Church, he proceeds to exclude from ecclesiastical art every story which 'piety may be allowed to believe, but which is not recognised as true', such as, for instance, that of the childhood of the Virgin Mary and her death, as well as that of a great many saints who, he declares, really existed, but not under the features given to them by the 'Golden Legend'. St. Christopher was not a giant; St. George never killed any dragons, and St.

Nicholas never raised three little children from a salting-tub. Anything which may provoke the derision of Protestant critics must be severely excluded; biblical characters must discard any picturesque or contemporary garment and don non-committal classical draperies; free interpretations of the Gospel, based on Franciscan literature, and more especially on St. Bonaventure's *Meditations*, are alike discouraged, while the Blessed Virgin must stand steadfast at the foot of the Cross, and no longer be overwhelmed by her sorrow.

In his anxiety to avoid the denunciations of the Puritans, Molanus condemns all free treatment in church pictures of such episodes as the Marriage at Cana, 'which must not look like a banquet of epicures'; Salome's dance, which may lead to indecency; and David spying on Bethsheba, which is equally indecorous.

The consequence of this attitude of the clergy towards religious art is obvious. By considerably reducing the number of subjects and curtailing the imaginative scope of the designer with regard to picturesque details, it entirely upset long-standing traditions and encouraged new developments in grouping and composition in the 'grand manner'. By excluding from the churches all pagan figures or even all biblical stories which might lend themselves to sensuous treatment, it brought about the production of a large number of mythological works displayed in houses and palaces, and a gradual cleavage between religious and profane art.

Just as the Council of Trent's decisions were applied more strictly in the North than in the South, the effects of these decisions were more apparent in the works of Rubens than in those of any other contemporary artist. It is significant that, during the period from 1609 to 1615, in which he established his reputation as an ecclesiastical decorator, he produced almost as many secular as biblical pictures. There was no essential difference in the style of these two kinds of works, but the former were destined for private galleries and the latter for churches. The cue to this apparent contradiction between an ardent, if somewhat pompous, piety and the free expression of Renaissance sensuousness, must then be found in the reaction of the Church when faced by the attacks of the Reformers. Rome would not and could not renounce ecclesiastical decoration, which for centuries had contributed to the teaching and edification of the faithful. On the contrary, she went on employing the greatest artists of the period and surrounded church ceremonies with more brilliance and glamour than ever before. But, at the same time, she was constantly on her guard against adverse criticism and kept all ecclesiastical artistic activities under severe and almost austere control.

The Counter-Reformation had a positive as well as a negative aspect. It appeared in the late sixteenth and early seventeenth centuries in most of the Catholic countries of Europe, and it was nowhere more active and enthusiastic than at the Court of Archduke Albert and Archduchess Isabella, the Netherlands being considered as a kind of Catholic outpost wedged between Protestant countries. The study of this movement may not be as inspiring as, for instance, that of the Mendicant Orders in the thirteenth century, but it reveals similar motives: the introduction of a new moral and social discipline following the attacks of heretics, which in their turn had been provoked by abuses. The Franciscans and Dominicans had fought for more simplicity, austerity and missionary zeal in the thirteenth century, just as the Jesuits fought for greater earnestness, purity and Catholic propaganda in the seventeenth. The early movement had produced the frescoes of Giotto and his pupils, just as the later one produced the large canvases painted by Rubens and the assistants who crowded his studio.

* * *

Quite apart from any comparison between the personalities of St. Francis and St. Ignatius, the methods used by both religious orders and the works of art created under their inspiration, it cannot be denied that the seventeenth century revival was pursued with a disinterested fervour and an enthusiastic zeal which justify and explain its remarkable success. It is not enough to say that it served the interests of Spain and was fostered and encouraged by the local sovereigns. Such results cannot be achieved at the instigation of civil authorities. Within ten years of the occupation of Antwerp by Farnese, the town which had been for so long the centre of Calvinist activities was completely reconciled to the Church, and what was true of Antwerp was still more true of the rest of Belgium. This result was partly due to the pressure of public opinion and the threat of persecution, but far more to an intense propaganda carried on in the Sunday-schools to which the parents were persuaded to send their children. There was, no doubt, a certain amount of censorship of Reformist pamphlets and some rare instances of sentence of banishment on obdurate Calvinists, but the Spanish authorities had learnt their lesson, and persuasion had taken the place of persecution.

Inside the Church, reforms were carried out in a drastic manner. No cleric could follow any trade or profession apart from his ministry; he was forbidden to enter taverns or gaming-houses or to wear coloured clothes and jewels. Baptisms, marriages, burials and the administration of the sacraments were strictly regulated, and the churches, which had so long been used by certain people as meeting-places where loud conversation and even singing were to be heard, were now entirely devoted to prayer and worship.

This restoration of austerity was combined with outward manifestations of an almost Revivalist character. Under the rule of Archduke Albert and Archduchess Isabella, the Jesuits alone succeeded in building twenty-four churches. Practically all of these were designed by Jesuit Fathers and lay-brothers, in the characteristic baroque style of the period. The finest of them—that of St. Ignatius at Antwerp—was planned by François d'Aguilon and finished by Huyssens, with the help and advice of Rubens, who provided sketches for the altar and the vaults of the Lady-chapel and apse. The building was completed in 1621 and consecrated by the Bishop of Antwerp, Jean Maldeus. The ceremony was followed by popular festivities which lasted for a week. These rejoicings, however, were as nothing compared with those which, in the following year, succeeded the canonisation of St. Ignatius, founder of the Society of Jesus, and of St. Francis Xavier, its great missionary.

In the evening of the 23rd of July, the whole town was illuminated. To the sound of guns and the pealing of all the bells of Antwerp, a long procession went from the new church to the Cathedral, carrying busts of the two saints, made of silver and adorned with festoons of pearls and diamonds. When the procession came back from Notre-Dame, thirty barrels of pitch were set alight simultaneously and the tower of the new church appeared in the light of thousands of candles, while trumpets and flutes were heard from every window. A wooden structure labelled 'Envy's Citadel', which had been erected in the middle of the square, was set on fire by rockets while, as a grand finale, a set-piece revolving on itself exhibited the monogram of Christ and the words: '*Sancte Ignati, ora pro nobis*'.

The next day, a great cavalcade left the Cathedral after mass. It included the representatives of twenty-six trades and six armed corporations, as well as the pupils of the Jesuit schools and colleges. A large triumphal chariot, drawn by twelve plumed horses, represented the Triumph of St. Francis Xavier. This was preceded by several groups of neophytes in their national garb, led by guardian angels, and followed by the emperors and kings of the converted countries, who played the part of vanquished prisoners in a Roman triumph. A similar display surrounded the car reserved for St. Ignatius, which in its turn was escorted by thousands of members of the congregation, carrying tapers. Although the route was short, the procession took many hours to reach its goal, owing to twelve halts made in various parts of the town, at which special tableaux were represented, to the great delight of the crowd.

Thus the Jesuits not only succeeded in bringing back the immense majority of the Belgian people to the fold, but they stirred up among them a genuine religious enthusiasm. The situation prevailing in the sixteenth century, when Calvinist preachers penetrated to the Southern Netherlands, while the Church stood on the defensive and contented herself with repressive measures, was entirely altered, and Catholic missionaries began to venture at great risk into the territory of the United Provinces. The various religious orders, which increased in number and importance under the protection of the Archduke and his wife, were animated with a new evangelistic spirit. They were not imported from abroad, but recruited from the ranks of the Belgian people, and the gulf which had formerly separated the clergy from the rest of the nation was rapidly being obliterated. This was partly due, no doubt, to the severe reforms introduced among the clergy, but also to the fact that, since the separation of the Northern from the Southern Provinces, Catholic and national interests, instead of being opposed, now coincided.

Under the oppressive rule of Philip II, Spain had appeared as the common enemy, and Belgian Protestants and Catholics had endeavoured to bridge their differences in order to unite against foreign domination. Under the enlightened rule of Albert and Isabella, on the contrary, the main danger came from Holland, whose armies had for years ravaged the countryside and whose fleet continued to hold the mouth of the Scheldt, even after the conclusion of the Twelve Years' Truce, thus ruining the trade of Antwerp. It had become increasingly difficult to remain at the same time a Calvinist and a good patriot, so that a number of Reformers, whom the Jesuits might otherwise have failed to bring back to the Church, were reconciled to Catholicism for political rather than religious reasons.

It is sometimes argued that the realistic character of Rubens' religious art is to be attributed to a degenerate faith. Such a statement scarcely tallies with the facts. Although the master was reluctant to expound his beliefs, we know from his correspondence and from the records of his daily life that he was a devout Catholic, who attended mass every day and took his religion most seriously. But his was not an isolated case, and a similar religious zeal pervaded the whole nation. The Counter-Reformation was anything but degenerate. It may appear to have been somewhat gaudy, or even blatant, but it was essentially vigorous and vital. It yearned for spectacular effects and sensational results, and its voice resounds almost like the trumpet-call of a seventeenth-century Salvation Army. Instead of exaggerating these tendencies, Rubens endeavoured to curb them with the discipline of his scholarship and classicism. It is often said that he was frequently carried away by his temperament, but the more one studies the period in which he lived, the more one feels that such excesses must be attributed rather to the spirit of his time than to his own individual character.

*　　*　　*

Helped, no doubt, by the position held by his father-in-law, who was, as well as Philip Rubens, Secretary of Antwerp, and possibly by his personal acquaintance with Nicholas Rockox, burgomaster of the town, Rubens obtained an important commission from the municipality, to decorate a large wall measuring 16 feet by 11 feet 4 inches, and occupying a prominent position in the Town Hall. This was no 'little curiosity', and the thirty-two-year-old artist seized his opportunity and threw himself heart and soul into this new undertaking. The most casual comparison between the 'Adoration of the Kings' and the 'St. Gregory' painted in the previous year for the Chiesa Nuova shows the transformation undergone by the artist's genius, under home influences.

The first impression is that of a rich confusion. In spite of its size, the picture is overcrowded and the attention is dis-

tracted by the wealth of detail.[1] It is as if the painter had wished to bring all races, ages and classes of mankind round the infant Child: the old kings and their young pages, and the chubby angels in the clouds; the black-skinned, the white-skinned and the yellow-skinned; the great kings draped in their brocades, and the naked slaves bending under the weight of their burdens. Animal-kind too is represented by a large group of horses, mules and camels. There are too many lights: one radiating from the Child, in the foreground on the left, another from the sky, in the background, others again from burning torches flickering against the dark clouds on the right. The muscular efforts of the slaves, unloading presents and bringing them to the Holy Family, are over-emphasised. There is a profusion of turbans, armour and feathers. Like all Belgians, Rubens was evidently particularly fond of pageantry, and he arranged his 'tableau', not so much in the manner of an artist who wishes to create an eternal work, as in that of a 'master of ceremonies', stage-managing a great procession.

But for all that, we find ourselves for the first time before a picture which is unmistakably a 'Rubens', and which is intimately connected with the master's finest productions. The work stands out, among all the great paintings of that period, as an arresting and original creation. It is full—almost too full—of vigour, rich—almost too rich—in colour and contrasts of light and shade; but there is a certain order in this confusion, and the eye comes to rest on the imposing figure of the old king, in the centre, who knits the whole composition together and connects the dark group on the right with the bright group on the left.

[1] See pl. 10, p. 101.

The friendship of a rich bourgeois, Cornelius van der Geest, master of the Mercers' Guild, was also responsible for the production, in the following year, of the 'Erection of the Cross' (now in the Cathedral), which was painted originally for the Church of St. Walburga. This wealthy citizen was the owner of one of the finest picture-galleries in Antwerp; he contributed generously to the funds collected for the erection and decoration of the high altar of St. Walburga, and introduced Rubens to the parish priest and churchwardens. We are told that the signing of the contract took place in a hostelry, and was celebrated by libations to the tune of nine florins ten sous, while the artist himself was promised a sum of 2600 florins on completion of the work. This was to be a triptych of a new kind. Instead of being formed by the juxta-position of three separate pictures, it was really to be only one picture, divided into three sections: on the left, St. John and the Virgin and a group of weeping women; on the right, the centurion on horseback issuing his orders; and, in the centre, a group of men striving to raise the Cross to which Christ is fastened.

That these three pictures were conceived as a whole is sufficiently proved by the various sketches still in existence,[1] which show the gradual development of the master's conception, the origin of which is to be found in one of the panels of the triptych painted for Santa Croce eight years before. The diagonal position of the Cross, which is being raised with the help of a rope, is already shown in this early work, which, however, lacks all the qualities of power and imagination that characterise Rubens' later creation.

There is far more unity of composition in the 'Erection of

[1]See pl. 11, p. 108.

the Cross' than in the 'Adoration of the Kings', but over-emphasis is at first perhaps still more apparent. If we try, however, to understand the master's conception of Christian art, this over-emphasis is not entirely unjustified. We may have a certain difficulty in believing that the weight of the presents brought by the Magi to the Child-Christ was enough to bend the backs of their slaves, but we have no difficulty in imagining that the raising of such a Cross should necessitate the combined efforts of a gang of powerful executioners. It may appear strange that the tragedy is expressed rather in muscular than in spiritual values, but this is the natural consequence of Rubens' realistic methods, which led him to transform the classical conceptions of Italian art into a series of human epics. A similar picture from the brush of Raphael would have been more graceful, and Michaelangelo would have avoided certain contorted attitudes and have adopted a more majestic outline; but, though Rubens remained throughout deeply influenced by Italian classicism, he was prompted to go a step further towards a purely naturalistic expression of the Gospel story. For him, Christ was not only God made Man, but Man raised to the dignity of God. He painted Him under the features of a powerful hero, by no means ascetic, Who might have been perfectly well able to defend Himself against His persecutors without calling upon the hosts of heaven, but Who had preferred to die the most ignominious of deaths for the salvation of mankind. There is no hint of sentimentality in the eyes raised to heaven, and the whole figure is expressive of the sacrifice, not only of life but of something greater: the joy of fighting for life. We may not agree with such a conception, but we must recognise that, from a purely religious point of view, it is more edifying than the graceful creations of the late Italian Renaissance. It may not express the divinity of the Saviour, but it expresses at least His healthy and vigorous humanity, and frees us from the conventional type of the bearded sentimental Apollo, favoured by seventeenth-century Italian art and which has had such a disastrous influence on modern religious imagery.

Rubens' methods are very much the same in all the branches of his art. When we speak of his realism, or rather of his realistic tendencies, we do not mean that he had entirely forgotten his pre-Italian and Italian education or that he devoted himself in his most characteristic works to a close portrayal of life, dwelling particularly on the individualistic or unsightly features of his models. Jordaens perhaps goes farther in that direction, and there is no doubt at all that Rembrandt does. But, while Rembrandt's methods are eminently suited to etchings and small pictures, they could not possibly be applied to a decorative scheme. What we mean is that Rubens discarded convention as far as it could be discarded in his days and for his purpose, and carried realism as far as it could be carried on a large scale, thus succeeding in founding a new style and giving a fresh lease of life to decorative art, at a time when it seemed condemned to irremediable decay, and when the attention of artists was turned more and more towards portraits, landscapes or genre scenes.

Just as he had infused another spirit into the conception of the 'putto' and the Madonna, by imagining them under the features of Clara, Albert, Nicholas and Isabella, so he renewed the type and the story of Christ by insisting on its heroic and human aspects. Fra Angelico in Italy, and Van der Weyden in Flanders, had been able to suggest, two centuries earlier, the supernatural character of the Crucified Saviour. Now that their mystic vision appeared to be lost, it was left to Rubens to assert at least the natural aspect of the incarnation. In so doing, he was bound to insist on the material rather than the spiritual features of the drama; but he remained, nevertheless, the sincere interpreter of a great and popular religious movement and, as such, may be considered as one of the greatest religious painters the world has known.

In order to take the true measure of his greatness, it is necessary to compare the overwhelming display of energy in the 'Erection of the Cross' with the disciplined restraint of the 'Descent from the Cross', which was painted between 1611 and 1614 for the Chapel of the Guild of Arquebusiers, in the Cathedral.

The tradition of three separate pictures on the same theme forming the triptych—namely, the 'Visitation', the 'Descent from the Cross', and the 'Presentation in the Temple'—was this time preserved. Instead of devoting the work to St. Christopher, patron of the Guild, Rubens contented himself with depicting the saint on the outside of the shutter, while, in the main pictures, he showed episodes concerned with the bearing and carrying of Christ.

Italian classicism and Flemish realism combine to give to the central panel a vigorous harmony. There is, doubtless, the same insistence on physical effort as in the 'Erection of the Cross', but this display of muscular energy is tempered by the restful attitudes of St. John and the holy women supporting the body, while the realistic contrast between the flesh and the white sheet is so delicately indicated that, instead of giving the composition what might have been a sordid and sensational aspect, it becomes a source of pure spiritual beauty. In insisting on this particular feature of the famous work, Sir Joshua Reynolds remarks that the idea of such a contrast was not likely to enter the mind of any Italian painter, and that only a great colourist could achieve it successfully. If we did not know from external evidence the date of the triptych, this feature alone would suffice to place it after Rubens' return to Antwerp, when the master had been for some time in close contact with his native land and had become the interpreter of the religious ideals of his fellow-countrymen.

Reynolds' comments on the 'Descent from the Cross' must retain our attention, for the great English master's appreciation shows the difficulties with which any critic trained in the worship of the Italian Renaissance is necessarily confronted in dealing with Rubens' art. While praising the noble expression of Christ's face in the 'Erection', and declaring that His figure in the 'Descent' is 'one of the finest ever invented', he strongly objects to 'the smooth fat face' of Joseph of Arimathea in the latter picture, and indeed to the whole appearance of this 'very unhistorical character'. In his general remarks on the master's work, he is equally outspoken regarding the drapery, which 'is not properly historical' for 'the quality of the stuff of which it is composed is too accurately distinguished'. He adds that Rubens 'never possessed a poetical conception of character'; and that 'in his representation of the highest characters in the Christian or the fabulous world, instead of something above humanity, . . . the spectator finds little more than mere mortals such as he meets with every day'.

There is an apparent contradiction between this strange mixture of blame and praise, but such contradiction is only apparent. Whenever the master is more classical then realistic in his interpretation, as in the figures of Christ mentioned above, his art receives the appreciation it deserves; whenever, on the contrary, he is more realistic than academic—or shall we say more Flemish than Italian?—he is accused of vulgarity and his characters or his draperies appear 'unhistorical'.

It might be remarked that, if the best way for a drapery to seem 'historical' is to conceal the stuff of which it is composed, the best means for a character to achieve the same quality is to lose all individualistic features and to conform to some conventional type. But criticism from such sources deserves more sympathetic attention. The fact is that, in spite of their popularity, Rubens' great creations remain very puzzling to the expert. If they are to be judged from the classical point of view, the realistic features must give offence; if from a realistic point of view—like a work by Breughel or Rembrandt, for instance—their classical features will appear out of place. We are led naturally to classify the works we study according to certain standards, and we have some difficulty in adopting two different standards for the same work or the same artist. The whole Rubens problem may be summed up in one question: Has the painter succeeded in creating unity out of such variety and in blending into one harmonious whole the classical conception he develops in his design and the realistic features he introduces into it? In other words, if we turn to the 'Descent from the Cross', do Joseph of Arimathea's 'smooth fat face' and the texture of the white sheet spoil the general effect of the composition, or enhance it? Are they obtrusive external elements, or do they find their appropriate place in the whole?

Reynolds seems to have been very near the truth when, discoursing on the special quality of Rubens' colouring, he explains that, thanks to it, the master is able to obtain effects which would thwart the efforts of any other. 'It is here', he writes, 'as in personal attractions; *there is frequently found a certain agreement and correspondence in the whole together which is often more captivating than mere regular beauty*'.

There is, in the Wallace Collection, a 'Holy Family', painted about the same time as the 'Descent from the Cross', which illustrates admirably Reynolds' remarks. Seen in a black-and-white reproduction, the picture is frankly disappointing, especially as regards the Madonna, who is of the Isabella type, with a particularly shallow expression, and the Child-Christ, a dark-haired heavy baby with a lowering brow. Seen in the gallery, in a good light, the picture appears to be a pure poem of colour. The Infant Christ, wearing a red coral necklace, and His Mother's smiling face are illumined by the reflection of the Madonna's red dress, while St. Elizabeth's grey cloak and the pale sallow complexion of St. John are still more emphasised by the fawn-coloured fur on which the latter is sitting. To these main contrasts must be added a series of secondary oppositions, such as that of the delicately modelled pink feet of the Child-Christ against the brilliant blue cloak of His Mother, and of the ivory hand of Elizabeth against the paler thigh of John. In a reproduction, it is the group on the right—formed by Elizabeth and the child resting against her, in a relaxed attitude—which immediately attracts the attention, while in the picture itself the miracle of colouring throws into relief the Virgin and Child. It seems almost as if the master had purposely given more interesting features to the characters he intended to paint in quiet tones, in order to preserve the balance of the composi-

11. Sketch for the ERECTION OF THE CROSS

Louvre, Paris.   *Photo, Bulloz, Paris*

tion. This is no doubt what Reynolds meant by the 'agreement and correspondence in the whole together', and Rubens' art depends on this agreement perhaps more than that of any other great painter.

* * *

The first result of Rubens' early successes was to attract the attention of art patrons in all parts of Europe and to bring to his studio many collaborators and young students, eager to work under his direction and to help him to execute the ever-increasing number of commissions which he received from all sides. It was a time when the new religious fervour stirred up by the Counter-Reformation was beginning to bear fruit. Princes, nobles and rich merchants vied with one another in eagerness to decorate the churches. There were not enough painters, sculptors and wood-carvers to satisfy the increasing demand for pictures, statues, monumental altars and other embellishments. Rubens received a great number of these commissions and organised his studio, dividing most of the work between his collaborators, and designing numberless pictures of the most varied size and character.

Apart from the small Madonnas to which reference has already been made, the master's religious works can roughly be divided into two categories: large panels (often triptychs) or single canvases for the decoration of high altars or the altars of important side-chapels, and pictures of medium size (usually half-length figures) painted either for memorials or for private chapels.

The second class includes a fairly wide range of subjects, mostly incidents from the New Testament, such as the 'Resurrection' (Antwerp Cathedral), 'Jesus and Nicodemus'

(Brussels), 'Christ and Repentant Sinners' (Munich), the 'Tribute Money' (Berlin), the 'Woman taken in Adultery' (Brussels), 'Feed My Lambs' (London), a number of 'Pietàs', the best known of which is perhaps the monument to Jan Michielsen in Antwerp, 'The Incredulity of St. Thomas' (Antwerp), for the Rockox memorial, and many others. Most of these half-length pictures were painted at the same time as, or even before, the 'Descent from the Cross', and, though designed by Rubens, are seldom entirely by his hand.

The first category is far more important, but it comprises a relatively small range of subjects. This is partly due to the fact that, after the striking success of such works as the 'Adoration of the Kings' and the 'Descent from the Cross', the master received a great number of orders for works dealing with the same episodes of Christ's life. It seems as if most of the principal churches had wanted pictures by Rubens, but pictures similar to those which had acquired such extraordinary fame. The painter had no sooner finished an important decorative work, than he was compelled to design a number of replicas in order to satisfy his patrons.

This is not so apparent nowadays, because many of such works have been removed from the altars for which they were designed and stored in museums. Nor did the Spaniards, the Austrians and the French fail to make use of their opportunities while occupying Belgium, in the seventeenth and eighteenth centuries, to add a number of Rubens to their own collections. Other pictures came on to the market in the regular manner, and found their way to England, Germany, Italy, and as far as Russia, not to speak of recent exports to the United States.

If, however, we ignore these later developments and make

a cursory survey of the churches for which Rubens painted his principal religious pictures, we find that they are widely distributed in the Southern Netherlands, including Artois, in Germany, Spain, Italy and Bohemia. Antwerp, of course, is the most strongly represented, having many altar-pieces scattered over the Cathedral, the Carmelite, the Jesuit, the Récollets and the Capuchin churches, and those of St. Michael and St. Jacques. Then comes Brussels, with the church of La Chapelle, the Carmelite and Récollets churches, the church of the Annunciation and the church of St. Jacques. Malines follows, with the Cathedral, the church of St. John and Notre-Dame de la Dyle; Ghent with St. Bavon; Alost with St. Martin and, in the Walloon districts, Tournai, Valenciennes and Lille. Several altar-pieces went to Cologne and Neuburg in Germany, and an important triptych to the church of St. Thomas at Prague, while Rubens' old patrons applied to him from Genoa and many other orders came from Madrid.

This survey is far from complete, but it may at least give some idea of the intense revival of religious art which roused the Southern Netherlands in the seventeenth century. Every year, several Jesuit churches were consecrated in the presence of the Archduke or his representative and, thanks to the zeal and generosity of the sovereigns, the rich bourgeois and the corporations, many more altars were unveiled. The baroque in architecture, sculpture and painting, triumphed throughout the land and, whenever religious fervour showed signs of flagging, local pride led to further donations and ceremonies. The sight of these great works stirred public devotion and public devotion clamoured for more great works. Never, since the golden days of the Dukes of Burgundy and the Brothers Van Eyck, had such enthusiasm been witnessed in the Netherlands.

* * *

The strict rule formulated by the Council of Trent and enforced by the ecclesiastical authorities in the stern spirit of the Counter-Reformation, contributed also to reduce the variety of suitable subjects. Rubens, for instance, deals only quite exceptionally with those episodes in the lives of saints which were so frequently treated by the early masters, or with any story which might be considered apocryphal. He painted several representations of 'Perseus and Andromeda', but only one 'St. George slaying the Dragon', an early work now in the Prado. The 'Education of the Virgin' (1630-33), executed for the chapel of St. Anne in the Carmelite Church at Antwerp (now in the Museum), stands almost alone in depicting an incident in the early life of the Virgin; and in the 'Erection of the Cross' the Madonna is painted in the steadfast orthodox attitude, as opposed to the dejected appearance of the other women. We find, on the other hand, a large number of Adorations of the Kings and Shepherds, Crucifixions, Descents from the Cross, Holy Conversations of Saints surrounding the Madonna, Assumptions of the Virgin, and pictures relating to the miracles performed by certain saints, and the martyrdoms they suffered. The choice of the latter is also significant. It is only occasionally that we meet among them the most popular figures of the *Golden Legend*. The giant Christopher is relegated, as we have seen, to an inconspicuous place on the great triptych of the Arquebusiers; St. Ursula only appears in a small sketch now in Brussels, and St. Sebastian in an early picture now in Berlin. Most of the other saints are either well authenticated by their connection

12. THE FALL OF THE DAMNED [1618–1620]

Pinakothek, Munich

Photo, Franz Hanfstaengl, Munich

with the Gospels, such as St. Peter, St. Paul, the two St. Johns, St. Thomas, St. Andrew, St. Mary Magdalene; or the founders of religious orders, such as St. Augustine, St. Theresa, St. Francis, St. Ignatius, St. Benedict; or saints closely connected with local tradition, such as St. Roch, St. Bavon, St. Liévin, and other more obscure heroes of Christendom whose deeds were not likely to be subjected to adverse criticism.[1]

It seems, therefore, as if Rubens had done his best to conform to the dictates of Molanus and to adapt church decoration to the spirit of the Counter-Reformation. In spite of this, he experienced certain difficulties with some Church dignitaries who no doubt found his style of painting too bold or too picturesque. We know, for instance, that the canons of Antwerp Cathedral objected to the nude figure of St. Christopher, on the outside of the triptych of the Arquebusiers, and agreed to send delegates to the bishop to formulate their protest on the eve of the unveiling. The sequel to the story is unfortunately left unrecorded.

Another incident which provoked the painter's anger occurred in the same year. As early as 1612, he had made a finished sketch of a picture destined for the high altar of the Ghent Cathedral, depicting in two scenes the conversion of the Church's patron-saint, St. Bavon: below, the Saint distributing his wealth among the poor, and above, his entrance into a monastery. This sketch (now in the National Gallery) had been approved by Mgr. Maes and the Chapter, and the

[1] It is worthy of note that the master designed the frontispieces for several works by his friend, the historian Rosweydus, who conceived the original plan of the well-known collection of the lives of the Saints, the *Acta Sanctorum*, begun by Jan Bollandus in Rubens' time and continued to the present day.

artist had further been commissioned to design the marble altar above which the picture was to be hung. After Mgr. Maes' death, however, his successor—who did not approve of Rubens' vigorous style—refused to confirm the commission. Peter-Paul wrote to Archduke Albert a strong letter of protest, dated March 19, 1614, in which, after telling him of these difficulties and of the 'most preposterous high altar without pictures of any kind', which the new bishop proposed to erect, he added:

'Moreover, which is most important to tell you, his Lordship the Bishop has resolved to expend upon this object the same sum that his predecessor had agreed to pay, so that, seeing so fine an undertaking go to nothing, I am filled with the deepest regret, not on account of my personal interest, which matters little, but on account of the great loss the town will suffer, . . . unless Your Highness should resolve to inform the Bishop of Ghent that Your Highness has seen my design, that you consider it good, and that his Reverend Lordship would do well to keep to it. . . . I assure Your Highness that I have no thought of the profit which would accrue to me from this work (for at the moment I am busier with important orders than ever before), but I may say, in all Christian conscience, that this design for Ghent is the fairest thing I have ever conceived in my life. . . .'

In spite of the Archduke's intervention, Rubens had to wait another ten years until a more sympathetic bishop came to the see of Ghent, before being able to carry out his scheme; and a comparison between the finished St. Bavon picture and the highly imaginative sketch devised by the master, shows that the latter had to water his wine a good deal before getting the work accepted.

Rubens found himself in a far more congenial atmosphere among the Jesuit fathers, who had begun to build at Antwerp a new church, in the baroque style, dedicated to their founder St. Ignatius. They had secured the painter's advice and help for the design of certain parts of the building, and, as soon as it neared completion, they asked him to undertake its decoration. This unique example of baroque style was, unhappily, wrecked by fire in 1718; but we may get some idea of its general aspect from pictures of the interior of the church painted by contemporary artists before its destruction. The great building, which was supposed to rival in size and luxury the church of the Gesù in Rome, had a long nave leading to the high altar and two aisles, with galleries above them. The floor was of black-and-white marble; marble columns supported the vault and the galleries, and the high altar was enriched by coloured marble columns, sculptures and precious ornaments. The treasures accumulated in the church were so valuable that they had to be guarded night and day, the night watch being kept by four lay-brothers posted in various parts of the building and provided with muskets and bells, that they might defend themselves and call for help at the same time.

The directors of the 'maison professe' were so keen to secure Rubens' services that they signed the contract in March 1620, several months before the building was finished. The master undertook to deliver by the end of the year thirty-nine pictures for the decoration of the ceiling of the aisles and galleries, as well as two large pictures, representing the 'Miracles of St. Ignatius' and of 'St. Francis Xavier', which were to be hung alternately above the high altar. It was stipulated that Rubens should make all the sketches himself and either give them to the church, or paint another picture for the Lady-Chapel. He was evidently so pleased with these sketches that he preferred to keep them, and accordingly designed the 'Assumption of the Virgin', now in Vienna. To complete the scheme, the master's munificent friend Rockox commissioned a fourth altar-picture for the chapel of St. Joseph. This was the 'Return from Egypt', now in the United States.

Both in the altar-pictures which have been preserved in Vienna, and in the ceiling decorations, of which we can obtain a fair idea from the sketches at Gotha, Paris, Dulwich, Vienna, Brussels and Düsseldorf, Rubens found ample scope for his love of pomp and display and for his uncanny technique in foreshortening. The great paintings dealing with the 'Miracles of St. Ignatius' and 'St. Francis Xavier' measure almost 18 ft. by 13 ft. The former scene is staged inside a huge Renaissance basilica, the latter outside some curious pagan temple supported by baroque columns. Of all Ignatius' miracles, the painter has of course chosen the most sensational: the curing of people possessed with devils, while behind St. Francis Xavier preaching to an amazed crowd, the enthroned Virgin surrounded by radiant angels appears amid the clouds.

Such works are the faithful expression of the revivalist spirit displayed in the pageants which accompanied the consecration of the church and celebrated the canonisation of the two saints. They may very well have been inspired by the tableaux shown in the historical procession already described. Most of the sketches, such as 'The Prophet Elias carried up to Heaven', 'The Coronation of the Virgin', 'The Ascension', and 'The Fall of the Rebel Angels', are equally bold in conception and design. The whole scheme must have meant to

Rubens the realisation of the dreams he had conceived while admiring Giulio Romano's decorations in Mantua. It required all the master's virtuosity thus to transform the Italian classical methods of decoration and adapt them to the realistic spirit of Flanders.

It appears as if Rubens had reached the limit of his exuberance and imaginative power in the decoration of St. Ignatius, and, if we compare these pictures with the admirable portraits which he painted at the same time, we realise that few masters have ever excelled in works so utterly different and combined qualities apparently so much opposed to each other. There were, however, limits to his genius, as there are to every human genius, and these limits must have been apparent even to him when he attempted to deal with certain subjects, such as apocalyptic visions, in which his realistic trend of mind cramped his imagination.

Ever since his visit to the Sistine Chapel, he must have cherished the ambition of creating some work similar to Michaelangelo's 'Last Judgment'. According to his usual methods, he may very well have made sketches at the time, though there is no evidence that he used them later. He must have felt that this was a subject not only worthy of his power, but for which he was remarkably well equipped by his knowledge of anatomy and his skill in translating swift and violent movement. It is therefore quite natural that he should have endeavoured to realise this dream when, in 1615-16, the Duke Wolfgang of Neuburg commissioned him to decorate the Jesuit Church of that town. The result was a huge picture measuring 19 feet by 14 feet, in which the master was able to display his technical skill, but in which the almost life-size figures in the foreground are far too prominent not to disturb the mysterious atmosphere of an apocalyptic vision. While conforming to the main theme adopted by Michaelangelo—that is to say, a group of nude bodies falling to Hell on the right, while another group ascends to Heaven on the left—Rubens brings his whole composition so closely together that the result is heavy and almost oppressive.

Another picture painted for the Duke of Neuburg, a few years later, is scarcely more convincing. The master mentions it in a letter dated October 11, 1619. It was intended for the altar of St. Michael, and represents the Archangel casting the rebel angels from Heaven. Rubens insists on the difficulty of the subject, adding that 'he doubts whether he will be able to find among his pupils anyone capable of painting it, even from a sketch by him'. The composition is evidently suggested by a well-known picture by the sixteenth-century Italianist Frans Floris. Apart from copies which Rubens made for the sake of testing his skill, it is perhaps the only evident example of Flemish-Italianist influence to be found among the works belonging to his mature period. It is significant that he should have thought of this early picture at a time of difficulty, when dealing with a theme which was uncongenial to him. It is still more significant that his own design should reveal the same defects of heaviness and lack of atmosphere so noticeable in Floris' painting.

Besides the 'Great Last Judgment', originally painted for Neuburg, there is in the Munich Pinakothek another work which, for a long time, was considered to be a reduced replica of the former. It is a rectangular panel (55 in. by 47 in.), surmounted by a semicircle faintly showing Christ and the Blessed, while the group of the damned, pouring downward

like a cascade of entangled bodies, is given far greater pro-
minence. It has been suggested that this 'Small Last Judgment' was originally a rectangular painting by Rubens, dealing with the Fall of the Damned, or of the Rebel Angels, and
was transformed by his pupil Boeckhorst into a Last Judgment, the semicircular part at the top of the picture being
added at a later period.

There is, also in Munich, another *Hoellensturz*, as the Ger-
mans call it, including an even larger number of smaller
figures and still farther removed from the original conception of the great decorative canvas painted for Neuburg.
Here, the figure of Christ, and those of the Blessed, disappear
altogether, and Rubens creates an awe-inspiring design,
sufficiently remote from the observer to suggest enormous
heights and abysmal depths.[1] The same remark applies to two
paintings on a smaller scale and displaying, if possible, an
even greater imaginative exuberance. The first, now at
Erlangen, represents the 'Ascension of the Blessed', and the
other, at Aix-la-Chapelle, is a replica of the 'Hoellensturz' at
Munich. It seems likely that the 'Ascension of the Blessed' is
an original sketch by Rubens—perhaps for the picture which
he intended to paint for the Duke of Buckingham—somewhat modified and enlarged by Boeckhorst.

There is no doubt that the master attached great importance to the subject, and the drawings preserved in the British
Museum, the National Gallery, and the Albertina, and which
refer generally to the Munich 'Hoellensturz', show clearly
enough that he was haunted with the idea of creating some
definite image of the Apocalyptic Vision. Confronted with
this array of sketches and pictures, the uninitiated might be

[1]See pl. 12, p. 113.

inclined to ascribe them all to a period before 1616, the year in which the 'Great Last Judgment' was completed. They would naturally think that the sketches, dealing separately with the 'Ascension of the Blessed' and the 'Fall of the Damned', and the 'Small Last Judgment', in which both themes are imperfectly combined, are mere experiments prior to the creation of the definite work in Neuburg. If they were at all acquainted with Rubens' methods, they would know that the master usually proceeded in this manner and that the number of preparatory sketches is generally in proportion to the importance he attached to his design. It is true that, when once an important work was completed, a number of replicas were usually prepared in the studio, in order to satisfy the public demand, but these replicas were more often than not on the same scale as the original, and Rubens admitted quite frankly that they had neither the same artistic quality nor the same material value. We seem, therefore, at first sight to be faced with a set of highly imaginative sketches showing, in spite of later alterations and additions, a visionary power almost unique, not only in Rubens' productions, but in Renaissance art—leading up to a work of large size, the 'Great Last Judgment', in which the model becomes more and more obtrusive and realism asserts itself to such an extent that all illusion is destroyed.

If, however, we are to believe the conclusions of modern criticism, the smaller apocalyptic pictures, instead of preceding it, followed the 'Great Last Judgment' and were designed between 1615 and 1620. There are strong arguments in favour of this opinion, one of them being that, in his correspondence with Sir Dudley Carleton, Rubens mentions, on April 28, 1618, a small replica (149 in. by 103 in.) of the

'Last Judgment' painted for the Duke of Neuburg. This replica has been lost, but the fact remains that the master and
his pupils dealt with the subject, on a smaller scale, after 1616.
Instead, therefore, of concluding that a series of sketches led
to a disappointing result, we may be nearer the mark in saying that Rubens himself, if not positively displeased with his
large picture, endeavoured nevertheless to give the theme
a different treatment after its completion, and that he succeeded only when he depicted a crowd of thousands of small
figures moving through the clouds of his dream and night-
mare, and not real men and women whose size cramped his
imagination.

Michaelangelo, steeped as he was in classicism, could ideal-
ise a full-size figure, which appeared to him more as a carved
statue than a man; whereas Rubens could only translate his
vision by withdrawing himself far away from it and by looking at it from a distance.

In his admirable description of Rubens' personality, Fromentin writes that the master's lack of self-criticism allowed
him to proceed with his task without ever being discouraged
by his failures or carried away by his successes. The study of the
apocalyptic pictures seems to suggest that, in this case at least,
he must, perhaps unconsciously, have realised his limitations
and been spurred to new efforts by the feeling that he had not
entirely overcome the difficulties with which he was faced.

It is impossible to examine attentively Rubens' treatment
of the Fall of the Rebel Angels without thinking of the description given by Milton at the end of the Sixth Book of
Paradise Lost:

> Hell heard th' unsufferable noise, Hell saw
> Heav'n ruining from Heav'n, and would have fled

Affrighted; but strict Fate had cast too deep
Her dark foundations, and too fast had bound.
Nine dayes they fell; confounded Chaos roard,
And felt tenfold confusion in thir fall
Through his wilde Anarchie, so huge a rout
Incumberd him with ruin; Hell at last
Yawning receavd them whole, and on them clos'd,
Hell thir fit habitation fraught with fire
Unquenchable, the house of woe and paine.

The similarity between these lines and Rubens' creations may be a coincidence, though this coincidence appears still more striking if we remember that in the same passage the vanquished host is compared to a 'herd of goats or timerous flock, together throngd', and that when, according to Milton, the wall of Heaven opened to disclose the abyss, this monstrous sight

Strook them with horror backward, but far worse
Urg'd them behind; headlong themselves they threw
Down from the verge of Heav'n, Eternal wrauth
Burnt after them to the bottomless pit.

The suggestion that, if Milton did not see the Flemish master's original work before the days of his blindness, he might very well have seen some of the engravings which were widely spread throughout Europe during the seventeenth century, is no doubt interesting, but the similitude between the paintings and the poetry is not so close as to justify it. What seems far more enlightening is the fact that the 'master of the commonplace' (as Rubens has been called), who is supposed by so many to have grasped only the external aspect of life, should have been impressed by such imaginary scenes in the same manner as the great English religious dreamer, whose mind was so intensely introspective. That the works of the blind Puritan poet and those of the keen-sighted Catholic painter should have anything in common is in itself a wonderful testimony to the universal character of true genius. Just as it is impossible to grasp the wide range of Milton's poetry unless we dwell on his sensitive and acute perception of natural beauty, sound and colour, so it is impossible to appreciate the strength of Rubens' personality unless we remember that this great painter succedeed not only in expressing the religious spirit of the Counter-Reformation, but even, in a few striking instances, the purely imaginative visions which are looked upon as the exclusive privilege of the mystics, and in forcing open a door which, according to all plausible beliefs, ought for ever to have remained shut against him.

CHAPTER V

RUBENS' WORKSHOP

THE EXTRAORDINARY reputation acquired by Rubens within two years of his return to Antwerp had an important and not always favourable influence on his works, or at least on those which bear his name and which modern critics have begun to classify, in order to discriminate between the hand of the master and that of the student. This is not always an easy task, since, of the three thousand pictures which are said to hail from the studio, a large majority are the result of collaboration, Rubens having in most cases provided the sketches and touched up the paintings before their final delivery.

The visit paid to the master by Otto Sperling has already been mentioned. The Danish doctor was evidently much impressed by the great man's activity and declares, no doubt with some exaggeration, that the latter talked to him while working and managed at the same time to dictate a letter 'as if to give proof of his powerful faculties'. Sperling's party was conducted round the house by a servant, and shown the Greek and Roman statues:

'We also saw a vast room without windows, lighted by a

large opening in the middle of the ceiling. A number of young painters were gathered there, each engaged on a different work, for which Monsieur Rubens had given him a pencil drawing touched with colour here and there. These young people had to carry out these pictures in paint, after which Monsieur Rubens will finish them off.'

The number of those who wished to work under the master's guidance was so large that, as early as the spring of 1611, he was obliged to refuse the application of a young man who had been recommended to him by his friend, the well-known engraver Jacques de Bie. In a letter addressed to the latter, Rubens says that he is unable to grant his request, explaining that he has already rejected over a hundred candidates, some of whom were members of his own family and of his wife's, while a protégé of Rockox was working in another studio until a vacancy occurred.

The master found himself, at the age of thirty-three, in the full strength of his body and mind, placed between a great number of patrons who were constantly ordering, urging, and begging him to paint more and more pictures of all kinds, altar-pieces, hunting scenes, battle scenes, allegories, pagan subjects and portraits—and a great number of artists and students who were only too eager to help him to fulfil these commissions and to carry out his instructions. He did not hesitate to avail himself of the proffered help, partly because it was the only means of satisfying his clients, some of whom he could not afford to disappoint, but also because the direction of a large studio had long been an established tradition both in Flanders and in Italy.

As early as the fifteenth century, master-painters had had students to help them, but these were more in the position of apprentices, that is to say they learned their trade while at the same time helping their master in the shop and the house. As soon as a student had finished his masterpiece, he was received into the Guild of St. Luke, after which he started on his own and no longer subordinated his personality to that of his teacher.

The Middle Ages never knew the large groups of artists who crowded Raphael's 'bottega' and Rubens' 'workshop'. The minute nature of fifteenth-century technique did not allow of such vast associations, for the originality of the work lay quite as much in its execution as in its conception. The distinction established in the sixteenth century between the sketch or cartoon and the finished painting was a new development.

Antwerp had known important studios before Rubens' time. We learn, for instance, that Frans Floris had a great many pupils, and that he himself used to prepare sketches of heads which he ordered his assistants to use in their compositions. This new method, which was the natural consequence of the increased size of pictures and of the substitution of bold brushwork for the painstaking technique of the miniaturist, modified people's ideas concerning artistic originality. For a picture to be considered as a great master's work, it was enough that it should have been painted in his studio.

Compared with his contemporaries and his famous Italian predecessors, Rubens seems to have been particularly careful to discriminate between school work and original work. His correspondence with Sir Dudley Carleton is enlightening on this point. Carleton combined diplomacy with scholarship and the hobby of collecting. He had been English Ambassador to Venice, and had recently been transferred to The Hague. Through the agency of Toby Matthew, son of the Archbishop of York, he had already purchased in Belgium a certain number of contemporary Flemish pictures, but could not well afford Rubens' prices. Hunting scenes had just come into fashion, and Carleton was bent on purchasing a 'Fox and Wolf Hunt', measuring 18 feet by 11 feet, for which the artist asked eighty pounds. Toby Matthew could only offer a diamond necklace belonging to Carleton's wife, who seems to have shared her husband's hobby, and which was valued at fifty pounds. In spite of pressing requests that he should reduce his price, Rubens remained adamant, and finally sold the picture to the Duke of Aerschot.

In a message dated 30th of December, 1616, from Louvain, Toby Matthew reveals to Carleton the fact that Rubens, 'for the gusto which he takes in that peece of huntinge', is making another picture of it, much smaller in size: 'This later picture, if you like to have for your chaine, you may; and he undertakes to make it of as much perfection as the other, if not more.'

Carleton evidently hesitated to clinch the bargain, as he thought that the second picture might have been painted by Snyders. The arguments used by Matthew to reassure him may be criticised by the expert, but they prove at any rate how far higher Rubens' name stood than those of his best known collaborators:

'In this Peece the beasts are all alive and in act eyther of escape or of resistance, in the expressing whereof Snyders doth infinitelie come short of Rubens, and Rubens saith that he should take it in ill part if I should compare Snyders with him in that point. The talent of Snyders is to represent beasts, but especiallie Birds altogether dead, and wholly without anie action. . . .'

After a year of negotiations, the picture found its way to The Hague, together with a few others by Jan Breughel, Snyders and Sebastian Vranckx.

A few months later, Rubens heard of the wonderful collection of antique marbles which Carleton had gathered together during his stay in Venice, and which he was willing to sell, partly because it was a considerable impediment to his diplomatic travels. This time the position between the two collectors was reversed, for Rubens, by his own confession, was 'mad about antiques' and as keen to purchase the diplomat's marbles as the latter was to secure his pictures. Carleton frankly confessed that, besides the practical inconvenience of travelling with such cumbersome property, his inclination had 'changed from sculpture to paintings, and especially those of Signor Rubens'. He used as an apology the well-known saying *Homo sum, humani nihil a me alienum puto,* which applies not only to him but also to his correspondent and to the group of 'Humanist' friends by whom the latter was surrounded.

As neither collector was anxious to pay in cash, Rubens explaining that the heavy expenses in which he had been involved by the building of his house forbade him to 'pass the bounds of wise economy for a luxury', they resorted to an exchange. The master was too busy to go to The Hague, so he sent a friend to inspect the collection and, on his favourable report, agreed to supply Carleton with a number of pictures which he valued at 6000 florins, the price paid by the diplomat for his marbles. This total seems a very small one, when we remember that one hundred florins was the equivalent of about nineteen pounds sterling. Rubens was careful

13B. THE FALL OF ICARUS [1636]

SKETCH FOR THE TORRE DE LA PARADA

Museum, Brussels

13A. THE FALL OF THE REBELLIOUS
ANGELS [1620]

SKETCH FOR THE JESUIT CHURCH, ANTWERP

Museum, Brussels

to discriminate between the paintings which he calls 'original by my own hand' and those which were 'begun' by his pupils and 'retouched' by himself. The former, in proportion to the size, were of course estimated at a higher price.

Carleton very wisely limited his choice to the original works and it was finally decided that, after adding three other pictures by his own hand, bringing the total price up to 4000 florins, the painter should make up the difference of 2000 florins by the purchase of tapestries on Carleton's behalf. Even among the pictures labelled original, the artist acknowledged that he had had recourse to collaborators. There was, for instance, a 'Prometheus in chains on Mount Caucasus, with an eagle tearing at his liver', in which the eagle had been contributed by Snyders; also 'Leopards painted from nature, with Satyrs and Nymphs', of which the landscape had been executed by 'a man well-skilled in this branch of art'; so that only the 'Daniel among numerous lions painted from nature', the 'Leda with a swan and Cupid', a 'Christ on the Cross' (life-size), the 'St. Peter taking the stater from the fish to pay the Tribute', and the 'St. Sebastian'—that is to say, five pictures out of twelve—could be said to have come from Rubens' brush alone.

As the English diplomat was a connoisseur somewhat difficult to please, we may take it that Rubens did not include in his list any picture only based on his sketches, so that, even when there is sufficient evidence that a painting came from the workshop, the expert is faced nowadays with the arduous problem of determining whether it is merely studio-work, or studio-work retouched by the master, or original work completed by collaborators specialising in landscapes, flowers, animals or still-life, or, finally, a picture in which no one but

Rubens had any part. It must also be remembered that the master made some distinctions among his students, and that when he says, for instance, in the case of 'Achilles with the Daughters of Lycomedes', that the picture was carried out by the 'best of his pupils', we must understand that he entrusted the work to the young Van Dyck, who already held a prominent position in the studio.

This most instructive list, submitted to Carleton, also shows that, to satisfy the public demand, the master was already in the habit of allowing his pupils to make replicas of some of his well-known paintings of earlier date. He mentions, for instance, a copy of the 'Twelve Apostles and Christ', in the Duke of Lerma's possession, dating from 1603-1604; a replica of a 'Hunt' painted for the Duke of Bavaria, and especially the reduced replica of the Neuburg 'Last Judgment' (1615-1616), to which reference was made in the last chapter.

* * *

We can now visualise our artist painting most of the time in his private studio, which was probably situated on the ground-floor of the new house, reading, or dictating his numerous letters and sometimes combining these occupations. From time to time, seeking a moment's relaxation, he would wander through the larger studio upstairs and inspect a score of pictures on the easels or against the walls; passing from a new student engaged in reproducing one of his old works to a trusted pupil enlarging his latest sketch; discussing some fresh plan with Van Dyck, examining the setting given to his own figures by Jan Breughel, Wildens or van Uden, and the animals and still-life introduced into his compositions by Snyders or De Vos; giving a word of encouragement here, a counsel there, or himself seizing the brush and re-establishing harmony in a colour-scheme, strengthening an effect of light, animating a shadow, and, by a few touches applied with unerring precision, transforming what might have been a conscientious study into a living masterpiece.

The first result of this kind of mass-production was naturally a great deal of repetition. Even during the first Antwerp period, that is to say up to 1625, quite apart from studio copies, we find a number of variations on popular themes, such as Judith and Holofernes, Lot and his Daughters, Susanna at the Bath, hunts of various kinds, bacchanals, battle-scenes, and, about 1620, at the time of Wildens' return from Rome, a series of landscapes peopled with cattle and small figures.

It is noticeable that, up to 1615, there is in the majority of the works produced by the studio a marked return to a calm and almost classical style, an avoidance of that tumultuous energy so prominent in the 'Erection of the Cross'; it would seem almost as if the master had realised that his pupils were not yet equipped to follow him along the original road he had opened out to them. It is only five or six years after his first great success that he allows his energy a freer scope in a number of hunting and battle-scenes, in which animals, not men, play the most important part; perhaps because some of his best collaborators were less likely to go wrong in dealing with animals than they might have been in dealing with human figures. For Rubens was not only a great painter, but also a great organiser, and he knew exactly how to extract the best service from those who enlisted under his banner. The fashion for mythological scenes was a heritage of Italian art, but the hunts and battles became henceforth one of the main features of the Flemish school.

If we examine these pictures side by side, we do not notice the same contrast in style according to the subject treated as that found in the productions of the Italian Renaissance. Rubens' religious paintings have to be examined apart, because they raise certain vital problems in the study and understanding of religious art. But otherwise, they might very well be assimilated to those which deal with more familiar themes. Realism is a stern leveller, and the realistic tendency —though always kept within bounds by Italian classicism— asserts itself in narrative, mythological or historical, as well as in religious paintings. It is worthy of note that, though the master no doubt possessed in his portfolios a large number of sketches from antique marbles, he made a much wider use of them in his allegories than in his mythological scenes. His goddesses, nymphs or satyrs are only exceptionally Greek statues. As has already been remarked, some of these look more like sturdy peasant men and women taking part in a kind of pagan pageant. The same remark applies to episodes from the Old Testament.

This direct contact with nature explains how Rubens is able to reproduce the same story almost indefinitely, without ever repeating himself (this, of course, refers only to his original compositions). To a classical artist, each episode becomes associated with some general ideas, which in their turn correspond to a certain definite design and colouring. But as soon as behind prophets and patriarchs, gods and heroes, sirens and dryads, real manhood and womanhood transpire, all combinations become possible and many designs may fit the same story.

The comparison made above between Rubens' methods

and those of a musical composer, who weaves any number of variations around the same theme, is a more appropriate one than might appear at first sight. When we compare all these hunting-scenes, bacchanals, battles—and, for the matter of that, the many Descents from the Cross, Pietàs, Adorations of the Kings, and the like—we feel that the painter's creative faculty follows very much the same lines as the inspiration of a musician, with the difference that he deals with design and colour instead of with rhythm and sound. After hearing the Christmas carol of the Epiphany, he can paint it in the grand and flamboyant style of the early work in the Prado, or in the picturesque and almost humorous style of the later work in Antwerp, or in some more intimate and quiet style, as in the Louvre picture; after hearing the huntsman's horn, he may dwell on the fierce struggle between horsemen and lions, or depict the boar overwhelmed by its foes, or, again, insist on the mad race between hunters and hunted; after hearing the bugle call, he may evoke the great clash of two opposing armies, or concentrate his attention on the crucial duel between two leaders, or show us heaps of wounded and dead rolling from a height or crushed under the hooves of struggling horses. There is no definite shape to his conceptions, they are inexhaustible as Nature herself, because they are in the closest possible contact with her.

An artist of a more classical or intellectual turn of mind is guided, first of all, by his conception of the subject with which he is dealing. The Conversion of St. Paul, for instance, will not mean for him, as for Rubens, a stampede of horses and a flash of light in the sky: it will mean exactly what the story of the road to Damascus suggests to his mind, according to his own beliefs, his habit of thought and the ideas of his age and the land in which he lives. He may be uncertain as to the image which will eventually translate this conception, and may try again and again—as Leonardo did, for example, in his sketches—to achieve an adequate result; but, all through his searchings, he is guided by a fixed idea which prevents him from straying from his path. No doubt the work produced by such careful cogitation has qualities often lacking in Rubens' more impulsive paintings, but, on the other hand, his direct and vivid method may lead to endless developments.

It is possible to go even further, and to suggest that his genius was to such an extent devoid of preconceived ideas, so exclusively bent on pictorial expression apart from all intellectual meaning, that, instead of subordinating his design to his subject, he subordinated his subject to his design; instead of submitting his eye and hand to his mind, he submitted his mind to the colours he saw and to the lines he drew. To return to the musical simile, it seems that, in some cases, not content with embroidering endless variations around certain subjects, he adopted leading themes very similar to the Wagnerian *leit-motiv*, that is to say, he reproduced designs for which he had a certain predilection when treating incidents which, in themselves, had nothing in common.

A few examples may help us to realise this curious correspondence between two great creators of realistic epics in art and music. Rubens took a special delight in painting his women models in certain attitudes. The crouching 'Venus Frigida', in Antwerp, evidently inspired by an antique statue of the goddess, has already been mentioned;[1] the same attitude is noticeable in 'Susanna and the Elders' and in one of the

[1] See pl. 5A and 5B, p. 56.

nymphs in the 'Bath of Diana' (both in Munich). Sometimes the position is more upright, as in the 'Hero crowned by Victory' (Dresden) and the 'Toilet of Venus' (Vienna); sometimes, again, the body is bent backwards, as in the 'Rape of the Daughters of Leucippus' (Munich) and the mermaids in the 'Arrival of Marie de Medici at Marseilles' (Louvre). This special feature becomes a *leit-motiv* which occurs again and again, irrespective of subject or date. More striking still is the conception of the rearing steed with its falling rider, often lighted from above by some heavenly vision. It appears in the 'Lion Hunt' (Munich), in the 'Conversion of St. Paul' (Berlin), and, quite at the end of Rubens' life, in the 'Martyrdom of St. Liévin' (Brussels). The same horse is also the central figure of the 'Overthrow of Sennacherib', and of another version of the 'Conversion of St. Paul' (both in Munich), only here the horse is smaller and surrounded by a crowd of fighting or fleeing men, while in both pictures a great light shines from the clouds, showing the angels of the Old and the New Testament. It almost seems as if, instead of painting the rearing horse to illustrate a hunt, a battle or a miracle, the master had painted these scenes for the sake of introducing that particular effect.

Admirers of Rubens might take as much delight in the discovery of such themes as students of Wagner have found in the unravelling of his entangled scores. The series of pictures dealing with triumphal processions (the 'Decius Mus' series, the 'Triumph of Julius Caesar', the 'Entry of Henry IV into Paris') would afford a fruitful hunting-ground, as would the works connected with the fall from Heaven (compare, for instance, the sketch for the 'Fall of the Rebel Angels' for the Jesuit Church, Antwerp, with the 'Fall of Icarus' for the

Torre de la Parada),[1] or the series of apotheoses (such as the 'Coronation of the Virgin' for the Jesuit Church and the 'Apotheosis' of James I in the Whitehall Banqueting-House), or again, the number of rectangular pictures, having as their main theme one recumbent and one kneeling figure ('Lot and his Daughters', 'Jupiter and Callisto', 'Cimon and Perus', 'Venus, Bacchus and Ceres').

* * *

Such investigations would doubtless show that the purely pictorial quality of Rubens' genius cannot be overestimated. There have been deeper thinkers, profounder psychologists, artists better able to express the mystic or mysterious side of life, but there never lived a greater painter. Not that, as is often suggested by superficial observers, he was exclusively temperamental and only able to express the external side of life. Anyone who is acquainted with his letters will realise that he possessed a most sensitive soul and an intense intellectual life. He was also a painstaking scholar, who took a vital interest in the interpretation of classical texts or in the most trifling detail of allegorical lore. But he was so constituted that he visualised his pictures almost before thinking of them, so that no reflection could alter his vision-thoughts.

This must, to a great extent, account for the amazing rapidity with which he was able to execute his works. If we are to believe his friend Balthazar Moretus, he estimated the value of his pictures by the time he had devoted to them, one day's work being worth a hundred florins, which corresponds roughly to nineteen pounds. On the Carleton list, there are several paintings entirely by his own hand, such as the 'Leda' and the 'St. Peter', which are priced at five hundred florins.

[1]See pl. 13A and 13B, p. 128.

Must we infer from this that Rubens only spent five days on them? This seems scarcely possible, though some accounts exist of his methods which are truly disconcerting.

A letter written from Antwerp by a dependent of the Earl of Arundel to his master, on July 17, 1620, informs us that, in the course of one sitting, Rubens managed to sketch the portrait of 'Lady Arundel with Robin her Dwarf, her Jester and her Dog'. This sketch would have to be copied again, because:

'It happened that, when Rubens wished to set to work, he could not find a canvas large enough; therefore, having drawn the heads in their definite form, he only sketched the attitudes and the draperies on paper, and made a separate drawing of the dog; but he has had another of the proper size prepared, and will himself execute the copy of what he has just done, to send it to your Lordship, with the original sketches.'

As Lady Arundel had left to spend the night in Brussels, and as no mention is made of any further sitting, it must be concluded that the fine portrait now in Munich is based on these separate sketches, which were afterwards enlarged to the required size. It seems strange that the composite character of this picture should not be obvious to the observer, especially as Lord Arundel himself was only included a year or so after the work had been finished. The Earl necessarily holds a less prominent position than his wife, but he belongs to the whole scheme just as if he had given a sitting to Rubens in 1620, and not in 1621.

This patch-work method was too bold to be always equally successful. There are several examples of enlargements and alterations, which show that it would sometimes have been better to leave well alone, instead of complying with the wishes of a difficult patron. True, it is not always easy to discover whether such changes were in accordance with the master's intentions or not, yet, on the other hand, there are definite instances in which Rubens preferred to oblige a customer, or to get some picture off his hands, rather than safeguard his artistic reputation for centuries to come, such as his letter to the Duke of Neuburg, on learning that, through faulty measurements, two of his paintings did not fit the frames that were ready for them:

'I console myself with the hope that the distance is not so great that one cannot easily remedy it, by adding at the top or bottom some little thing or other which will cover the gap without spoiling the symmetry of the whole.'

Surely, even in those easy-going Renaissance days, the idea of fitting the picture to the frame instead of the frame to the picture, was unusual and entailed heavy risks.

The temptation to entrust important commissions to second-rate assistants must have been irresistible in times of stress. In this respect, the Duke of Neuburg, who was perhaps less discriminating than others in his admiration, does not seem to have always been fairly treated. Neither the 'Adoration of the Shepherds' nor the 'Descent of the Holy Ghost' (now in Munich), ordered for the Jesuit Church in Neuburg, are worthy of the master's studio. As for the 'Fall of the Rebel Angels', Rubens was so little pleased with the general composition that he altered it considerably before allowing an engraving of it to be made.

The incident which occurred with regard to a 'Lion and Tiger Hunt', which the master sent to Lord Danvers in London in 1621, is probably another example of the carelessness with which certain commissions were executed. Carleton acted as go-between, and this miserable affair was the occasion of a lengthy exchange of letters. Lord Arundel, that 'evangelist for the world of art', to use Rubens' own expression, had succeeded in persuading Van Dyck to pay a visit to England, and the Prince of Wales, later Charles I, was naturally anxious to secure for his collection a good painting by the master of so remarkable a pupil. It happened that Lord Danvers owned a picture by Bassano, the 'Creation', which was too large for his house and in a bad state of preservation. This he sent to Rubens, in the hope of securing in exchange one of the master's paintings, which he could offer to the Prince. A good deal of haggling ensued, for Rubens did not value the Bassano at more than ten pounds and was unwilling to deliver one of his own pictures unless an extra sum was paid. Toby Matthew explained all these difficulties to Carleton, hinting at the same time that the 'Lion and Tiger Hunt' (a replica of the picture painted for the Duke of Bavaria) was not entirely original:

'Rubens confesseth in confidence, [he wrote] that this is not all of his owne doinge and I now thanke him for this confession, for a man who hath but halfe an eye, may easily discerne it; but he protests that he hath touched it over all, in all the partes of it. I must confess a truth to your Lordship (though I know he will be angry at it, if he know it), that it scarce doth looke like a thinge that is finished and the colorito of it doth little please me, though upon the whole matter it be a gallant peece, for the desseigne of it is precious.'

The master grew tired of this bargaining, and finally declared that he would abide by Carleton's decision. But when the 'Lion and Tiger Hunt' arrived in London it met with a cold reception, Danvers' advisers saying that it was unworthy of the master, and Danvers again appealed to Carleton, in a letter from St. James's, dated May 27, 1621:

'But now for Ruben in every paynters opinion he hath sent hether a peece scarce touched by his own hand, & the postures so forced, as the Prince will not admitt the picture into his galerye. I could wishe, therefore, that the famus man would doe soum on thinge to register or redeem his reputation in this howse . . . for from him we have yet only Judeth and Holifernes, of littell credite to his great skill, . . . and I will be well content to showte an other arrow of allowinge what monye he may aske in exchaynge, and theas Lions shall be safely sent him back for tamer beastes better made.'

Carleton transacted these fresh negotiations with his usual tact, and Rubens, who considered him more as a friend than as a patron, gave way with a good grace and promised to paint a hunt 'less fierce than that of the lions', adding that Danvers had not clearly explained that he required an original and not a studio picture.

It is unfortunately impossible to say whether the criticisms of the 'Lion Hunt' were entirely justified, but Rubens' repeated admission that he had allowed a second-rate work to leave his studio is significant. The whole discussion seems to suggest that he sometimes treated his patrons as a merchant might treat his customers, and not as a great artist should treat art lovers. Whenever we are faced with a so-called Rubens of inferior quality, we should bear in mind the experiences of Danvers and the Duke of Neuburg, and remember that the expression 'touched' is a very loose one, and that the master was at times too indulgent with regard to some of the paintings produced in his workshop.

This method of mass-production had other drawbacks. True, it involved collaboration with artists such as Van Dyck and Snyders, who, each in his own sphere, were so steeped in Rubenian art as to be able to blend their style with his own. But some older painters, such as Jan Breughel, whose technique was entirely different, went on painting for Rubens as they had painted before their association with him. Far from subordinating their personality to that of the master, they were inclined to overestimate the services they rendered him. Allusion has already been made to the series of Madonnas in which Rubens softened his style to harmonise the figures with the frames of flowers and birds delicately executed by Breughel; but it is somewhat surprising to read a letter from the latter to Ercole Bianchi, dated September 5, 1621, in which he announces the despatch of 'the fairest and most lovely piece I have ever made in my life'. This 'piece' is the Rubens 'Madonna' surrounded with flowers, now in the Louvre. That Breughel pictured in his mind very large flowers and a very small Madonna, may be fairly inferred from one sentence in his letter: 'Rubens too has given proof of his talent in the middle picture'.

From a purely artistic point of view, it is perhaps to be regretted that the master should have humbled his genius to suit his old friend's talent. At the same time, this eagerness to enlist Breughel's valuable services shows both Rubens' practical sense and his lovable artistic modesty.

* * *

By making so great a use of the Renaissance workshop system, there seems no doubt that Rubens lowered the average quality of the works attributed to him. It would be useless to try to found our appreciation on the relatively small number of pictures which are undoubtedly entirely by his hand, for this would at once place out of bounds all his great decorative paintings, which are the most characteristic of his works. Just as the man must be taken as a whole, with his domestic, diplomatic and artistic sides, if he is to be properly understood, the painter must be held responsible for the larger proportion of the paintings with which he had anything to do.

Rubens was not the kind of genius who spends a whole lifetime on the production of two or three masterpieces, and expects eternity to worship him on the strength of this meagre output. We hear again and again that quantity does not count against quality, that one perfect production is better than a hundred less perfect ones. This may be true of nature's works, but it does not apply to human effort. When all is said, no human creation can ever be perfect; there is always a certain proportion of failure to be detected somewhere. The greatest man is never a god, but he can be, and often is, a demi-god or a giant; and giants are apt to combine tremendous strength with startling weaknesses. In them everything is exaggerated, and a defect which might appear insignificant in a smaller man may assume surprising dimensions. The great giants of art, literature and music have been, · when we come to think of it, responsible for curious blunders. Shakespeare would seem to have patched up some very inferior plays; Balzac wrote l'*Histoire des Treize*; Dickens begot a good many Florences, and Wagner made havoc of his characters in the latter part of his *Ring*.

Such weaknesses are not so apparent in Greek art and literature of the best period, but this may be due to the fact that we appreciate Greek civilisation from a small proportion of the works which it produced, and that, our chronology being by no means complete, all the finest productions are naturally grouped together. Besides, if the Pagan world appears more perfect, it is also more limited; the failure is proportionate to the aspiration. It seems as if the greater effort required of Christian art needed an almost superhuman strength which even the most powerful creators are unable to muster. Rubens is no exception to this rule; he is, rather, a typical example of the very type of artist who, in his eagerness to seize every opportunity of expressing himself, and to undertake the performance of tremendous tasks in too short a time, lays himself open occasionally to the reproach of hastiness and negligence. In his voracity for work, especially for great decorative work, he seems to have been reluctant to refuse a commission, even when his day was so crowded that he could scarcely call his life his own.

If he could not always keep pace with the calls made on his powers, it was not for lack of industry, for he rose, summer and winter, at four o'clock in the morning and, after hearing Mass, worked relentlessly till night, snatching here and there a few hours of relaxation which he spent with his family or intimate friends, or in riding through the neighbouring countryside. Only a man of his iron constitution could have stood the strain, and indeed, in spite of his sensitive face, he was abnormally strong physically. There is a strange correspondence between his physical appearance and his works, so that anyone who had met him after seeing his pictures must have felt that he alone could have created them. That imaginative brow and those strange eyes, at once keen and pensive, tell their own tale; so does that extraordinarily powerful hand, which handled pencil and brush with amazing rapidity and realised in record time what the eyes had seen and the brow conceived.

⋆   ⋆   ⋆

Against the drawbacks of the workshop should be placed its obvious advantages. If some of the pupils were not worthy of their master, others achieved greatness through their association with him. From Van Dyck downwards, almost all the great representatives of the seventeenth-century Flemish School benefited directly or indirectly by his teaching. Jordaens is perhaps the only exception, and even Jordaens, though working on independent lines, reaped some of the sheaves of the great sower. For the studio, besides being a workshop, was also an academy, and it is more than likely that, if some of Rubens' patrons occasionally suffered from the master's over-indulgence, some of his pupils profited by it. Greater severity might have prevented certain disappointments outside the workshop, but it might also have discouraged some hopeful youth, whose later work justified Rubens' leniency. We must not forget that Antwerp had by this time, and largely through the master's influence, become the artistic centre of Northern Europe, and that it was to this centre, and no longer to Rome, that promising students flocked eagerly, in the hope—and often in the forlorn hope—of being among the chosen few who were allowed to enter the sacred premises on the Wapper.

Antonius Sanderus, the penitentiary of Ypres, was so elated by Rubens' triumph that he condoled with Italy on the decadence of Rome, who had been robbed of her supremacy by the Flemish master's skill:

> Roma dole: vicit nostro Rubenius oevo,
> Aduatica latiam dexteritate manum.

By comparing the pre-Rubenian to the post-Rubenian situation of art in the Southern Netherlands, we shall be able to estimate the great teacher's influence. On the one side must be placed Pourbus, Vaenius, Martin De Vos and other 'Italianists'; on the other, Jordaens, Van Dyck, Teniers and a number of portrait and genre painters, who maintain the reputation of the school up to the end of the century. By making Italian traditions his own and adapting them to the light and temperament of his country and people, Rubens may be said to have lifted the car of national art out of the ruts of cold convention and awkward imitation, and to have sent it rolling among the green fields and bright villages of Flanders. The impulse given by that strong hand was felt forty years after the hand itself had become still, and a combination of political and economic calamities was needed to bring that powerful movement to a standstill.

Again, if in the case of Jan Breughel the spirit of true partnership was not always maintained, there were other instances in which the close collaboration between Rubens and his fellow-artists was fertile in its results. The case of Van Dyck, who was entrusted with the complete execution of a large number of designs, need not be stressed. The younger artist's debt to his master has often been acknowledged. No doubt his genius would have manifested itself even had he not found a Rubens to help him—such a portrait-painter could not fail to produce fine portraits in whatever circumstances he was placed—but, when he dealt with religious subjects, Van Dyck was not always able to free himself from the sentimentalism which prevailed at the time in the Italian School. What would have happened if, instead of submitting to the virile influence of his great teacher, he had tried, from the first, to follow his own line?

In the Carleton correspondence, Rubens refers to certain cartoons on the story of the Roman Consul Decius Mus, which he was preparing for tapestries ordered by some Genoese patron. These cartoons have apparently been lost, but the Liechtenstein collection in Vienna contains six finished pictures in oil dealing with the same subject, which are supposed to be copies by Van Dyck from the original designs. If this is the case, there are few examples of a happier artistic collaboration. Rubens followed the story as it stands in Livy, dividing it into six episodes,[1] just as Shakespeare might have divided up the action of an historical play. As a matter of fact, a curiously Shakespearean feeling runs right through the series, from the oration in the first picture to the triumphal funeral in the last. These muscular and dignified heroes and soldiers combine classical with Renaissance features, as do the characters of the 'Roman plays'.

The 'Decius Mus' series, together with a score of historical pictures, such as the 'Reconciliation of Romans and Sabines' (Munich), 'St. Ambrosius and the Emperor Theodosius' (Vienna), 'Mucius Scaevola before Porsenna' (Budapest), and the series of cartoons on the 'Life of the Emperor Constantine' prepared for Louis XIII as designs for tapestries, represent the reaction of Northern Europe to Roman tradition in art, just as *Coriolanus*, *Julius Caesar* and *Anthony and Cleopatra* represent this reaction in the drama.

Another painter whose help appears to have been invaluable to Rubens was Wildens. The return of that talented landscape-painter from Rome in 1618 coincides with the production of the first notable landscapes to issue from the

[1] 1. Decius Recounts his Dream. 2. Decius Consults the Haruspices. 3. Decius Devotes himself to the Gods of the Lower World. 4. Decius sends back the Lictors. 5. Decius mortally wounded. 6. The Funeral of Decius. 7. Rome Triumphant. 8. Trophy of War.

studio. Rubens begins by introducing figures of peasants and cattle into Wildens' scenery, but there are certain works in this first group of landscapes, such as the 'Return of the Prodigal Son' (Antwerp), which are considered to be entirely by him. In 'Philemon and Baucis' (Vienna), on the other hand, the influence of Elsheimer is distinctly noticeable. The admiration which Rubens had for the German artist and his regret for the loss which the latter's death caused to art, has already been mentioned. The memory of this friend's work seems to have haunted him, even during the busiest years of his career. There is a 'Flight into Egypt' (Cassel), painted in 1614, which also recalls Elsheimer's manner.

* * *

It must not be imagined that, because Rubens was considered to be the first painter in Northern Europe and was surrounded by a crowd of admiring friends and pupils, he lost for one moment the appetite for learning and for fresh experiments which had characterised the Italian period. He had undoubtedly asserted his originality as a great decorator in religious, mythological and historical subjects, but even that was not enough, and his inexhaustible curiosity and interest prompted him to wander through many new byways, some of which had only the remotest relationship to his main work.

That he should try his hand at landscape-painting is comprehensible, since it was the only department of his art which he had not yet explored. But that this great colourist, whose happy and vivid temperament could only express itself in brightly lighted scenes, should have experimented in chiaroscuro in the manner of the Dutch painter Honthorst is more surprising. There is an 'Old Woman with a Brazier' at

Dresden,[1] which must be attributed to Rubens, because it is known from an old copy that the picture was once joined to the 'Venus at Vulcan's Forge' now in Brussels. But, if we had to judge this picture entirely on internal evidence, Rubens is the last master whose name would come to our minds.

Again, Honthorst was, after all, a contemporary of Rubens, and we may suppose that the latter was attracted by the novelty of his night effects and, in his search for fresh material, endeavoured to reproduce them, just as he copied and interpreted so many contemporary Italian paintings. But how are we to explain the fact that an artist who belonged so essentially to his time and who applied himself so indefatigably to express the spirit of the late Renaissance, should have gone out of his way to copy an old sixteenth-century portrait by Scorel, the 'Paracelsus' (Brussels),[2] and even to reproduce, in 'St. Pepin and St. Bega' (Vienna), a lost picture in the style of Quentin Massys? The idea that, in these years, when he was engaged on most important and pressing commissions, this 'prince of painters' and 'modern Apelles' found time to indulge in such exercises, suggests anything but an attitude of self-satisfaction. To combine an admiration for Caravaggio and Giulio Romano with a practical interest in Scorel and Massys, and to associate a hunger for the late Italian Renaissance with a thirst for Flemish and Dutch 'Primitives' shows not only an exceptional catholicity of taste, but an extreme modesty of artistic opinion.

Any other artist's production would, no doubt, have been delayed by outside experiments such as these, but Rubens took everything in his stride and went on seeking and seeking new treasures while the whole world was dazzled by

[1]See pl. 14B, p. 148.　　　[2]See pl. 14A, p. 148.

14A. RUBENS AFTER SCOREL
PORTRAIT OF PARACELSUS
[1615–1618]. Museum, Brussels

14B. RUBENS AFTER HONTHORST
OLD WOMAN WITH A BRAZIER
[1616–1618]

Gallery, Dresden. *Photo, Franz Hanfstaengl, Munich*

those he had just unearthed. He was ambitious, of course, but the achievements he dreamed of were before not behind him. His true humility was not founded on a false sense of self-abasement, but on the hope of doing much better in the future than in the past, so that every new work was only a stepping-stone leading to fresh efforts. This was no doubt why he so frequently declares, in his letters, that his latest production is also his finest. The tendency to set oneself a new goal as soon as the last one has been reached is characteristic of the race of giants to which Rubens belongs. It is only the small man who ever rests content.

* * *

The master was soon to engage on a work as important as, and, from the purely pictorial point of view, even more important than the decoration of the Jesuit Churches at Antwerp and Neuburg. Thanks to the diplomacy of the Abbé de Luçon, later Cardinal Richelieu, peace had been restored between Louis XIII and the Queen-Mother. For six years, Marie de Medici, as President of the Council, ruled supreme in France, and, having inherited the Medici tradition of patronising the arts, she wished to leave behind her a worthy memorial of the bright period which her courtiers were pleased to call her 'prosperous reign'. She had bought the old Hôtel de Luxembourg and had ordered her architect de Brosse to build a Renaissance palace in its place. When the time came for decorating the large gallery of the new palace, she selected Rubens for this task, in spite of the jealousy which such a choice could not fail to arouse, not only in France but in her native country.

It is doubtful whether she still remembered the young 'Fiamingo' who had accompanied her brother-in-law the

Duke of Mantua at the time of her marriage by proxy in Florence. What is more probable is that she was well acquainted with the European reputation of Rubens, that she had had some opportunity of appreciating his work, and that, as a true Medici, she could distinguish greatness when she saw it.

Both the Archduke and his wife were too anxious to secure the good-will of the Queen-Mother to place any obstacle in the way, and, in January 1622, Rubens left for Paris, carrying with him several presents from Isabella to Marie. He spent a few weeks there, discussing preliminary plans with de Brosse and the Abbé de Saint Ambroise, the Queen's representative, concerning the number of pictures, their subjects and the places they were to fill on the walls. He managed, at the same time, to make certain purchases for the Infanta and for himself—among which, a picture by Titian and another by Tintoretto—and to spend many hours with a well-known French antiquarian, who combined this absorbing hobby with the functions of Councillor to the Parliament of Aix, Nicolas Claude Fabri de Peiresc. This great traveller and scholar, who had been introduced to Rubens through their common friend, the Flemish Humanist Gevartius, was a man after the painter's own heart, and a long correspondence followed this first visit to Paris, a correspondence which contains an enormous amount of information not only as to Rubens' work and the antiquarian interests of both friends, but also as to Court intrigues and European politics.

Peiresc was in close touch with the Abbé de Saint Ambroise and, needless to say, shared the latter's admiration for the Flemish master. He took good care to inform Rubens of

the protests which the offer of so important a commission
had provoked in French artistic circles and of the firmness
displayed by the Queen in silencing them. The argument
used by the Abbé de Saint Ambroise to justify Marie's choice
is characteristic. Rubens was the only European artist capable of carrying out such an important task within a few
years: 'The painters of Italy would not accomplish in ten
years what he would do in four, and would not even think
of undertaking pictures of the necessary size.' Such were the
advantages of mass-production.

Peiresc's letters are full of practical details of the measurements of the panels in the Luxembourg, and of the long discussions which took place concerning the choice of subjects.
Until the final achievement of the great work, this devoted
friend acted as Rubens' agent at the Court of France; but the
interests of the antiquarian are not forgotten and the painter
finds time to send his friend imprints in wax of some of his
marbles. Among these was a bust of Demosthenes which
seems to have puzzled Peiresc a great deal, for he discovered
that half the head was hairless, as if the great orator had suffered from partial baldness. It is strange that so learned a man
should not have heard of the tradition according to which
Demosthenes, when he wished to retire from society,
shaved half his head in order to avoid all temptation to break
his vow. There are several references to this curious problem,
which are mixed up with further information as to the
Luxembourg commission, and with news from the Court.
It was at this time that Rubens first used his artistic connections to obtain political information, and began to combine
diplomacy with art.

An incident occurred in 1622 which seems to have caused

a good deal of anxiety in Paris. The rumour spread in that city that Rubens had been the victim of an attempt upon his life. The painter was able to reassure the Queen, through the agency of Peiresc, but he had evidently had a narrow escape. He had been attacked by Luke Vorsterman, the engraver to whom he entrusted his most important work, who had shown signs of mental derangement. This man appears to have been obsessed with the idea that he, as an engraver, was really a far greater artist than Rubens as a painter, and that the latter had robbed him of his fame.

Marie de Medici had given Rubens a commission to decorate two galleries, for which he was to receive fifty-four thousand francs, with an extra six thousand if the Queen-Mother was entirely satisfied with the work. One series of pictures was to illustrate the story of her own life, and the other that of her husband Henry IV. The first series alone was completed; it included two narrow pictures placed between the windows on either side of the entrance; sixteen pictures each measuring 13 ft. by 9 ft. placed between the nine windows looking on to the garden and the nine windows looking on to the courtyard; and three larger pictures, measuring 13 ft. by 23 ft., decorating the wall opposite the entrance and the two spaces between that wall and the windows on either side. Finally, an 8 ft. portrait of the Queen-Mother was to be placed over the mantelpiece, while large portraits of her father and mother filled the spaces above the doors.

The Queen's life having been an uneventful one, the material at the painter's disposal was remarkably poor. He started, in the first narrow panel on the left of the entrance, by depicting the 'Three Fates' spinning Marie's destiny.

Next came her 'Birth', then her 'Education', presided over by Minerva, Mercury, the genius of Music playing the 'cello, and the Three Graces (the latter being one of Rubens' favourite themes). The next four pictures dealt with Marie's marriage to Henry IV: 'Henry receiving Marie's Portrait', while Jove and Juno look down on him propitiously; the 'Marriage by Proxy' in Florence, which is referred to in Chapter II; the 'Arrival at Marseilles', with the delightful group of mermaids by Rubens' own hand, in the foreground; and the actual 'Marriage of Henry and Marie', who pose as Jupiter and Juno, while the town of Lyons appears below, drawn by two symbolical lions. Then comes the 'Birth of Louis XIII', also referred to above, with the Spirit of Health holding the baby in his arms on the right, and Fruitfulness on the left, showing to the happy mother the small effigies of other children yet to come.[1] The group of four which follow, including the three long central panels, concern the regency of the Queen before the majority of Louis XIII: 'Henry IV conferring his Authority upon Marie', when he leaves for the German wars; 'Marie's Solemn Coronation', in the Gothic Abbey of St. Denis; the 'Apotheosis of Henry IV', and the 'Queen's Happy Rule', supported by the sword of Mars, Minerva's lance and Apollo's archery. The first quarrel with Louis is tactfully hinted at in the 'Ride to Pont-de-Cé', where Marie's forces met those of her rebellious son. A delightful interlude is provided by the 'Exchange of the Princesses', in which Elizabeth of Bourbon, who married the Infante of Spain, and Anne of Austria, Louis XIII's bride, dance a quadrille with the symbolical figures of France and Spain, under a shower of gold.[2] Then back again to the

[1]See pl. 6, p. 61.   [2]See pl. 15, p. 157.

'Prosperous Regency of the Queen', who poses as the figure of Justice, with Time, France, Minerva, Prosperity and Comfort on the steps of the throne, while Ignorance, Calumny and Hatred lie in chains on the ground. The 'Majority of Louis XIII' is represented by a ship rowed by Strength, Religion, Justice and Loyalty, bearing appropriate symbols on their shields; while the last five pictures of the series refer again to the quarrels between mother and son: 'Marie's Flight from Blois', her 'Reconciliation and Interview' with Louis, the 'Conclusion of Peace' and the 'Triumph of Truth' (the narrow panel facing the 'Fates').

As an artistic achievement, posterity has endorsed the judgment of the Court of Brussels, which had an opportunity of admiring some of these pictures when Rubens brought them to Paris early in 1623, and the enthusiasm of the Queen-Mother herself and of the great Cardinal, when they saw them in the gallery a few weeks later. With the exception, perhaps, of the library of the Siena Cathedral, in which Pinturicchio depicted episodes from the life of Pope Piccolomini, there is no example of biographical decoration to compare with the Luxembourg series as regards vigour of composition and brilliancy of colouring. No work better illustrates the master's faculty of adapting himself to any subject or circumstance and of discovering opportunities for the display of his imaginative power, where perhaps even a greater man might have felt discouraged by the shackles and restrictions imposed upon him. After reading in the Peiresc letter those long discussions about the position of the pictures on the walls, the advisability or non-advisability of introducing a figure or an episode which might give offence to the King, or provoke the sarcasm of the Queen's enemies; after

following the arguments as to the submission of preliminary
sketches for the Queen's approval, and the fresh difficulties
that cropped up almost every month, one wonders how the
master had the patience to continue his work unperturbed,
complying with his patrons' requests whenever possible, but
remaining firm when compliance might entail failure.

Rubens was not devoid of a sense of humour, though this
tendency is only occasionally manifested in his art. It is,
however, difficult to believe, with some critics, that he deliberately made fun of the Queen's self-satisfied vanity by
introducing an ironic motive into certain pictures, such as the
gnome putting out his tongue in the bottom corner of the
'Prosperous Regency of the Queen'. We must not lose sight
of the fact that this figure, or rather this head, represents
Calumny and that Rubens took his allegories very seriously.
He was far too much of a courtier to indulge in jokes of the
kind at the expense of his admiring patroness, though he may
well have felt somewhat impatient at her unquenchable
thirst for flattery. If there is any irony in the Luxembourg
series, it is of a far more subtle kind, and the artist may have
been almost unconscious of it. He was entrusted with the
decoration of an imposing room, and he made it as brilliant
as he possibly could, using bright crimson and amber-yellow
most lavishly. He had to glorify the career of a Queen who
was by no means an example of all the virtues, and naturally
avoided any episode which would have revealed her blem-
ishes. He accepted this challenge to his clear-sightedness in
the same spirit as that in which he accepted the technical
difficulties of his task, and called upon the gods of Olympus
and the paraphernalia of allegory to help him to overcome
all obstacles. He considered himself a painter, not a scrupulous

historian, and, in a true practical spirit, desired above all to carry out successfully the work he had undertaken. He may have smiled to himself when piling up a great deal of undeserved praise, but these very exaggerations were essential to the gorgeous effects he wished to obtain. Assuming that the Queen-Mother was on the side of Light, she must be escorted by a pageant of heavenly Virtues, protecting her from the vain attacks of human Vices. To the uninitiated, the result may appear to be the undeserved glorification of Concini's protectress, but to Rubens it was first of all the justifiable apotheosis of Renaissance decorative art, and it is as such that posterity appreciates it.

The Medici series raises the whole problem of Rubens' allegorical style. Strangely enough, the master's realistic tendencies, which are so apparent in his mythological, historical and even religious pictures, are not so conspicuous when he deals with allegories. Nowhere else does he approach so near to classicism. True, his vigorous style asserts itself again and again in certain ornamental incidents, such as the group of mermaids in the 'Arrival of Marie de Medici at Marseilles', the shackled Vices in her 'Prosperous Regency', or the vigorous oarswomen in the 'Majority of Louis XIII', but there is, on the whole, an ordered dignity and an exceptional restfulness in the series. The familiar outbursts of the master's temperament could not be reconciled with the pomp of Court etiquette and, with his usual versatility, he kept these in the background and had recourse to his portfolios and memories of antiquarian lore to help him to adapt himself to these new circumstances. We have already noticed the use made of antique statues in the 'Birth of Louis XIII' and in the 'Happy Reign'. Further examples of such borrowings might

15 . THE EXCHANGE OF THE PRINCESSES
[1621-1625]

Louvre, Paris.　*Photo, Bulloz*

doubtless be discovered in the Luxembourg pictures, and, though the various interpretations given to the hundreds of emblems and symbols which Rubens scattered so lavishly among them are often contradictory, there is no doubt whatever that the master attached a definite meaning to each one of them, and could have given good reasons for his choice.[1]

* * *

After five weeks in Paris, Rubens returned to his workshop in Antwerp, to complete the fifteen remaining pictures. These he was able to place in position in January 1625, and, working incessantly with his pupil Justus van Egmondt, he managed to have the great hall ready by May 11th, the day of the marriage by proxy of Henrietta-Maria, the King's sister, to the Prince of Wales. The Abbé de St. Ambroise's prediction was thus realised, for Rubens had succeeded in executing in three years a task which would have overtaxed the powers of any other painter of the period. It is characteristic of the master that, after launching almost lightheartedly into a vast undertaking of this kind, and carrying it through with relentless energy, he nearly always suffered a reaction. In the case of the Medici series, he felt that the material reward was not in proportion to the time he had given to the work, and that he had wasted too much of his energy on the petty obstacles placed in his way by the jealousies and rivalries which divided the French Court.

In a letter to Peiresc, written on May 13, 1625, Rubens

[1] The same remarks apply to a series of religious allegories painted a few years later (1625-28) for the Infanta, on the 'Triumphs of the Eucharist'. The thirteen sketches (now in various public and private galleries) were enlarged in the studio to serve as designs for the series of tapestries still preserved in the Convent of the Descalzas Reales, Madrid.

admits that he is only too ready to leave the Court and be at home again:

'I am therefore resolved, as soon as I can obtain payment for my work, to go at once, and to leave to him [Cardinal Richelieu] and M. de Saint Ambroise the task of acquainting me with the decisions taken, even if they should mismanage them in their usual way. . . . In fine, I am weary of this Court, and if I do not obtain satisfaction with as much readiness as I myself used in the service of the Queen-Mother, it may be—I say this in confidence—that they will not find me eager to return; although, truth to tell, I have little to complain of up to the present in the conduct of Her Majesty; for the delays have been legitimate and excusable. But meanwhile, time passes and I am far from home, which does me no good.'

As the master feels compelled by circumstances to take a more active part in politics and wanders to Holland, Madrid and London, in the service of his country and his Princess rather than in that of his reputation and his art, he gives vent again and again to similar expressions of disappointment. He longs to go back to Antwerp and his studio, and to resume the active and happy life he has led since his return from Italy. This glow of happiness is darkened for four years after Isabella's death, and is only to be rekindled when Helen enters his house, inaugurating a second period of peaceful work, undisturbed by politics and the petty quarrels of Court life.

CHAPTER VI
DIPLOMACY

IN ORDER to understand the drift of the diplomatic negotiations in which Rubens became involved after 1625, it is
necessary to retrace our steps as far back as 1609, when the
Twelve Years' Truce between the Northern and Southern
Netherlands allowed the work of economic and artistic re-
construction to take place.

Europe was, at that time, divided between Roman Catholics and Protestants—if we can include under this heading
such different conceptions of religion as those of the English
Church party, of the German Lutherans and of the Dutch
and French Calvinists. That religious differences were in
most cases the cloak under which political rivalries for supremacy in Europe hid themselves, does not concern us here.
The fact is that orthodox Spain, with the Southern Netherlands under Albert and Isabella as an outpost, and Hapsburg
Austria as an ally, looked askance upon all countries in which
'heresy' had made considerable progress or entirely domi-
nated politics. This group included Northern Germany, Holland, England, and even France under the ex-Huguenot king,
Henry IV. The true conflict, as it was to develop during the

159

Thirty Years' War, was between the House of Hapsburg and the France of Cardinal Richelieu.

In the very year when the truce between Northern and Southern Netherlands was signed at The Hague, the Duke of Cleves and Juliers (whose possessions occupied an important strategic position in the Rhineland) suddenly died, and the Emperor, anxious to exclude from the succession the Protestant Elector of Brandenburg, John-Sigismund, and the Duke of Neuburg, Wolfgang-William, sequestrated the Duchy. Henry IV of France seized this opportunity to interfere in German affairs by upholding the rights of the claimants. His hostility to the Hapsburg party was increased by the fact that the Prince de Condé, seeing his wife Charlotte de Bourbon pursued by the assiduities of the old king, had gone with her to Brussels to seek protection, and that Archduke Albert had succeeded in thwarting a plan for the abduction of the 'new Helen', as she was called at the time. In May 1610, the Archduke received a kind of ultimatum from the French king, asking leave to pass with his army through Luxemburg on his way to Germany. This would inevitably have provoked another 'Trojan War', had not Henry IV been assassinated a few days later. The latter's death, however, did not put an end to the vexed question of Cleves and Juliers. Four years later, the Duke of Neuburg—whom we have already mentioned as an enthusiastic patron of Rubens—was converted to Catholicism, while the Elector of Brandenburg abandoned Lutheranism for Calvinism. The fight between the two factions continued covertly, supported by Spinola at the head of the Spanish forces in the Netherlands, on the one side, and by Maurice of Nassau, at the head of the forces of the United Provinces, on the other. The two enemy generals went on manœuvring for position along the frontier, without however breaking the truce.

In 1618, the revolt of Bohemia against the Emperor brought about a new conflict between the Catholic and Protestant parties. After the Protestant Elector Palatine Frederick, James I's son-in-law, had accepted the crown of Bohemia, the King of Spain decided to interfere and, in September 1620, a small army under Spinola crossed the Rhine at Mayence on their way to the Palatinate, which they were to occupy in conjunction with the Austrian forces, after the repression of the Bohemian revolt.

Archduke Albert, on the other hand, wished above all to prolong the truce with the United Provinces. Although Philip III had his own reasons for desiring to resume hostilities as soon as possible, the Court of Brussels started negotiations with Maurice of Nassau, who was believed to be open to persuasion. Being misinformed as to the intentions of the Republic, Albert sent his representative Chancellor Pecquius to The Hague, in the spring of 1621, but his proposals met with a scornful refusal and the populace showed itself so hostile that the ambassador had to give up all hope of coming to terms.

A few weeks later, on July 13, 1621, the Archduke died in Brussels, and was solemnly buried, clad in a Franciscan habit, in the Church of Ste. Gudule. So great was the sorrow of Isabella that for weeks she remained in her darkened apartments, refusing to see anyone. She donned the habit of a nun, sacrificed the tresses which had been her pride in happier days and even talked for a time of relinquishing the task of government. She may also have been discouraged by the death of her brother, Philip III of Spain, which closely followed upon that of Albert. This death meant that the main power in Madrid passed from the hands of her old friend the Duke of Lerma, into those of Philip IV's new adviser, Olivarez, who pursued an aggressive policy detrimental to the interests of Belgium.

Meanwhile, fortune continued to favour the Catholic party in Germany. After the occupation of the Palatinate, Spinola had invaded Juliers, in February 1622, and Mansfeld, who had attacked the Southern Netherlands on behalf of the United Provinces, had been completely defeated at Fleurus in August. In the following year, England and Spain concluded an arrangement concerning the disputed Palatinate occupied by the Austro-Spanish armies. The possessions of Frederick were, for the time being, placed under the guardianship of Isabella, who was *persona grata* with James I as well as with the Hapsburg party. Finally, the death of Maurice of Nassau, in April 1625, and the taking of Breda by Spinola, gave the Catholics a reasonable hope of bringing the war to a successful conclusion.

*　*　*

It has already been noticed that, in his letters to his French correspondents, Peiresc, Valavez and the brothers Dupuy, Rubens makes several references to these political events. As a matter of fact, since the death of Archduke Albert, he had become one of the most trusted confidants of Isabella. He had been for some time a close friend of Spinola, and was therefore particularly well placed to play a prominent part in all negotiations undertaken by the Court of Brussels. Nor were his services entirely gratuitous, for we know that the Infanta gave him a grant of 10 écus per month 'for the services he had rendered to the King'. This grant was to be paid not by the Belgian Government but by the Citadel of Antwerp, and was therefore taken from the money sent to the Netherlands by Madrid for the upkeep of the army. When we remember, however, the value of the master's time, we realise that this allowance did not in the least compensate him for the commissions he lost through his diplomatic activity.

Why did Rubens sacrifice himself in this way, and abandon the quiet life of his studio and the congenial work on which he was engaged, to undertake a series of tiring and sometimes dangerous missions during eight years of the most productive period of his life? No doubt he was devoted to the Infanta. While, in his correspondence, he can be particularly outspoken with regard to other princes and criticises freely life in the Courts of Paris, Madrid and London, there is nothing but praise for Isabella, whom he certainly considered to be a model sovereign. Witness his letter to Pierre Dupuy, written on the 26th October, 1626:

'I am sorry not to have any interesting matter to offer you in return for your news. Our Court is short of that commodity compared to the Court of France, which, by its greatness, is subject to the most important changes. Here we go on in the ordinary way, and every minister serves as best he can without pretending to other favours than those of the rank he occupies. And so everyone grows old—and dies even —in the same office, without having hoped for extraordinary honours or feared disgrace. For our Princess shows neither great love nor great hate; she is sweet and kind to all.'

Two years later, in a letter to Jacques Dupuy, he expresses an even greater admiration for Isabella: 'She is adorned with all the virtues that are to be found in woman! Long experience has made her skilful in the art of governing and has shown her the fallacy of the new theories which come to us from Spain.'

He entirely shared Isabella's views and believed with her that peace and prosperity could not be maintained in the Netherlands if Spain engaged in fresh European conflicts. He fully realised the vulnerable position of his country, insufficiently defended by Spain and surrounded on all sides by her enemies. He therefore wholeheartedly espoused the cause of peace, not only between the Southern and Northern Netherlands but also between the European Powers.

When, however, we read in the correspondence the series of letters in which Rubens expresses regret at being away from home and wasting his time and energy on these lengthy negotiations, we are inclined to think that, in spite of his loyal devotion to his sovereign and his sincere patriotism, nothing would have induced him to embark on such adventures had he realised from the first whither they would lead him. But he had been drawn gradually into the vortex, beginning doubtless by carrying messages for the Infanta, as any courtier was bound to do; becoming more and more interested in the progress of the drama in which he was taking a small part; witnessing with impatience the blunders of other agents less wary and skilful than himself; being obliged to put right what they had so sorely mismanaged; feeling that it would have cost less time and energy to take the whole responsibility of the negotiations on his own shoulders; and realising at last that he had become so deeply involved that he could not withdraw his collaboration without harming the cause he wished to serve.

He possessed the kind of genius which fits in with Carlyle's theory. He might have turned his hand or his mind to almost anything, and have left his mark on the world—not so deep a mark as the one he did leave as a painter, but nevertheless a mark bearing the stamp of genius. He must have felt this unconsciously, and have been tempted to abandon his art, if only temporarily, to rush into other pursuits, just as he was incited to imitate old or modern paintings, very different from his own, to test his powers. This is no doubt why he became a scholar, a collector, an antiquarian, a skilled linguist, and finally a diplomatist. In the latter career, as in the others, he started as an amateur, but diplomacy can scarcely be considered a hobby and it did not take many months to give Peter-Paul so strong a taste for it, that only some great achievement could satisfy him.

The death of his wife in 1626, at a time when he was being drawn farther and farther into politics, must have favoured this new inclination; for we know that he sought relief in travel, feeling her absence harder to bear among the familiar surroundings of the old home. In this matter, he very wisely followed the advice of his friends; his new diplomatic work afforded him an excellent excuse for seeing the world.

The Infanta's choice of Rubens is more easy to understand. After the loss of her devoted consort, she was more than ever in need of a loyal and trustworthy adviser who shared her views, not as a means of promoting his own interests at Court, but because he sincerely believed that the policy she followed was the only one which could save the country from wrack and ruin. The fact that Peter-Paul was an outsider rather helped than hindered her purpose, since he did not share the prejudices of the Spanish grandees and Belgian aristocrats who surrounded her, and, at the same time, enjoyed through his artistic reputation a prestige which the humbler agents she might have used in his stead did not possess.

*   *   *

The beginnings of Peter-Paul's activities are shrouded in mystery. Apart from the grant of money referred to above, the first proof we have of his share in international affairs is a letter written from Antwerp on September 13, 1623, to Chancellor Pecquius. In this letter, the artist tells of a visit he has paid to Jan Brant (not the father but the cousin of his wife), a Belgian agent residing at The Hague, and who is mentioned under the mysterious name of 'el Catolico'. Jan Brant was apparently engaged in secret negotiations carried on by the Infanta with the United Provinces, unknown to Spain. This is made clear by the postscript in which Rubens expresses the fear that Brant's visit to Brussels might arouse the suspicions of Cardinal de la Cueva, Spanish Ambassador at the Court of Isabella.

Rubens' activities were sufficiently noticeable a few months later, since, on August 30, 1624, de Baugy, French Ambassador at Brussels, thought it necessary to draw his government's attention to them:

'Allusions to the Truce [with the United Provinces] are not disagreeable to the Infanta, whatever their source; she lends every day a favourable ear to the suggestions made to her on this subject by Rubens, a celebrated Antwerp painter known in Paris by his works in the Queen-Mother's palace. The latter goes to and fro between here and the camp of the Marquis Spinola, letting it be understood that he has some special intelligence with regard to this matter with Prince Henry of Nassau, whose disposition is, he declares, rather favourable to the Truce, by the conclusion of which he might insure his own fortune, and to the Prince of Orange peace in his old age.'

It was already Richelieu's policy to keep Spain busy in the Netherlands, and Baugy, understanding his master's wishes, loses no opportunity of jeering at the pacifist efforts of the painter-diplomat. A few weeks later, he writes again: 'The painter Rubens is here. The Infanta has ordered him to paint the portrait of the Prince of Poland; in which I deem that he will succeed better than in his negotiations concerning the Truce, to which he can only give superficial colours and shadows without any solid body or foundation.'

It was also known that secret negotiations went on between the Court of Brussels and the United Provinces, in spite of Spinola's military offensive. Rubens undertook fresh parleys in August 1624, during the siege of Breda (as is testified by a letter from an English agent to Secretary Conway), without however achieving any definite result.

Owing to the secret nature of these negotiations, it is impossible to know the exact proposals made by the trusted agent of Isabella and Spinola to the Dutch Government, but it is most probable that he endeavoured to take advantage of the military successes obtained by the Genoese general, to lay the foundations of a peace acceptable to Philip IV. All through these years, Isabella was bent on a practical policy of peace by negotiation, which did not suit the King and his minister Olivarez, who had not yet given up hope of bringing the whole of the Netherlands under the Spanish crown; and Peter-Paul was working under great difficulties, since he propounded a policy which was subjected to constant attacks from Madrid and could not therefore be taken very seriously at The Hague. It was no doubt to reinforce his prestige that he asked Philip IV to confer upon him a patent of nobility, which he received in June 1624.[1]

This diplomatic activity forms the background of the artistic work executed between 1622 and 1625, in connection with the decoration of the Luxembourg Gallery. It is easy to understand that Rubens had more than personal reasons for making himself agreeable to Marie de Medici, since she was inclined to adopt a neutral attitude between the Catholic and Protestant parties. The climax was reached when the marriage by proxy of Henrietta-Maria of France to Charles I of England brought to Paris a great gathering of European princes, among whom the Duke of Buckingham cut a brilliant figure. The fact that Rubens had been entrusted with the decoration of the great gallery, which was visited by most of these lords, was a particularly happy coincidence, for it gave the painter-diplomat an excellent opportunity to make a favourable impression on the man who directed the course of English policy, and to try by this means to improve relations between England and Spain.

For the arrangement concluded in 1623 between the two countries, concerning the Palatinate, had only lasted a few months, and complete estrangement had followed the unfortunate visit of 'Steenie and Baby Charles' to Madrid. James I had promised to send reinforcements to Holland in July 1624 and, under the influence of Cardinal Richelieu, Louis XIII had, in the same year, undertaken to grant an annual subsidy of one million pounds to the United Provinces.

The diplomatic task of Rubens during the Paris festivities

[1]In the following year, Isabella herself raised Rubens to the ranks of the nobility and, in 1627, she made him a 'gentleman of her household'.

was a delicate one, for, besides preserving the Queen-Mother's favour, he had to discover and, if possible, to thwart the Cardinal's plans and to seize every chance of getting into touch with Buckingham. He was greatly helped in this by Balthazar Gerbier, confidential agent of the Duke, who accompanied the latter during the nine days he spent in Paris to greet the new Queen of England. Gerbier too was an artist, and the fact that he was a native of Antwerp was another bond with his compatriot. In this short time, Rubens managed to do the honours of the royal galleries to the Duke, and to make sketches for his portrait and for that of the Duchess.[1] No doubt he also described the collection of pictures and antiques which he had gathered together at Antwerp. Buckingham, still dazzled by the splendours of the Luxembourg, was so deeply impressed by this description that, either immediately or soon afterwards, he offered to purchase the whole collection in the house on the Wapper —marbles and pictures—for the sum of one hundred thousand florins. After insisting on retaining a few marbles with which he could not be induced to part, the artist finally accepted the Duke's proposal; but further discussions served as a cloak for the diplomatic negotiations which Rubens really carried on, during the following years, with Balthazar Gerbier. There is little doubt that the master was prompted to part with his cherished possessions by his desire to obtain Buckingham's favour and to make the most of an excellent opportunity. Since he came to a final decision before the death of his wife, it would be a mistake to suppose that he gave up his treasures because he was too much depressed by this loss to take any further interest in them.

[1] The sketches are now in the Liechtenstein Collection, Vienna.

By that time, Rubens was evidently fascinated by the diplomatic enterprises into which he had been drawn. A long letter written to the Infanta from Paris, on the 15th of March, 1625, shows that he had succeeded in gathering up into his hands all the threads of information and influence, and that he did not hesitate to criticise any measure taken by Madrid or Brussels which seemed to him unwise or ill-considered. We have no record of his first conversations with Gerbier, but, from the correspondence which followed, we may infer that he informed his colleague of the peaceful inclinations of the Court of Brussels towards London and of Isabella's sincere wish to re-establish friendly relations between England and Spain.

Meanwhile, military events scarcely favoured this pacifist policy. Charles I had, with the United Provinces, France and Denmark, formed a coalition against the Hapsburg party, and an English fleet commanded by Viscount Wimbleton attacked Cadiz on November 1, 1625, while Mansfeld invaded the Palatinate. Both expeditions failed, but they provoked the wrath of Philip IV, who no longer followed Isabella's counsels, and threatened reprisals. He withdrew his representative in London and succeeded, in the following year, in concluding a treaty with France. No English military success having retrieved this diplomatic reverse, Buckingham decided to reopen negotiations with Spain, through the semi-official Gerbier-Rubens channel.

Having obtained a passport from his friend, Gerbier arrived in Brussels in January 1627, bringing with him a proposal for a truce between Spain, England, Denmark and the United Provinces. He suggested that this truce might be prolonged from two to seven years, during which the basis of a lasting peace could be established. The Infanta answered expressing the fear that difficulties might arise on the Dutch and Danish sides, and hinted that negotiations would be more likely to succeed if they involved only England and Spain. This was accepted with some reservations by Buckingham a few weeks later. Soon afterwards, at the beginning of May, another diplomat, who was to play an important part in these negotiations, reached Antwerp. This was the Abbé Scaglia, the representative of the Duke of Savoy, who had a special talent for mixing himself up in the affairs of others. Scaglia declared that, while in London, he had heard of the Anglo-Spanish negotiations carried on through Rubens, and that, as he desired their success, he had hastened to Belgium to warn the painter that France and England were negotiating a new treaty of alliance which, if concluded, would wreck the whole scheme. Rubens brought Scaglia to Brussels, and the Infanta was so impressed by this news that she sent an urgent message to Philip IV to obtain the necessary powers for treating with England.

The Spanish king was much embarrassed when he received Isabella's letter, for he had just ratified an alliance with France which aimed at nothing less than the invasion of England. He sent the necessary powers to the Infanta, however, but was careful to date them March 24, 1626, in order to avoid France's anger should the document fall into French hands. He also warned his aunt that he could conclude no treaty at the moment, but that he might try to gain time by discussing the conditions of a truce. In a letter dated June 15, 1627, he criticises the Court of Brussels for entrusting such important affairs to a 'painter': 'It is easy to understand that the reputation of this monarchy will necessarily suffer if a man of so little importance must be approached by ambassadors concerning such proposals'.

The Infanta retorted that Gerbier, like Rubens, was a painter, and that the Duke of Buckingham having sent him with an autograph letter for the aforesaid Rubens, it was impossible to negotiate without the latter.

Since we do not possess all the documents relating to these negotiations, it cannot be said whether Peter-Paul's next move was justified by the actual circumstances. In view of the evidence at our disposal, he certainly seems to have been somewhat hasty in his eagerness to obtain definite results. Not knowing that Philip IV was paralysed by the French treaty, he suggested to Gerbier that they should meet in Holland, thus taking the initiative of resuming the pourparlers. This move was bound to fail and it very nearly alienated Gerbier's sympathies, for, after coming to Holland and spending a week with Rubens at Delft, Buckingham's agent discovered that his friend could only give him vague assurances of the good intentions of the Infanta and Spinola, pending the arrival in Brussels of Don Diego Messia, Marquis of Leganes, with definite instructions from the Spanish king.

The only result of Rubens' visit to Holland was to cause some alarm to the French ambassador in that country and to his Venetian colleague and close ally; so that Carleton, who was still English representative at The Hague, was obliged to reassure them.

The master had paid several visits to some Dutch painters of his acquaintance, which gave colour to the assumption that his journey had been prompted by purely artistic motives. He had first called on Honthorst in Utrecht, who gave a great banquet in his honour, and had then proceeded to Amsterdam and other places where he saw Abraham Bloemaert, Cornelius Poelenburg and other painters of repute. He met everywhere with the most cordial reception, and a young German painter from Honthorst's studio accompanied him from town to town as far as the frontier of Brabant. This painter, Sandrart by name, who later became a writer on art, has left us an account of this journey. He recalls how happy he was 'to be able to enjoy the society of an artist who could so widen his knowledge of art by his conversation, his advice and his works':

'I could tell a great deal about this journey and of his [Rubens'] worthy conduct, but I shall sum up all by saying that, as he has excelled in his art, so I found that he was perfect in every other way, and that he was greatly esteemed by persons of the highest and the humblest rank.'

He adds that the master, on several occasions, praised Honthorst's 'perfect style of painting in his night effects', Bloemaert's 'noble drawing' and Poelenburg's 'charming little figures accompanied by delightful landscapes, ruins, animals and other accessories'.

In this way Rubens sought comfort for his unsuccessful meeting with Gerbier, treating as equals artists who are now only remembered because they happened to interest him, and magnanimously giving the benefit of his knowledge and wisdom to the admiring youth whom chance had placed in his way, while they cantered together along the avenues of the Dutch plain.

Don Diego Messia's arrival having been delayed, Gerbier, who had already spent six weeks in Holland without result, wrote a pressing letter to Rubens on September 6th, in which he begged him to obtain at least an autograph document from the Infanta and Spinola, to show that there was some solid ground for pursuing the negotiations. He was evidently anxious to save his face, and hinted strongly that both Rubens and himself would lose all credit in England if the business they had so carefully engineered should come to nothing.

Messia arrived in Brussels almost at the same time as Gerbier's letter reached Antwerp; he had come from Madrid through Paris, and been delayed in that city by the illness of Louis XIII. He had brought with him to the French Court a plan for a joint attack upon England by Spanish and French forces, the idea being to operate a landing on the southern coast and to march straight on London. Since the Spanish envoy had obtained the approval of Louis XIII and Richelieu, it goes without saying that Rubens could give no further encouragement to Gerbier. In a non-committal letter which he evidently intended that his friend should show to Buckingham, he declared that no written assurance could be given, since Don Diego Messia had 'enlightened the government of the Netherlands with regard to the understanding existing between the Kings of Spain and France for the defence of their kingdoms', but he assured him that both the Infanta and Spinola remained favourable to peace and that, if the Duke of Buckingham did the same, their correspondence might continue to be useful. This letter is written in Italian, as is most of the Rubens diplomatic correspondence, but shortly afterwards the master sent two personal letters to Gerbier, one in French and one in Flemish, in which he expressed himself much more freely and frankly, speaking of the Franco-Spanish aggressive scheme as of 'thunder without lightning, which will make a great noise in the air to little effect, for it is a component of divers humours gathered in one body, more by anger than by reason'. He was particularly bitter against Olivarez who, he said, allowed himself to be carried away by his passion while the majority of Spanish statesmen wished to come to terms with England, being convinced that the Franco-Spanish alliance would never mature. He adds:

'For myself, I am filled with regret for this ill-success, which is against all my best intentions, but I find this comfort in my conscience, that I strove sincerely and industriously to reach the goal, which I might have done had God not decided otherwise.'

Once more Rubens found himself thwarted by Spanish arrogance. Though he was not inclined to be quickly offended, he must have chafed bitterly under this disappointment, knowing full well that his enemies and even his friends would hold him partly responsible for the failure of the negotiations. Carleton and Gerbier, however, seem to have spent their anger on the unfortunate Leganes. The former wrote that this famous Messiah, after keeping everyone waiting so long, had at last arrived in the Netherlands, without fulfilling any of the hopes which had been centred upon him; while the latter declared more bluntly that the 'Messiah' had turned apostate.

*   *   *

Rubens was beginning to realise that it is not quite so easy, even for the greatest genius, to deal with men in real life as in pictures, and that it takes far more time and trouble to bring harmony into the world than to decorate a thousand churches and palaces. He knew already, from his Italian and French experiences, that princes were not always what they should be, and that their councillors sought their own interest more than that of the people they ruled. In his correspondence with his French friends (1626-27), he deplores the fact that nations should be 'governed by men without experience and incapable of following the advice of others'.[1] He laments the evils of war, wishing that he could live 'in an age of gold, instead of an age of iron' and 'that all the world should be at peace'. The distress in Flanders is insignificant compared with that which prevails in Germany and France, 'but truly we are tired, and so hardened to suffering that the war seems to us endless'. As for Antwerp:

'She languishes like a body stricken with consumption, and dying little by little. Each day the number of her inhabitants diminishes; our unhappy people cannot support themselves by their habitual industry or commerce. We must hope for some amelioration of these evils which our own imprudence has caused, unless we work according to that tyrannical maxim: It matters not if our friends perish, so our enemies be destroyed. But even that plan does not succeed, for our misery far surpasses the little harm we do our enemies.'

This intense sympathy for the people is rather exceptional on the part of a courtier, at a time when, in most European countries, the lot of the common folk did not greatly preoccupy the elect. It is all the more worthy of notice that, Rubens having had little opportunity of painting genre scenes (apart from the great 'Kermesse'), this feeling is

[1]Rubens had more particularly in mind the Spanish and English Courts. 'When I consider the caprices and arrogance of Buckingham', he wrote to Valavez, 'I pity this young king who, without need and through bad advice, throws himself and his people into such an extremity. . . .'

scarcely reflected in his pictures. But he was a Humanist in the full meaning of the term and made his own the motto *Homo sum, humani nihil a me alienum puto*, in more senses than one. His interest in the world was not merely that of an aesthete, a scholar or an antiquarian, but also that of a good citizen and, it may even be added, of a good European; for he understood far better than most of his contemporaries that the prosperity and happiness of his own country depended on the welfare of her neighbours and, above all, that aggressive war never provides a satisfactory and lasting solution of national troubles. No doubt the peculiar situation of the Southern Netherlands at the time helped him to reach this lofty point of view, but the fact remains that many casual remarks which slipped from the great painter's pen three hundred years ago, have to-day an almost prophetic sound.

The man was far too practical to be called a pure idealist, either in art or politics. He began painting no doubt because he felt that he could handle the pencil and the brush with exceptional skill and was therefore happy in his work. He was drawn later towards diplomacy because he discovered that he possessed a special aptitude for the task, but, just as his artistic achievements brought him to realise the eternal value of beauty, his political activities taught him the infinite worth of political wisdom as a cure for human sufferings. He was a painter before becoming an artist, and a diplomat before becoming a peacemaker.

If the aggressive plans of Olivarez against England had brought to naught Peter-Paul's efforts in 1627, the failure of the expedition led by Buckingham against the Island of Ré for the relief of La Rochelle paved the way for the renewal of negotiations in the following year. Towards the middle of December, Rubens received in Antwerp some letters from Gerbier and also from the Abbé Scaglia, who had returned to London. These letters suggested that the moment was particularly favourable for bringing about a reconciliation between the two countries, and that the Duke was well disposed towards such a proposal. By that time, both Madrid and Brussels had lost a great deal of confidence in the French alliance, for Louis XIII had not fulfilled his promise to withdraw the support in men and money which he gave to the United Provinces. When, therefore, Rubens communicated to Spinola in Madrid the purport of the messages he had received, the latter in his answer did not discourage the English offers, mentioning only that some reasonable basis for negotiations ought to be decided upon from the start, and this time he authorised Rubens to send a copy of his answer to Gerbier. The latter's reply was delayed owing to the sudden death of the messenger who carried it, and only on March 30, 1628, was Rubens able to communicate the correspondence to Spinola. Gerbier declared in substance that the King and Buckingham persisted in their intention of coming to an agreement, in spite of the small encouragement they had received from the Spanish side, and that, if Madrid gave full powers to the Infanta or her delegates to conclude a general treaty with the allies, or a special treaty with England, they would, on their part, hasten to choose suitable representatives. Before writing to Spinola, Rubens had of course consulted Isabella, who had no doubt approved the scarcely veiled suggestion contained in the covering letter. The painter had expressed the wish to pay another visit to Italy, adding that he would carry out or give up this plan according to the

King's decision. He apparently expected to be entrusted with this mission, but his hope was to be once more delayed by the cautious and hesitating policy of Philip IV.

On hearing from Spinola, Philip, who evidently wished that the negotiations should be carried on from Madrid and not from Brussels, ordered Isabella to obtain from Rubens all the Gerbier correspondence, on the pretext that the painter might have omitted certain important passages. Peter-Paul naturally demurred, not only because he did not wish to see the slight fabric which, for many months, he had so patiently and carefully woven with Gerbier, roughly handled by some Spanish grandee of the type of Messia, but also because the correspondence contained some very outspoken opinions on Spanish policy in general and on Olivarez in particular, which might bring about his undoing. He asked the Infanta to answer that the letters would be unintelligible without his personal explanations and that it would therefore be preferable for him to communicate them in Brussels to some person in whom the King had entire confidence, or else for him to bring them himself to Madrid. If Philip IV suspected the painter's good faith, Isabella's letters to her nephew show that she preserved entire confidence in him. 'As for me,' she wrote on May 31st, 'I do not doubt that Rubens has faithfully conveyed Gerbier's proposals.'

This question had assumed such importance that Philip wished to obtain the advice of the Junta on the matter. That august body met on July 4th, and proposed that Rubens should be asked to come to Madrid. 'It will thus be possible', declared the King's advisers, 'to delay negotiations, if it is considered necessary. If they must be pursued, Rubens's visit will in any case be rather advantageous than harmful.'

On receiving this invitation, Peter-Paul travelled post-haste to Spain, scarcely stopping in Paris, where he did not visit any of his friends, but making a slight detour to obtain a view of the siege of La Rochelle, which seemed to him a 'spectacle worthy of admiration'. This opinion may appear to be somewhat inconsistent, considering the trend of the writer's political activity. But Rubens was a peacemaker rather than a pacifist, and did not allow his spontaneous impressions to be influenced by any theories. He had his very good reasons for fighting war with all his might, but this did not prevent him from appreciating the colour of uniforms and the stirring bustle of warlike preparations.

★   ★   ★

Another feature of the master's character was his faculty for altering his opinions when new experiences proved them to have been unduly prejudiced. Under the stress of his negotiations with Gerbier during the previous months, he had declared that, 'when anyone who is dealing with the Spaniards turns his back, they profit by it to defer carrying out their promises', and had chafed against what he called 'the profound lethargy' which seemed to oppress the King and ministers of Spain.

Soon after his arrival in Madrid, at the beginning of September 1628, when he had had some opportunities of estimating Philip IV's character, he wrote to Gevartius:

'Personally, I have nothing but pity for the King. He is gifted by nature with all qualities of mind and body. In the daily intercourse I have had with him, I have learnt to know him thoroughly well: this prince would certainly be capable of governing under any difficulties, if he did not distrust himself and too much respect his ministers. Now he must suffer the blame of his own trustfulness . . . and be the victim of a hatred which should really be directed elsewhere. . . . *Sic visum superis cum nobis.'*

When in Antwerp or Holland, the painter-diplomat's plans had been thwarted by the policy of Madrid, and he had naturally held both King and ministers responsible for the mistakes he considered to have been made. But now, at close quarters, he was able to discriminate between them and to apportion blame where it was due.

Rubens' presence at the *Corte* naturally provoked a good deal of interest in the diplomatic world, and all kinds of conjectures were made by the various ambassadors. Alvise Mocenigo, for instance, wrote to Venice mentioning Rubens' secret meetings with Olivarez. His information was that the painter had come straight from England, where he had pursued mysterious negotiations with Buckingham, but he was doubtful whether the purpose of this visit was the truce with Holland, the peace with England, or both things at once.

Meanwhile, Scaglia and Gerbier did not remain inactive. They arrived in Brussels from London soon after Rubens' departure for Spain, accompanied by Endymion Porter, one of Buckingham's favourites who had been entrusted with a mission to the Spanish Court. Savoy played, on the Spanish side, more or less the same part as Venice on the French side, and, when received by the Infanta, Scaglia enlarged upon the excellent dispositions of both Charles and Buckingham towards peace. The latter had even declared, according to him: 'Let us treat with Spain and arrange the affair of the Palatinate; the Dutch will then have to agree to what we have decided.'

Gerbier was able to confirm these favourable tidings, and

the Infanta, finding Philip IV inclined to pursue the negotiations, delivered the necessary passports to Porter, who proceeded to Madrid while Scaglia and Gerbier took the road to Italy. When therefore, on September 28th, Olivarez assembled the Junta and summoned Rubens to appear before this council and give an account of the negotiations he had pursued, he was able to confirm the painter's declarations by the messages that Porter had brought with him and by several letters which Sir Francis Cottington, the English Secretary of State, had recently sent him, stating that he (Cottington) intended to come very shortly to Spain.

The murder of Buckingham caused some dismay to Olivarez, who had been the Duke's greatest antagonist in former years but who had lately considered him to be a powerful influence for the cause of peace. Madrid, however, was soon reassured by Sir Francis Cottington's letters to Don Carlos Coloma, formerly Spanish Ambassador to London. Cottington maintained that Buckingham's death did not alter King Charles' leanings towards peace, and that the Grand Treasurer, Sir Richard Weston, who was at that time the most influential man at the English Court, pursued the same policy. Several weeks passed, nevertheless, before matters came to a head. Endymion Porter left Madrid, but Cottington did not appear. Scaglia arrived at the beginning of January 1629, without, however, bringing Gerbier with him, and rumours spread that these delays were caused by new Anglo-French negotiations.

At last, at the beginning of April, the Infanta sent to Madrid the copy of a letter from Weston to Coloma, in which the Grand Treasurer declared that the English government, aware of the good intentions of Spain, had resolved to begin negotiations, and that, if the King of Spain sent an ambassador to London, the King of England was ready to send one to Madrid. This last news determined Olivarez to ask Rubens to go to England on a mission similar to that which Endymion Porter had fulfilled in Madrid. Though the master's artistic reputation insured him a worthy reception, Philip IV made him Privy Councillor for the Netherlands, and gave him besides a diamond ring in token of personal regard. He informed Isabella of this decision and of the painter's instructions in a long letter dated April 27, 1629.

★   ★   ★

That Rubens does not seem to have taken a very important share in the course of events during the nine months he spent in Madrid is no doubt due to the fact that no record is left of his letters to the Infanta during that period. It is certain, however, that his prestige increased every month, and that his advice carried more and more weight, even with those who had originally opposed his pacific policy.

From a 'mere painter' he had almost become one of the King's intimates. Philip seems from the very first to have lost all prejudice against him. He had assigned to Peter-Paul an apartment in the royal palace, and there he visited him almost daily, at first in order to sit for him and later for the pleasure of seeing him at work and of enjoying his conversation.

Even the grandees of the Junta had changed their minds. Olivarez, who, since his rise to power, had favoured the alliance with France against England, was gradually veering round. Rubens seems to have escaped criticism either because his correspondence with Gerbier, which he had been ordered to produce, had not been carefully examined, or because the most compromising of the letters, being written in

Flemish, had passed unnoticed. Don Diego Messia himself had become one of the master's most enthusiastic admirers and patrons. Don Jaime de Cordona commissioned him to paint a picture representing St. John the Evangelist. At no time perhaps did diplomacy and art walk hand-in-hand to better effect than during those Madrid months. The diplomat seems to have taken his work somewhat leisurely, being ready to help whenever his advice was sought, but retiring to his studio as soon as public affairs no longer required his attention.

The master's production increased considerably. According to Pacheco, Velasquez' father-in-law, who has left us an account of Rubens' work at the Court of Spain, the latter painted no less than five portraits of the King, among which one of Philip on horseback, with five other figures, was considered to be a masterpiece. He also executed several portraits of the Infanta Marguerite, daughter of Emperor Maximilian II, a Carmelite nun who had a great reputation for saintliness. Again, for the Archduchess Isabella, he made half-length portraits of the King, the Queen (Elisabeth of Bourbon), the Infante in his Cardinal's robes, Don Carlos, and the Infanta Maria Theresa. This is confirmed by a letter from Rubens to Peiresc, and most of the portraits are still preserved in Genoa, Munich, Vienna and Madrid; others have only reached us through engravings.

Pacheco adds that, besides these royal commissions, Rubens painted five or six private portraits and that, in spite of the fact that he suffered several times from attacks of gout, he copied 'all the pictures by Titian in the Royal Gallery'. This seems an exaggeration, since there must have been from sixty to seventy Titians in the King's collection; but the Spanish critic was none the less justified in saying that 'it seems incredible that, in so short a time, and amid so many occupations, Rubens should have managed to execute such a number of works'. Pacheco might have added: away from his workshop,—for, as far as we know, Rubens did not use the help of any other painter while he was in Madrid. He did not associate with his Spanish colleagues, with the sole exception of Velasquez, who was then twenty-nine years of age and had already established his reputation. Pacheco gratefully acknowledges the praise which the Flemish master bestowed upon the work of his son-in-law. In Spain perhaps even better than in Italy, Rubens was apparently able at once to distinguish genius from mere talent, and generously to recognise a brother in art whenever he met one.

A few of these 'Titian copies' have been preserved, among which 'Adam and Eve' and 'Europa' (Madrid). Like all copies by Rubens, they are not, of course, exact reproductions of the original designs. They might, indeed, more fitly be called Rubens variations on Titian themes, but the influence of Venetian colouring is very marked and this influence is henceforth to appear again and again in the master's later works, whenever he deals with a subject or design more or less akin to Titian's style.

We have seen how, during the Italian period, Rubens was drawn in various directions towards Raphael, Michaelangelo, Caravaggio or Correggio, but only now, twenty years after his departure from Italy, does he fully realise that, in the hierarchy of art, Titian is really his spiritual father, and understand that it is given to him to adapt to northern climes the realistic conceptions of the Venetian School.

By a curious coincidence, when Philip IV invited the

painter-diplomat to come to Madrid, the latter was already contemplating a second voyage to Italy. This was not a mere pretext for inducing the King of Spain to make his invitation more pressing, since before leaving Brussels for Madrid, where he had only expected to spend a few weeks, he had obtained permission from the Infanta to prolong his absence in order to pay another visit to Rome. There seems to be no doubt that, soon after the production of the Medici series, Rubens felt the need of stimulating his inspiration by fresh contact with the masterpieces he had so much admired in the past. This desire for a change of atmosphere was doubtless increased by the loss of his wife Isabella, which rendered a prolonged stay amid the familiar Antwerp surroundings particularly painful at the time. When diplomacy interfered once again with art and the master was requested to leave Madrid for London, he felt obliged to give up his Italian journey. But he had already found in Spain what he really wished to find in Italy. Philip IV's collection of Titians was perhaps the finest in Europe, and if the master did not copy them all he certainly used this unique opportunity to steep himself so deeply in Titian's conceptions and colouring that some of those conceptions never left his memory and that some of that colouring stuck to his palette to the last.

★ ★ ★

The intercourse established in Madrid between Rubens and Philip IV is only another example of the connection of the master's portrait-painting with his diplomatic and artistic activity. If it were possible to consult a full list of his portraits, we should find among them almost all the sovereigns, statesmen, collectors and scholars with whom he came into close contact, besides of course his personal friends and his own

16A. PORTRAIT OF JAN BRANT [1635

Pinakothek, Munich

Photo, Franz Hanfstaengl, Munich

16B. PORTRAIT OF GEVARTIUS
[ABOUT 1627]

Museum, Antwerp

family. Practically every one of these pictures has a story, and it is nearly always possible to explain how and why Rubens was led to paint it.

Several passages from the correspondence show that the master did not attach as much importance to his portraits as to his other works. Many of them were finished hastily after one or two sittings, or even from sketches. Rubens discriminates between those he painted 'from nature' and 'with great care' and . . . the others. The inferior quality of some of these works may also be due to the fact that a number of them are copies wrongly taken for originals and that, to satisfy his patrons, Rubens was several times induced to paint posthumous likenesses of their dead relatives or ancestors.

For all these reasons, Rubens' portraits are perhaps more unequal than any of his other productions, and this is all the more worthy of notice that, apart from the copies, the workshop methods could obviously not be applied to the same extent to this kind of painting. Some of them, such as 'Spinola' (Paris), the 'Self-Portrait' in Vienna, 'Jan Brant'[1] (Munich) and the admirable 'Bishop Yrsselius' (Copenhagen), challenge comparison with Velasquez' strongest characterisations. Others, such as 'Charles de Cordes' (Brussels), 'Helen Fourment as a Bride' (Munich), 'Anne of Austria' (Madrid), and 'Gevartius' (Antwerp[2]), have all the qualities of refinement and finish of the best Van Dycks. But Rubens' greatest admirers must recognise that a certain proportion of his portraits, though apparently by his own hand, are unworthy of his brush.

Fromentin attributes such weakness to the fact that the master was too self-centred to subordinate his own person-

[1]See pl. 16A, p. 186.   [2]See pl. 16B, p. 186.

ality to that of his model, and that he was better equipped to express a person's external aspect than his or her inner soul: 'We must distinguish in Rubens', he says, 'two observers: one who puts the lives of others to his own use, subjects his models to his own personality, and takes from them only what suits his purpose, and the other who remains beneath his task, because he ought to subordinate himself to his model, and is incapable of so doing.'

These reflections are evidently inspired by an unconscious comparison between Rubens and Rembrandt, and might also, to some extent, be applied to the great Italian masters; but Rembrandt's earliest works date from Rubens' mature period, and it is somewhat unfair to reproach the latter for failing to combine the exuberant life of the Renaissance with the deep feeling for atmosphere and the psychological penetration which appear for the first time in the history of Art in the works of his Dutch colleague.

The weaker specimens of Rubens' portraiture must not be attributed to any fundamental deficiency. In his best works, he certainly did subordinate his own personality to that of his model, as much as any other great artist of his day, with the sole exception of Rembrandt. But when time was short, or when the type of the sitter did not interest him particularly, he was apt to content himself with a good likeness, and did not trouble, as Van Dyck did, for instance, to add dignity and refinement to his work by a skilful treatment of costumes and accessories. We have already seen how, during the Italian period, he chafed against Duke Vincenzo's commissions for portraits. They were for him the 'small curiosities' he mentions rather scornfully in the correspondence with Carleton and, unless his model was particularly interesting to paint, he allowed his mind to wander while his hand worked almost mechanically. He was gloriously independent of his subject where large decorative painting was concerned, as is sufficiently shown by the Medici series. Had he applied himself in the same way to interpret the features of some of his sitters, he might easily have succeeded in imprinting on all his portraits the characteristic features so conspicuous in his masterpieces. But he was essentially a decorator, and the portrait is almost the only kind of painting for which he sometimes appears to lack enthusiasm. It was not only a question of size, for Rubens never complained when he had to prepare drawings from his pictures for the engraver's use, or when he provided his friend Moretus with designs and ornamental devices for his books. The work only appeared 'small' when the subject was uninspiring.

The criticism aroused by some of Rubens' portraits may lead us to revise any hasty conclusions concerning his realistic attitude of mind. The fact that the master insists so forcibly on the human aspect of religious, mythological or historical scenes does not in the least imply that his vision was limited to the observation of nature. If such were the case, the portraits would have been the kind of picture most, and not least, congenial to him. What he wished to do—consciously or unconsciously—was to infuse fresh blood into the decadent Italian conventions prevalent in his time by bringing such imaginative compositions into closer contact with reality, and more particularly with the realities of Flemish type and colouring.

Though he gave new life to the portraiture in the Southern Netherlands, as his contemporary Frans Hals did in the

North, he never considered that his main work was to carry on and perfect the fine tradition established in the sixteenth century by such portrait-painters as Floris, Moro or Pourbus. Flanders had always been rich in such works. The best of his energies must be devoted to making her the heiress of Italy and to raising her style from small specialised painting to the 'grand manner' of decorative composition. Whenever he has an individual likeness to introduce into such compositions, he never fails to rise to the occasion. The Medici series, for instance, is full of magnificent portraits. The Queen herself appears there at all ages and in every guise; Henry IV cuts such a living figure that some critics have wondered whether Rubens had not seen him during his earlier travels; Anne of Austria and Elisabeth of Bourbon, in the 'Exchange of the Princesses', are among the most exquisite full-size portraits ever painted.[1] The same power of individual characterisation is revealed in the marriage-scenes at Florence and in the great coronation-scene in St. Denis. But, while painting all these portraits, from life or from imperfect documents, Rubens was always conscious that he was painting history, and that these characters were playing their parts on the stage of the world, and he painted them with the same gusto as that with which Titian, Raphael, Pinturicchio and all the great Italian masters had introduced their own distinguished contemporaries into their decorative schemes.

[1]See pl. 15, p. 157.

CHAPTER VII

ENGLAND

WHAT EXACTLY was the situation of the two contending parties which divided Europe at the time of Rubens' departure for England?

The successes of the Imperial and Spanish armies, which had led to the occupation of the Palatinate and to the taking of Breda in 1625, had soon been checked by Richelieu's policy. The great Cardinal was by now the real master of France's destiny and, though he fought the Huguenots inside the realm because they threatened the principle of absolute monarchy which he desired to establish, he upheld Protestant interests outside France in order to weaken the power of Spain and Austria,—the only serious rivals which stood in his way. As has already been mentioned, he had promised regular subsidies to the United Provinces as early as 1624. James I followed suit, after the failure of the projected Spanish marriage between the Infanta and Charles, and, when the latter succeeded to the throne, he formed with France, Denmark and Holland a powerful league against Philip IV and the Emperor.

Such a combination would no doubt have proved fatal to

the Catholic party had the allies been loyal to one another. But Richelieu was all the time playing his own game and, to prevent any agreement between Madrid and London, or for still subtler reasons, he soon induced Philip IV to sign the secret treaty aiming at a joint attack on Charles which wrecked the pacific negotiations pursued by Rubens with Gerbier, with the approval of the Infanta, in 1627. So England and France found themselves once more in a state of open hostility. The French alliance soon proved as disappointing to Madrid as it had been to London. Richelieu did not cease to subsidise the United Provinces which, after the recall of Spinola, took the offensive under the leadership of Frederick-Henry of Nassau, brother of Maurice, who proceeded to blockade Bois-le-Duc. A diversion caused by Henri de Bergh, Spinola's successor at the head of the Spanish troops in the Southern Netherlands, was successfully checked; but the Republic was so exhausted by this effort, and her finances were so depleted, that negotiations for the renewal of the truce were continued with the Infanta, during the military operations.

We are not told what were the personal feelings of Rubens when he was asked to undertake his mission to England; but, from the general drift of the correspondence, it may be inferred that he did not accept it with alacrity. As has already been said, he had wished to take once again the road to Italy, and his artistic activities during his stay in Madrid show that the spell of his calling had again been cast upon his life.

In spite of his success, he was growing tired of Court intrigues and of the subtleties of seventeenth-century diplomacy, which did not suit his frank and outspoken nature.

But he had gone too far to draw back now without harming his reputation both at Madrid and Brussels, and the natural tenacity of his Flemish temperament prevented him from wasting the labour of several years just at the time when he had a chance of reaping the fruits of his previous efforts.

He had, besides, personal reasons for complying with his patrons' wishes. He had reached an age when a father who realises his responsibilities begins to think of his children's future; and the fact that he had been so long absent from Antwerp had tended to increase rather than weaken his solicitude. Writing from Madrid after an illness to his friend Gevartius, on December 29, 1628, he alludes with peculiar tenderness to his son Albert, who was then fourteen years old:

'I beg of you to take my little Albert, my other self, not into your sanctuary but into your study. I love this child, and it is to you, the best of my friends and Father of the Muses, that I recommend him earnestly, that you, together with my father-in-law and brother-in-law Brant, should care for him during my life or after my death.'

It is worthy of note that the appointment of Privy Councillor given to Rubens when he accepted the English mission, together with the emoluments attached to it, were to pass on his death to his eldest son, so that, by accepting the King's offer, he was securing at the same time a future and an income for his 'little Albert'.[1]

The painter-diplomat left Madrid on April 29, 1629. He passed through France even more rapidly than he had

[1] In another letter to Gevartius, written a few months later from London, after hearing of his son's illness, he says: 'God grant him life, *neque enim quam diu, sed quam bene agatur fabula refert*' (For what will be recorded of his life will not be how long but how good it has been).

done on his outward journey, only stopping a few hours in Paris to catch another glimpse of the Luxembourg Gallery, which was now completely furnished and which appeared to him 'more sumptuous than anything he had seen at the Spanish Court'. He stayed only a few days in Brussels, to see the Infanta and to take his final instructions from her. It was agreed that he should go to London as the official representative of Isabella and of the Spanish King, with full powers to arrange for a suspension of hostilities preparatory to the conclusion of a treaty,—the treaty itself being reserved for further negotiations as soon as diplomatic relations should be resumed and embassies restored in both capitals. The suspension of hostilities might be extended to the United Provinces and to Denmark if England so wished, but, since the Infanta was already negotiating directly for the same purpose with the United Provinces, through Jean de Kesseler, Rubens need not deal with this matter if Kesseler was able to settle it.

After a short visit to his Antwerp home, Rubens left for Dunkirk, accompanied only by his brother-in-law, Henry Brant, Secretary to the town of Antwerp, and sailed for England in the English warship the *Adventure*, on June 3rd. His haste was amply justified by events, for he had heard that, five days before his departure from Madrid, peace had been signed between England and France. Once again, the delays of Olivarez had seriously compromised Peter-Paul's efforts. The failure of the raid on the Isle of Ré and the fall of La Rochelle had greatly strengthened the position of France, and had deprived Charles of any excuse for interfering in French affairs. He was, besides, engaged at this time in a desperate struggle at home, and was only too ready to come to any arrangement which would not damage his prestige.

A few weeks before, after the vote of the Three Resolutions, Parliament had been dissolved *sine die*, and the King had declared that he alone possessed the power to call it together again, and that he alone was judge of the time when such a summons should be issued. Though the country was apparently calm, trouble was brewing, and Charles and the wisest of his advisers must have realised that the time for adventures was over and that any serious failure in foreign policy, leading to new wars and further public expenses, must necessarily strengthen the hands of the parliamentary party.

On his arrival in London on June 5th, Rubens went to the house of Gerbier, who had invited him to stay there. Buckingham's confidential agent, whose reputation had suffered by the loss of his master, was far too astute not to use this opportunity for attracting the attention of the Court by giving hospitality to the great painter-diplomat, whose fame had for years been established in England. Apart from the incident of the 'Lion Hunt', recalled in the Carleton correspondence, and which shows that Charles, while still Prince of Wales, had been most anxious to add a good picture by Rubens to his collection, we know that shortly after his marriage, in 1625, the King had specially asked Rubens to send him his own likeness—the well-known self-portrait which still exists in the Royal collection at Windsor.

Besides Carleton who, as Lord Dorchester, now held an important position at Court, we have seen that the master was also well acquainted with Lord Arundel, but the latter could not be very helpful to him, as he did not enjoy the King's favour and refused to take an active part in public affairs. Rubens knew, through the negotiations which he had previously carried on with Gerbier and Scaglia, that he could rely on the support of Sir Francis Cottington, Chancellor of the Exchequer, and he believed that the Earl of Carlisle was also well-disposed towards the Spanish peace. He was more doubtful as to the attitude of Sir Richard Weston, Lord High Treasurer, who, since Buckingham's death, had become the most prominent of the King's advisers. Among the foreign diplomats in London, Rubens possessed only one friend in Barozzi, the representative of the Duke of Savoy, with whom he was in daily contact, as he went to Mass in the Italian's private chapel.

It is through Barozzi's letters and the remarkable message sent by a certain Sir John Coke to an Antwerp merchant, who must have been in touch with the Infanta, that we are informed of the course of events after Rubens reached London.

Charles was evidently anxious to see the great man at once, for he commanded him to come to Greenwich on the morrow of his arrival. He received him very graciously and assured him that he would willingly sacrifice the French alliance, which was concluded but not yet ratified, if he could come to an understanding with Spain; but, when the painter mentioned a suspension of hostilities, the King did not even wish to discuss the point and advised him not to mention it to anyone, with the sole exception of the Lord Treasurer, since it would certainly be regarded as an artifice used by Madrid to gain time, in view of the critical situation at Bois-le-Duc. Such a temporary measure could be of little use, and he, Charles, would only consent to negotiate a treaty if Spain would undertake to give back the Palatinate to his brother-in-law Frederick. Rubens remarked that, as far as the question of the Palatinate was concerned, Philip IV, though willing to use all his influence with the Emperor, could not possibly break with him in order to be reconciled with Charles. He also hinted that Spain might renew her treaty with France, if the present negotiations should fail. Before parting, the King advised Peter-Paul to pursue these conversations with Weston in London, which the painter promptly did, bringing to the High Treasurer as well as to Cottington the letters which Olivarez had asked him to deliver to the English ministers.

The rest of the week was spent in festivities, which were highly gratifying to the painter's pride, but did little to further the success of his diplomatic mission. Both Carlisle and Dorchester gave receptions in his honour. There was a dinner at the Lord Treasurer's house, and a long conference at the same place between Rubens and the three statesmen with whom the King wished the negotiations to be pursued: Weston, Cottington and Pembroke. The painter regretted the exclusion of Carlisle, but it was explained to him that that nobleman was unable to keep any secret from his wife, and that the discretion of the attractive Lady Carlisle could not possibly be relied upon.

The three ministers were not more favourable than the King had been to the proposal for a suspension of hostilities; they understood that Spain could not break with Austria on the question of the Palatinate, but evidently thought that Madrid's influence at Vienna was such that she could obtain the necessary concessions without having recourse to extreme measures. According to Barozzi, Charles was still doubtful as to the sincerity of Spain's intentions and feared that the Rubens mission had only been used to gain time.

These doubts were fostered by certain foreign plenipotentiaries who had heard of the negotiations in spite of their supposed secrecy, and who did all in their power to bring them to naught. Joachimi, the representative of the United Provinces, declared that Rubens had brought with him no document worthy of mention and that his proposals were therefore futile. Alvise Contarini, the Venetian ambassador, who was entirely committed to France's policy, indulged in personal attacks upon the painter, whom he held to be 'an ambitious and greedy man who wished above all to be talked of and to obtain favours'. He suggested to the King that Rubens' arrival in London was bound to weaken his (Charles') friends and that the interests of Spain were entirely opposed to those of England; to which the King retorted:

'I have signed peace with France for the advantage of Christendom, and according to my constant principle with regard to the public weal. It is in the power of the French, if they so desire, to dissipate these shadows of painters (*queste ombre de pittori*) . . . , but I do not know what to think of them, for they have suddenly made open war upon the Huguenots.'[1]

In a letter to Olivarez written on June 30th, Rubens gives a very detailed account of a second interview which he had had with the King five days before. The trend of the conversation was similar to that of their first meeting, Charles showing the same kindness to the painter but being very emphatic on the question of the Palatinate, in which he was, he explained, in honour bound to receive some satisfaction in defence of his family interests. If Philip IV could not see his way to obtain the restoration of the whole of Frederick's estates, he could at least concede the towns held by his own

[1]Dispatch of Contarini in the Venetian archives.

garrisons. Rubens remarked that he was not empowered to treat such questions, which should be referred to the negotiators of the treaty, but that he had with him a proposal for a suspension of hostilities signed by Philip, which, if accepted by England, would give ample time for the two countries to come to an understanding. But again the King objected that he was prevented by his alliances with other Powers from agreeing to any proposals apart from them. He suggested that peace should be negotiated at Madrid, and that the Emperor and the Duke of Bavaria (who had by now ousted Frederick from his Bohemian throne and placed himself at the head of the German Catholic princes) should be invited to send representatives.

Unwilling to lose any chance of coming to terms, the painter undertook to send these proposals to Madrid and received, at the same time, a formal promise from the King that, pending the results of the negotiations, his relations with France should not assume an aggressive character towards Spain. In so doing, Peter-Paul was evidently overstepping the limits of his instructions and exposing himself to the criticisms of Olivarez (which did not fail to reach him in due course), but his peculiar position gave him greater authority, at least in England, than that of an ordinary agent, and the practice of art had taught him that no definite results can be gained if one is not prepared to take certain risks. As before, at the time of the Gerbier negotiations, he did not allow his loyalty to paralyse his initiative; neither did he forget that the policy of the Infanta was not exactly the same as that of Olivarez, and that the conclusion of peace with England was of even greater interest to Belgium than to Spain.

Having seen Weston and Cottington shortly after this conversation, and the latter having declared that the King had gone too far with regard to the Palatinate in conceding the principle of possible partition, Rubens returned the same day to Greenwich, in order to obtain from the King full confirmation of what the latter had said on the subject. Peter-Paul feared what he called the 'instability of the English temperament', and was also disturbed by the fact that no advantage which Charles might grant him could be of any use unless it were approved by his ministers. 'For,' he writes, 'if in other Courts affairs begin with the ministers and end with the King's sanction and signature, here they begin with the King and end with the ministers.' He also thought that if, before the arrival of the French ambassador, the Anglo-Spanish negotiations looked unsatisfactory, they would become hopeless after Chateauneuf had had opportunities of using his powers of persuasion.

'There are several parties in this Court; [he wrote] one, which is led by the Earl of Carlisle, wishes peace with Spain and war with France; the second, which is much larger, wishes peace with everybody; to tell the truth, I believe the Grand Treasurer is of this opinion and also Lord Holland. The third is the worst: this party wishes a war with Spain and an offensive league with France against her; it is much strengthened by the [imminent] arrival of the French ambassador, and it works mightily through the Venetian ambassador, a bad influence at this Court.'

The prospects appeared so unfavourable to Rubens that he wrote to the Infanta to ask permission to return to Brussels, and would have left immediately to make his report to her, had not Cottington insisted on retaining him in England and promised to draft a dispatch with him for Olivarez' information.

Twelve days later, the situation had improved considerably and Rubens was able to announce to Olivarez that, 'thanks to the good offices of their friends', Charles was persevering in his peaceful resolutions. He, Rubens, had urged the immediate nomination of the English ambassador to Madrid, and the King had just informed him that he had designated Cottington and had fixed his departure for August 1st, so as to leave sufficient time to obtain Olivarez' answer to the proposals included in Rubens' previous dispatches. This success was the more remarkable that Richelieu had recently written to Weston informing him of Chateauneuf's early arrival, and telling him that the French ambassador came with full powers to conclude an alliance for the recovery of the Palatinate. In the ordinary course of events, the King might have awaited Chateauneuf's proposals before making definite arrangements with regard to the Spanish negotiations.

Though the painter preferred to attribute these good dispositions to the favourable influence of Spain's friends at Court, it seems certain that his own personal charm was beginning to work in London as it had worked at Madrid, and that the keen interest which Charles took in painting was proving no less helpful than Philip's enthusiasm for pictures.

Charles could not be said to possess the art of government, but he had many other accomplishments which helped him to appreciate Rubens. He too was a good linguist, and understood the classics. He had the greatest respect for literature, delighted in Shakespeare's works and was a personal friend of Ben Jonson and of May, the translator of Lucan. He loved music and performed on the viol da gamba. He patronised at Mortlake a manufacture of tapestry which, had it been allowed to flourish, might have challenged all its rivals. He had lately purchased the entire collection of the Duke of Mantua, and, since his Spanish voyage in 1623, had acquired a number of works by Quentin Massys, Holbein, Titian, Raphael, Correggio and others. He had made Van Dyck welcome when the latter had been brought to his Court by the agency of Lord Arundel, and we know that it was on Rubens' advice that he bought Raphael's cartoons of the 'Acts of the Apostles', which are now preserved in the Victoria and Albert Museum. He was, in fact, with Marie de Medici and Philip IV, the greatest patron of art in Europe, and tradition will have it that he asked Rubens to correct some of his own drawings.

The latter may, in a moment of impatience, have written that the King's decisions were controlled by his minister's wishes, but it is rather remarkable that, whenever he succeeded in making any progress in his diplomatic work, this progress was invariably due to the King's interference. There were so many points of contact between the Flemish painter and the English King, that on more than one occasion their conversation must have wandered from the dreary affairs of State to the more congenial subject of art and antiquities; so that when 'serious business' was resumed the atmosphere was cleared of the clouds of former disagreement.

Within a month of his arrival in England, Rubens had thus succeeded in gaining the King's confidence and in obtaining a promise that negotiations should begin forthwith. The obstacles which now stood in his way were no longer in London but in Madrid.

On July 6th, the master was able to confirm the good news which he had sent to Olivarez a few days earlier:

'The King has bidden me to inform Your Excellency that he has appointed his ambassador to Spain. It is Sir Francis Cottington, and the 1st of August is fixed for his departure, on the condition, however, that in the interval His Catholic Majesty shall make a similar arrangement concerning his own ambassador and the date of his departure.'

Rubens had suggested to the King that he should go to Brussels and report to the Infanta, but Charles had objected that this report might just as well be made by letter, and that it was necessary that he, Rubens, should remain in London for the arrival of the French ambassador, in order to prevent any suspicion on the part of Spain and to 'make it impossible for the French to spoil the negotiations by spreading false and malicious rumours, according to their habit'. The King was evidently as satisfied with the painter as the painter with the King. There was no talk now on Rubens' part of the 'instability of the English temperament'. According to Barozzi, he was 'much pleased with the sincerity with which the King had spoken to him', and he even said that Spain might very well relinquish the towns of the Palatinate which James I had given in trust to the Spaniards in 1623. This pleasant state of mind was scarcely disturbed by the arrival of Chateauneuf, who was coolly received; the painter states with obvious pleasure that 'most of the coaches sent to meet him remained empty, although their number did not exceed twenty'.

But Olivarez and the Junta had grown restless on hearing

Rubens' news. His remarkable activity caused them some alarm, and they strongly objected to the interpretation he had placed on the strict instructions given him. The painter had been sent to London to settle a suspension of hostilities. This offer having been turned down, the only thing left to him was to withdraw from the scene, and not to compromise Spain by urging the conclusion of a treaty and even beginning to lay down the basis of negotiations.

We do not possess Olivarez' letter of criticism, but Rubens' answer, dated July 22nd, leaves no doubt as to its contents. The Spanish minister reproached him for overstepping the limits of his instructions, by dealing with a treaty when he had only been appointed to deal with a suspension of hostilities, and for giving an opinion as to the manner in which Charles' suggestions would be received at Madrid. Peter-Paul retorted that he had remained strictly faithful to his orders, but that he could not prevent the King from mentioning matters outside his instructions, and that he had never expressed any opinion with regard to the acceptance or refusal of Charles' proposals, but had merely undertaken to transmit them to Madrid. In so doing he was carrying out the express command given him by the Infanta, in view of the efforts made by Richelieu to wreck the negotiations.

Though couched in the most courteous terms, Rubens' reply is not lacking in a certain blunt firmness. He had extracted a promise that an English delegate should be designated to go to Spain and that a time should be fixed for his departure; he had also obtained a written document in which the King set forth his proposals (to which reference will be made later), in spite of the fact that Madrid had not yet nominated an ambassador to London, and that no answer whatever had been made to the English suggestions enclosed in his dispatches of June 30th. In short, everything that was necessary had been done in England, while nothing had been done in Spain. How could it be said that he had disregarded his instructions when the latter mentioned explicitly the simultaneous exchange of ambassadors, Philip's willingness to give some satisfaction to the 'friends and relations of the King of England' in Germany, and the desirability of preventing as far as possible the conclusion of the forthcoming Anglo-French agreement? Rubens annexed to his dispatches a ciphered copy of the document mentioned above, which he had received a week earlier and which need not be reproduced here, since its contents correspond exactly with Charles' verbal proposals, although—as Rubens remarks in his covering letter—certain terms are slightly attenuated. The possession of such a note, written and signed by the Grand Treasurer, under the King's orders, was obviously of great value to Spain, and the fact that the King had granted this document to Peter-Paul while an agreement with France was under discussion in London shows the absolute confidence he had in him. Charles had told Rubens to write to Olivarez that: 'he trusted his [Olivarez'] generosity and discretion far more than he should trust that of Cardinal Richelieu, to whom he would never deliver such a document, since he would immediately communicate it to the adverse party in order to derive some profit from it.'

It was not without a certain satisfaction that the painter was able to counter the criticisms of his Spanish master by sending him fresh proof of his diplomatic skill. To the same dispatches he also added Weston's and Cottington's answers to Olivarez' letters, which are glowing testimonials to the discretion and tact shown by Rubens since his arrival in London. Weston speaks of all the trouble Rubens has taken over the negotiations and adds that 'he has won the esteem of all, not only by his fine talent, but also by his great abilities', while Cottington declares that his choice as an envoy 'has been much approved here, not only because he is most able and skilful in dealing with public affairs, but also because he has gained the esteem of everyone and especially of the King my master'.

After presenting Olivarez with so many proofs of the credit he enjoys in London, Rubens elegantly begs to be allowed to return home, 'not that he prefers his own interest to the service of His Majesty the King, but because, seeing that for the moment there is nothing for him to do here [in London], he deems that a longer sojourn might be harmful to him'. In the meantime, with the abject politeness of the period, he recommends himself humbly to the minister's kindness, and 'with all his heart and all due respect, he kisses the feet' of His Excellency, of whom he is the most humble and devoted servant.

The main cause of trouble between Rubens and his 'master' was not that he had not exerted himself enough to bring his negotiations to a successful conclusion, but that he had exerted himself too much; not that he had been too slow and uncertain, but that he had been too quick and resolute. He had been sent to put out feelers and to prepare the ground, not to grasp every opportunity and ride straight to the goal. The Junta wished, above all, to gain time, and Richelieu's intrigues were not entirely discouraged at Madrid. If England did not prove amenable, there was still the resource of a new treaty with France, and meanwhile the wisest course was to sit on the fence and carefully examine on which side it would be more advantageous to jump. Olivarez must have been somewhat embarrassed on receiving Rubens' answer, for he could not possibly confess the true reason of his displeasure. The Infanta's straightforward policy was once again becoming inconvenient, and the London mission appeared as another aspect of the old conflict between the pacific policy of Brussels and the ambitious policy of Spain.

Chateauneuf, in the meantime, was striving hard to bring Rubens' efforts to naught. He was conferring with Carlisle, Holland, Pembroke, Arundel and Dorchester, concerning the possible alliance for the recovery of the Palatinate by Anglo-French forces and the 'freeing of Germany from the oppression of Austria'. He did not hesitate, according to Rubens' reports, to suggest to certain lords and more particularly to Lord Holland the necessity for calling Parliament together, saying that, as long as the King postponed this measure, he would never agree with his subjects or possess the money and troops necessary to help his friends and attack his enemies. In thus exploiting England's internal troubles and the jealousy existing between Weston and Holland, the French ambassador seems to have overstepped the mark, for 'many people considered that it was an odious and impertinent move on the part of the representative of a sovereign so lately reconciled with England to interfere in the internal and domestic affairs of the kingdom.'

As the date of Cottington's departure approached, Richelieu's efforts increased, and Rubens thought fit to warn Olivarez that the Cardinal would not hesitate to use the strongest means of persuasion at his disposal:

'At the moment it is right that you should be informed as to the state of things in this Court, in which connection it should first of all be mentioned that the greatest lords lead a sumptuous life and spend enormously, so that most of them are heavily in debt. Among the first of these are the Earl of Carlisle and the Earl of Holland, who hold their followers together and their position among the nobility by their table, luxury and generosity being highly esteemed in this Court. I cannot speak of all the other lords and ministers, who, for the most part, have insufficient revenues to support their rank, and are obliged to fulfil their needs as best they can, and that is why both private and public interests are sold here for cash down. And I firmly believe that the Cardinal de Richelieu is very liberal in gaining partisans by this means.'

Rubens had just learnt in strict confidence from Cottington that an English agent of Richelieu, named Furston, had recently arrived in London and, unknown to Chateauneuf, had brought to Weston a letter warning the King of England against the treacherous offers of Spain, and promising him to take the offensive on all fronts if he would only give the assistance of his fleet to ravage the coasts of Spain, in conjunction with the Dutch. If Charles abandoned the project of an 'infamous peace with Spain', Louis would give him any advantage within his power. He had urged his sister, the Queen of England, 'who is greatly opposed to Spain', to 're-spect her husband as it was her duty'. In conclusion, Richelieu offered a large sum of money to the Grand Treasurer, in the form of capital or pension, as he preferred. Cottington had brought this remarkable document to the King, who had laughed after perusing it, saying that 'the cunning and dis-loyalty of Cardinal Richelieu were well known to him and that he would rather make an alliance with Spain against France than with France against Spain'.

Although French diplomacy seemed to defeat its own ends in its eagerness to prevent Cottington's departure for Madrid, and in spite of the fact that the King remained constant to his peaceful intentions, Rubens must have congratulated himself on his foresight in procuring a written document confirming the latter. He knew that Cottington's departure might be delayed, as the minister might at any time be detained by some urgent affair of State, but the written and oral assurances which he had received allowed him to devote at least some of his time to visiting art collections and to the company of English art lovers and scholars.

The impressions he gathered from such visits are summed up in a memorable letter, dated August 8, 1629, to his French correspondent, Pierre Dupuy:

'If in my youth I had visited in so short a time so many different countries and Courts, it would have been much more valuable to me than it is now, when I am old. My body would have been more fitted to bear the inconveniences of post-travel, and my mind, by the experience and knowledge of such diverse people, would have been made capable of grander things in the future. Instead, my body uses up all the strength which is left to me, and I shall not have time to enjoy the fruits of so many labours. All I shall have won is to die knowing more.

'However, I console myself by thinking with joy on all the beautiful things I have met with on my journeys. This island, for example, seems to me worthy the consideration of a man of taste, not only because of the charm of the countryside, and the beauty of the people, not only because of the outward show, which appears to me most choice and to announce a people rich and happy in the bosom of peace, but also by the incredible quantity of excellent pictures, statues and ancient inscriptions which are in this Court.'

Rubens' praise of England to Dupuy is fully confirmed by another letter to Peiresc:

'If I were allowed to dispose of my affairs according to my wishes and to arrange my occupations as I like, I should have come to you long ago, or I should be with you now, but I do not know what spirit, whether good or bad, is always disturbing my projects and drawing me in opposite directions. My only pleasure is to see, during my pilgrimages, so many various countries, so many cities, so many peoples following different customs. I am far from finding in this island the barbarous ways which its climate might warrant, since it is so different from gracious Italy, and I must even confess that, from the point of view of painting, I have never seen such a quantity of pictures by great masters as in the Palace of the King of England and in the gallery of the late Duke of Buckingham. The Earl of Arundel possesses an enormous number of antique statues and of Greek and Latin inscriptions, which you have seen, since they have been published by John Selden,[1] with the learned commentaries which one might have expected from that talented and cultivated author. You have no doubt seen his treatise *De Diis Syris*, which has just been reprinted in a revised and enlarged edition. But I wish that he would confine himself to the bounds of science without

[1] Selden's treatise had been reprinted in Holland in 1627. He had been arrested for having denounced the illegality of the King's levy of the subsidies of Tonnage and Poundage. The Arundel Marbles are still to be seen in the Ashmolean Museum, Oxford.

mixing in political disorders, which have made him lose his liberty, with several other members of Parliament, who are accused of offending the King during the last session.

'There are also here the 'Cavalier' Cotton,[1] a great antiquarian, very remarkable for the variety of his knowledge, and the secretary Boswell,[2] and other people whom you must know perfectly and with whom you are no doubt in correspondence, as you are with all the distinguished men of the world. The latter (Boswell) told me lately that he had at his disposal and would communicate to me the text of certain omissions in Procope's history concerning Theodora's debauches; these passages were omitted in Allemannus's edition, no doubt for the sake of modesty and decency, and have since been discovered in a manuscript in the Vatican.

'I have only seen the famous philosopher Drebbel[3] in the street, and scarcely had time to exchange a few words with him. He is still in the country, in a place somewhat remote from London. He is like those things of which Macchiavelli speaks, which appear larger far off than near. I am assured that for many years he has produced only this optic instrument with a perpendicular tube, and which enlarges enormously the objects placed underneath it. . . . I do not wish to trust to hearsay against such a celebrated man, but I shall

---

[1]Robert Bruce Cotton owned one of the richest libraries in England. Peiresc had actually met him in London.

[2]Sir William Boswell was, at this time, secretary to Lord Carlisle. He was, as a matter of fact, in correspondence with Peiresc.

[3]A physicist and inventor, born in Alkmaar in 1572. He had obtained a pension from James I, and claimed the invention of an apparatus demonstrating perpetual movement, a submarine ship, and several scientific instruments. During his whole life, Rubens showed the keenest interest in science, particularly in physics and astronomy.

make a point of seeing him in his house and of speaking with him familiarly if at all possible. I do not recall having ever seen a man of more extravagant aspect than his: there is in this man, ill-clad in coarse clothes, something which surprises you and which would make anyone else look ridiculous.

'I hope, with the permission of my superiors, to be able to retire to my house, where I did not stop four days on my return from Madrid. After so long an absence, home must require my presence most urgently. I have not lost hope of accomplishing my pilgrimage to Italy. My desire to do so increases on the contrary, from hour to hour, and I assure you that, if fortune prevents me from going, I shall neither live nor die content. You may be sure that on the way there or coming back, but most probably the former, I shall come and present my compliments, in your fortunate Provence, and it will be the greatest happiness which can still come to me in this world.'

If we cannot follow Rubens week by week and month by month during the time he spent in England, we may, at least, understand from documents of this kind how deeply impressed he was by the beauty of the English countryside, as he wandered from one great house to the other; by the wealth of the English collections, which, in spite of the Revolution which followed, still remain one of the most characteristic traditions of English life; and by the knowledge and taste of English scholars and antiquarians.[1] He must also have been pleased with the elegance and perfect etiquette ob-

---

[1] He had a further opportunity of coming into contact with the latter during a visit to Cambridge in October 1629, when the Senate entertained him lavishly and conferred upon him the honorary degree of Master of Arts.

served at the Court of Charles, which provoked the admiration even of the most critical French courtiers of the time, and he doubtless had occasion to witness several of those gorgeous masques and comedies in which the King and Queen took an active part, and which were denounced so fiercely by the Puritans. It was hard, no doubt, for Rubens to be kept so long from home, but he seems to have found in England an atmosphere more congenial to him than that of Spain.

*   *   *

Meanwhile, the Junta had at last been stirred to take some action. At its meeting of July 24th, called specially to deal with Rubens' dispatches, it had been decided that, with the King's approval, Don Carlos Coloma should leave for London when Cottington embarked for Spain, and that the Emperor and the Duke of Bavaria should, at the same time, be invited to send representatives to Madrid; but the councillors were not optimistic, for they thought that the French successes in Italy and the critical situation of Bois-le-Duc would stiffen England's attitude.

Owing to some absurd misunderstanding, the date of Cottington's projected departure was allowed to pass without any news reaching London as to Spain's intentions. The French ambassador took advantage of these delays to press his demand for an aggressive alliance against Spain, urging again that France would assume the whole responsibility of the war if the English joined the Dutch in attacking the Spanish forces on sea and in threatening the Indies. The promise given by Charles not to take any steps against Spain was now almost the sole obstacle to the French alliance.

It was only on August 17th that Rubens heard that Don

Carlos Coloma had been chosen as future ambassador to London. He hastened to inform Sir Francis Cottington and the Grand Treasurer, and rode or drove seven leagues from London to Oatland, where the King was residing at the time. Charles showed great pleasure at this appointment, but remarked that Sir Francis Cottington could not leave at once for Madrid, owing to pressing duties, and that it was doubtful whether he would be free before the end of August or beginning of September.

The unaccountable tardiness of Spain had now provoked a corresponding postponement on the part of England, and Cottington himself, Rubens' most loyal and constant ally, showed some nervousness. He and Weston expressed their surprise that Olivarez had not thought fit to answer the English proposals. Weston insisted that it would be a mistake on the part of Madrid to imagine that further concessions could be obtained. In a private conversation with the painter, Cottington was most emphatic concerning the danger he himself was running in accepting this mission: he foresaw a thousand difficulties and his ruin seemed to him inevitable; 'he had wrought a miracle in obtaining from the King this document (sent by Rubens to Olivarez on July 22nd) and in having it approved by his Council, as the French offered *carte blanche* only to prevent the peace with Spain. The promise, contained in the last lines of the document, not to conclude any agreement with France which would be harmful to Spain, was of such importance that it sufficed to prevent and evade all the intrigues and machinations of the adverse party'.

Cottington further remarked that the absence of reply from Madrid regarding the English suggestions might lead

to the postponement of his departure; but Rubens endeavoured to turn the tables on him by insisting on the difficulties he himself had had in obtaining a written document
containing definite proposals. Had the English ministers
made up their minds earlier, he would no doubt have now
been in a position to inform them as to Madrid's views on
the subject.

In the same dispatches in which he relates this discussion,
the painter-diplomat—once again over-stepping the strict
limits of his instructions—emphasises the importance of the
negotiations from the Spanish point of view:

'I have neither the talent nor the position [he writes], to
give advice to Your Excellency, but I consider that this peace
is most important, as it seems to me the knot in the chain of
all European confederations. The fear alone of its conclusion
has already proved effectual, and the rupture of the negotiations would cause a great deal of emotion and acrimony. If
their issue should become hopeless, the whole face of things
would soon be changed. I admit that, for the King our Lord,
peace with the United Provinces matters even more, but I
doubt whether this can ever be concluded without the intervention of the King of England; whereas peace between
Spain and England is practicable, and its conclusion would
give the Dutch food for thought; it might even influence the
decisions of other Powers. Such a peace is in the hands of
Your Excellency, and a great result might be obtained by
the promise of restoring a few towns, for it must appear
evident to any prudent man that, if this peace were concluded,
all the others would follow.'

Rubens was obviously growing restless under Olivarez'
apparent apathy, and made desperate efforts to persuade him

that the interests of the Infanta and of Belgium were inseparable from those of Philip and of Spain.

A week later, on September 2nd, Rubens returns to the attack: The absence of answer from Madrid is discouraging to the friends of the Spanish peace; Cottington himself fears that as soon as he reaches Madrid he will be obliged to return empty-handed; and the French ambassador is growing so optimistic that, instead of placing obstacles in the way of the minister's departure, he does his best to hasten it. The Duke of Savoy, who had so long upheld the Anglo-Spanish negotiations, has now veered round to the opposite party, and Barozzi has become unreliable. The news of the taking of Wesel by the Dutch and of their successes near Bois-le-Duc are also having an unfortunate effect on the negotiations.

At last, on September 14th, Rubens received Olivarez' dispatches, approving all the steps he had taken and acknowledging the receipt of Charles' proposals. But by that time, Weston, who was loth to part with his most trusted colleague, had put forward the argument that Cottington could not leave before the receipt in London of a detailed and entirely satisfactory answer from Olivarez. Rubens appealed successfully to the King against this new objection, only to be countered by Weston, who urged that the duration of Cottington's absence should be strictly limited. This proposal was of course backed up by Chateauneuf who, finding himself unable to prevent the English mission to Madrid, was now trying his hardest to make its success impossible. Once again, the painter-diplomat was able to parry this thrust, and no time-limit was set to Cottington's activity, Charles declaring that he trusted the latter's discretion to carry out his instructions as quickly as possible.

Feeling his hands strengthened by the approval of the Junta, Rubens resumed his part of self-appointed adviser. His long dispatches of September 21st prepare the ground for Cottington's mission. He starts with an emphatic eulogy of the English minister, whose 'sincerity and good faith could not be greater if he were our King's own councillor', and explains in detail Cottington's proposed attitude:

'He will speak to you in two different manners: the first in his capacity of English ambassador, the second as if he were councillor of State to our Lord and King and the faithful servant of Your Excellency. First, he will explain clearly to Your Excellency all the advantages which will accrue from this peace and alliance, if—as the King his master wishes—it is concluded in such fashion as to produce the closest union possible, an indissoluble union between the powers and hearts of the two sovereigns. Secondly, he will make Your Excellency realise the serious inconveniences which must be feared if the King of England should find himself compelled to ally himself with France, the Dutch, the King of Sweden, the German princes (including the Duke of Bavaria), and in Italy with the Venetians, the Duke de Nevers and several others who, though they hide it at the present moment, would soon show their bad intentions against Spain in the event of a break with England.'

In order to drive his argument home, and to impress Olivarez with the importance of the peace with England, Rubens insists on the anger aroused in the French camp by the progress of the negotiations. The French ambassador seems to have lost his head, and declares to the King that, even if Cottington leaves for Madrid, Coloma will never come to London. Furston has appeared again with a secret message for the Grand Treasurer, dwelling on the Dutch successes in the Netherlands (Bois-le-Duc had fallen by this time) and on the Swedish successes in Germany; as his brother-in-law, Louis, must warn Charles against compromising all his interests in the Palatinate by sending Cottington to Madrid. Richelieu further promised that he would bring the Duke of Bavaria into the alliance against Austria—the only means of getting him to restore the Palatinate.

When this letter was communicated to the King, his only answer was: 'Let Cottington hurry, let him leave at once.'

Cottington only left a fortnight later, on November 4th. Rubens was expecting Coloma every day. Then occurred a last accident which very nearly wrecked the frail structure so carefully built up by the painter's skilful and persevering hands. The English representative in Brussels wrote on the 16th that he had seen Don Carlos Coloma, who had coolly told him that he had not yet received any instructions from Spain and that he could not leave for London before their arrival. Both Charles and Weston were evidently incensed by this news, which they considered to be a gratuitous outrage. The King sent an urgent message to Cottington, enjoining him to suspend all negotiations pending further instructions, and Weston vented his fury without restraint on Rubens:

'The Grand Treasurer spoke to me with great anger and emotion. . . . He declared to me that from this moment he looks upon the negotiations as broken, and that the French, and more particularly their ambassador Chateauneuf, were certainly right when they said that the Spaniards laughed at the King of England, that they had no intention of sending an ambassador to the Court and that their only aim was to entice Cottington to Spain by vain promises, hear his proposals and only decide afterwards whether they should send an ambassador to England or not. . . . I consider this delay in the present situation so bad that I curse the hour in which I came to this kingdom. Please God that I leave it safely!'

This appeal was sent to the Infanta by special courier. It reached Brussels at the same time as Philip IV's orders to Coloma to proceed immediately to England. These orders had only been sent from Madrid on November 5th. Both Isabella and Coloma advised Rubens accordingly, and the latter was once more able to calm the storm and to persuade Charles to allow Cottington to resume negotiations. The latter, who had remained some time in Lisbon awaiting further orders, arrived in Madrid at the beginning of January, while Coloma was received in the Banqueting-House on January 6th, with all the pomp and circumstance due to his rank and to the solemnity of the occasion.

With the arrival of Spain's official ambassador, Rubens' mission virtually ceased. If any further negotiations concerning the proposed treaty were to be transacted in London, Coloma alone was qualified to fulfil this task. Besides, the scene of operations had now been transferred from London to Madrid, where peace was signed at last between Spain and England, on November 15, 1630. Philip IV promised to use his influence with the Emperor to restore the Palatinate to Frederick, and undertook to give back to him the towns then occupied by Spanish troops, as soon as he, Frederick, should make his submission to the Emperor.

Thus Rubens' efforts had finally borne fruit; but the peace was not to bring about the wonderful effects he had so optimistically foretold to Olivarez. Political, economic and religious forces, against which no man could contend, were driving the whole of Europe towards division and strife, and the painter was soon obliged to recognise that all he had been able to do was perhaps to postpone for a few years the terrible ordeal which threatened the very existence of his country and caused such appalling suffering throughout Europe.

★　★　★

In the Rubens room of the National Gallery hang two pictures which indicate in a striking way the change in the master's political outlook from 1630 to 1637.

The first is entitled ' Peace and War',[1] or 'Minerva Protecting Peace from the Assaults of War'. From a comparison between the woman and children in this allegorical composition, and the various versions of the 'Gerbier Family', there seems little doubt that the painter's hostess and her family sat for the figures in the central group. The lady herself and several of the children, more particularly the dreamy-eyed little girl facing the spectator,[2] are easily recognisable in both the Fremantle and the Windsor groups. A leopard lies at the feet of Peace, beside Pan in a crouching attitude, holding a horn of plenty. On the left, stand Happiness striking a tambourine and Abundance dressed in green; on the right, Mars in a threatening attitude, repulsed by the strong arm of Minerva pressed on his shield; while against the stormy clouds of the background is discerned a figure impersonating the miseries of war. In its glowing Titianesque colouring, no doubt reminiscent of the months lately spent by Rubens with the works of the Venetian master in Madrid, the picture seems to radiate a sense of confidence and happiness. All its

[1]See pl. 17, p. 213.
[2]Who also appears in a small portrait, in Lord Spencer's collection.

18. THE HORRORS OF WAR [1637-1638]

Pitti Palace, Florence. *Photo, Alinari*

lines are restful and composed. It was not commissioned by Charles, but presented to him by the painter, probably as a parting gift in token of gratitude for the confidence and sympathy shown him by the King during the course of his successful mission.

The second picture hangs a few steps away from the other. It is much smaller, and is merely a very finished sketch for an allegory now in the Pitti Gallery, Florence, entitled the 'Horrors of War'.[1] We are particularly well-informed regarding the latter picture, for the master himself explained its somewhat complicated symbolism in a letter written in 1637 to his colleague the painter Sustermans, through whom he had received the commission from the Grand-Duke of Tuscany. Here Peace is replaced by Venus trying in vain to hold back Mars, who has stepped out from the Temple of Janus and is drawn forward by the tragic figure of Alecto, torch in hand. At his feet lie a woman with a broken lute, a mother clasping her child: 'showing that fruitfulness is threatened', and a prostrate workman still holding the tools of his trade (a builder's): 'to show that what is built in time of peace is destroyed by war'. Mars is treading on a book and on some sheets of paper covered with sketches. On the ground also lie a quiver with broken arrows (the shafts of love), a caduceus and an olive-branch (the despised emblems of peace). On the left, with hands upraised to the stormy heavens, and clad in mourning weeds, stands Europe 'who for so long has been plunged in sorrow'. She is followed by a child bearing a globe surmounted by a cross, symbolising the Christian world. The wise Minerva is no longer here to prevent War's onrush. All is distress and violence, the symbols

[1]See pl. 18, p. 220.

of civilisation and culture are trodden underfoot, and the lines of the picture, instead of swaying in graceful curves, cut across each other in fierce and almost cruel antagonism.

The European situation had grown from bad to worse during the interval of seven years which separates the two pictures, and, by the time the second was painted, the master had been compelled to realise that his efforts would be better employed in the pursuit of his artistic career than in endeavouring to obtain immediate results in the diplomatic sphere. Indirectly, he might still use the influence his reputation gave him in the cause of peace which he had so long defended in speaking and writing; but the brush was, after all, his most powerful instrument, and both the sketch in the National Gallery and the finished picture in the Pitti show that he could, when opportunity arose, place it at the service of his political ideals. This horror of war, for the sufferings it inflicted on its innocent victims—and the Thirty Years' War was, perhaps, the most fierce and cruel ever waged before the age of industrialisation—for the irremediable damage it wrought on the monuments of art and learning to which Rubens was so devotedly attached, for its brutal power of destruction, which hurt both the humanity and the humanism of this great 'builder', is perhaps the only idea (apart, of course, from his religious beliefs) that Rubens ever consciously defended in his paintings. In all other matters, he felt perfectly justified in complying with his patrons' wishes, as long as they gave him the opportunity of displaying his decorative powers. He glorified Marie de Medici on the walls of the Luxembourg, and James I on the ceiling of the Banqueting-House in Whitehall, without examining whether his heroes or heroines were really worthy of such apotheoses.

He had no scruple in indulging the taste which prevailed in his day for subjects of a sensuous character, and exploited lavishly both the Old Testament and classical Mythology for this purpose. He did not hesitate to depict fierce hunting scenes, and even battle scenes, in which he could show his extraordinary ability for expressing violent movement. But he never missed an opportunity of extolling the virtues of peace and denouncing the crimes of war.

This tendency appears in most of his allegories, which are not, like so many modern productions of this kind, the expression of a loose and conventional symbolism, but thoughtful compositions worthy of the most careful attention. His early 'Heroes crowned by Victory' (in Munich, Cassel and elsewhere) have not only won their glory by the strength of their arm, but because of their success in overpowering hatred, envy and all the forces of destruction. It is for the same reason that, deservedly or undeservedly, Marie de Medici sits enthroned, surrounded by all the virtues of peace, and that James I sails so loftily into Heaven on the ceiling of the Banqueting-House. Force may be extolled, but it is always the force of Minerva against the violence of Mars, constructive wisdom against destructive brutality.

★   ★   ★

Although the actual paintings for Whitehall were not finished before 1635 and several of the sketches were no doubt executed after Rubens' return to Antwerp, the original conception of this decorative scheme must have taken place during the last months spent by the master in London. The project vaguely alluded to in the Carleton correspondence eight years earlier had borne fruit. Charles' appreciation of Rubens' genius confirmed him in his wish to possess in London a reception hall which might equal and even surpass in brilliancy the Luxembourg gallery. He commissioned the master to paint three large compositions for the roof of the Banqueting-House, showing the 'Apotheosis of James I', 'James I nominating Charles to the Throne of Scotland', the 'Beneficent Reign of James I', surrounded by six allegorical panels emphasising the virtues of order and good government. If Charles had also been able to carry out the plan which he is supposed to have conceived, of commissioning Van Dyck to decorate the walls with pictures relating to the Order of the Garter, and if sufficient care had been taken to protect Rubens' work from the injuries of the London climate, his dream might have been realised. But the walls remained bare and the roof was allowed to deteriorate so badly that, in spite of recent restoration, the central panel showing the 'Apotheosis of James I' is now the only one which can give some idea of the original colouring. The designs (as they appear from the sketches in the Louvre, the Hermitage, Vienna, Cologne, Brussels and English private collections), with their powerful foreshortening effects, rank among the finest of Rubens' works, but the finished paintings must have suffered from the fact that the master was unable or unwilling to come to London in 1635, and entrusted to a pupil the delicate work of touching up the great canvases after they had been placed into position. There seems to have been a fate against the decoration of Inigo Jones' great hall, as against most of Charles' enterprises.

★ ★ ★

The months spent in London were among the least productive of Rubens' artistic career and in strong contrast, from this point of view, with his sojourn in Madrid. The position was entirely different. The master had been called to Spain to give an account of his conversations and correspondence with Gerbier and had not been required to take any active part in the deliberations which followed. He was sent to London on a special mission which, considering the interpretation he gave to his instructions and the obstacles he encountered, absorbed all his energies and left him little time for painting. The part he had played in Madrid may be compared to that of a witness, while in England he assumed the responsibilities of a barrister and had to plead his cause not only with Charles and his ministers but also with Olivarez and the Junta.

The peculiar position he held as the envoy of an enemy country must also have curtailed his activities. It appears startling at first that, while Van Dyck produced so many pictures of Charles I, the royal family and the principal lords and ladies of the Court, the only portraits by Rubens which can safely be attributed to the London period, apart from the 'Gerbier Family', are those of a curious character, the 'old Parr', on whom popular belief conferred the fabulous age of 145 years, and of Theodorus Turquetus Mayernius, the King's physician, whose services the painter, who was frequently afflicted by attacks of gout, no doubt required on several occasions. If we remember that every ruler with whom the master had been connected—the Duke of Mantua, Albert and Isabella, Marie de Medici and Philip IV—had commissioned him to paint a number of portraits, this can only be accounted for by the fact that, despite their admiration and esteem for the painter, the King and his ministers could not place themselves on so intimate a footing with an agent of Spain. Whatever their personal wishes may have been, they had to take into account the comments which such an action would most certainly have provoked among the partisans of France.

The only likeness of Charles and his Queen painted by the master during his stay in England, are very discreet indeed and scarcely recognisable. In the picture preserved in Buckingham Palace, Charles plays the part of St. George and the Queen that of St. Agnes, in a landscape which is said to be a view of the Thames Valley at Richmond. According to a letter written by an English contemporary, this work 'wherein, if it be possible, Mons. Reubens hath exceeded himself', was executed 'in honour of our nation, from whom he hath received so many courtesies'. The letter goes on to say that 'he [Rubens] hath sent the picture home into Flanders, to remain there as a monument of his abode and employment here',[1] but the writer probably alludes to a replica, since the original seems never to have left the royal collection. Apart from this work, and of course from the decoration of the Banqueting-House, which was to be carried out at a later date, the only other commissions that Rubens seems to have received from the King while in England are designs for a silver ewer and basin, which were executed several years later by a famous Antwerp silversmith. The grisaille sketch for the salver, representing the 'Birth of Venus', is to be seen in the National Gallery.

After attending a series of dinners and festivities given in honour of Coloma and himself, Rubens took leave of the King on March 3rd. Charles conferred a knighthood upon

[1] Rev. Joseph Mead to Sir Martin Stuteville, March 6th, in *The Court and Times of Charles I.*

him on this occasion, and, in token of special regard, presented him with the jewelled sword with which the ceremony had been performed, a diamond ring and a diamond hatband.

These last days in London were given up to farewell visits. Rubens showed his courtesy not only to the friends who had helped him during his difficult mission, but even to some of his most obdurate opponents. We know that he made a point of calling on the Dutch ambassador Joachimi, and that he took this opportunity to beg from him the release of thirty Flemish sailors who, after being captured by the English, had been handed over to the Dutch and imprisoned at Rotterdam.

The painter's departure from Dover was delayed until the 23rd of March, because he wished to extend his protection to a party of English boys and girls who were going to school at Douai and various convents. Such acts of kindness were no doubt part of his daily life, but it is rather a happy coincidence that the last news we possess of Rubens' peaceful mission in England should concern the protection of the weak and the relief of the oppressed.

CHAPTER VIII

HELEN

'WHEN ZEUXIS prepared to paint Helen, he chose five virgins and composed his heroine from their various beauties. But greater than Zeuxis is Rubens, of whom one knoweth not whether to say he excelleth in his eloquence or in his art; behold he possesseth the living image of the Helen of Antwerp, who far surpasseth the Helen of Greece.'

Thus does Gevartius sing the praises of his friend's bride, a few months after Rubens' return to Antwerp.

After the anxiety of diplomatic negotiations, the constant risks of Court life, its fickle friendships and stubborn hatreds, the long months passed in strange houses under foreign skies, the master must have felt a deep sense of relief at being once more at home among his books and collections, warmed by the admiration of his pupils and comforted by the sincere and open-hearted sympathy of his friends. The memory of Isabella was ever-present, but it no longer awakened those pangs of grief which had led the widower to wander about the world. He found Albert, no longer 'Albertulus', and Nicholas, much changed and ripened, under the guidance of good Gevartius and able now to share their

228

19A. HELEN FOURMENT IN BRIDE'S DRESS [1630-1631]

father's interests; the old circle of Romanists, Moretus, Rockox, and the two Brants among them, pursuing as keenly as ever their antiquarian studies; and every house in the town ready to receive him as a most honoured guest.

Among those houses was that of Daniel Fourment, a silk merchant whose son had married Clara Brant, Isabella's sister, and here the master, after his day's work, fell into the habit of spending his evenings. There were eleven daughters, one of whom—Susanna—had made a strong impression on Peter-Paul, who had used her likeness in various pictures and painted her portrait several times, notably in the so-called 'Chapeau de Paille' (National Gallery). But, as in the old stories, the youngest daughter was the fairest. When he married her on December 6, 1630, in the Church of St. Jacques, he was fifty-three and she was sixteen. Rubens was not in the habit of opening his inner soul even to his most intimate friends, and, if we were to believe his letter to Peiresc, written four years later, his motives would seem to have been anything but passionate:

'Being unable to make up my mind to live in celibacy [he writes], I took the step of marrying again; for, while placing continence above everything, it is permitted us to give our senses legitimate satisfaction, thanking God for the pleasures He grants us. I have, therefore, married a young woman of honourable, though middle-class birth, although everyone advised me to choose a lady about the Court. But I was chiefly afraid of finding my companion subject to pride, that plague of the nobility. That was my reason for choosing one who would not blush to see me take up my brush. And, to tell the truth, I loved my liberty too much to exchange it for the embraces of an old woman.'

Judging from this, the sole piece of self-confession we possess on the subject, the master would appear to have considered carefully whether his religion allowed him to give his senses some 'legitimate satisfaction', and, finding the answer to be in the affirmative, whether it would be wiser to take a young bourgeoise from the town or an old lady from the Court. But the score of portraits still preserved of Helen, in her bride's dress, her town dress, and no dress at all,[1] in her home and in her garden, as herself, or as somebody else, smiling and demure, serious and dreamy-eyed,—and the other score of paintings, which are haunted by her figure in all kinds of parts, heroic, mythological, allegorical, and even religious, such as Venus restraining Mars, a nymph pursued by a satyr, or the young Virgin taught by Anna—are perhaps more faithful interpreters of Rubens' real feelings.

No wonder that, in spite of those cool remarks, the master's second marriage is considered by posterity as one of the most passionate ever lived. Never has the brush inflicted a more emphatic contradiction on the pen. Had Rubens been a poet instead of an artist, had he been childlike and humble instead of prudent and wise, he would have confessed in writing what he so openly confessed in painting: that he was madly in love with Helen, that the whole world was Helen for him, that she had brought a new spring into his life, new children into his home and new inspiration to his art, that she had made him feel as young at fifty as he had been at twenty, and that henceforth the main purpose of his efforts was to lay his achievements, his reputation and his honour at her feet.

Considering that the mature and learned Humanist and philosopher had very nearly lost his head, one cannot help

[1]See pl. 19A and 19B, p. 229.

wondering how this robust beauty of sixteen kept hers and how, possessing as she did such power over such a man, she never yielded to the temptation of abusing it. In the course of this story, there have been several opportunities to point out that, besides being one of the greatest men who ever lived, Rubens was one of the most fortunate; and he was never so fortunate as when, on the brink of old age, he brought into his home this healthy, bright-eyed girl, who irradiated with her smile the last ten years of his life, and moved him to fresh enthusiasm and discoveries which led to the creation of some of his finest masterpieces.

Critics have endeavoured to distinguish various periods in Rubens' career, and to assign to each period a distinct character, but the chronology of his works is so elusive that some of these generalisations must perforce be questioned. The Italian period stands, of course, by itself as a time of experiments, while the 'Adoration of the Kings', following the first return to Antwerp, inaugurates a new and original style. But 1630 is certainly a date to be remembered, because there is no picture posterior to that date—apart from purely School works—which does not reach the highest standard of Rubenian art. These last ten years are flooded with a golden light, and its glowing colouring blends the crude reality of Flanders with the dreamy romanticism of Venice. The influence of the Titian worship in Madrid can be traced almost everywhere. It shows how sound was the master's instinct when, after the great effort of the Medici series, he wished to go back to Italy. This new baptism in Renaissance classicism conferred upon his later work a poetical quality sometimes lacking in earlier days. There had been strength, sincerity and an unsurpassed wealth of imagination, but one often missed the supreme mark of genius, the touch of the magic wand which conjured up atmosphere. It is impossible to say to what extent the beautiful Helen of Antwerp was responsible for this transformation, but there is certainly a strange coincidence in the fact that the two tendencies, realism and classicism, which contended for supremacy in Rubens' art, never reached such perfect harmony as when her conquering beauty appeared in his life.

★　★　★

In the same letter to Peiresc in which Rubens mentions his marriage to Helen Fourment, he gives an account of his life during the years which followed his return to Antwerp and congratulates himself on having 'renounced all employment likely to draw him away from his dear profession: *experti sumus invicem fortuna et ego*'. He explains how he took the fateful decision to devote himself entirely to his art, without allowing politics to interfere any further with his work:

'When I found myself lost in this labyrinth, obsessed night and day by a host of importunate affairs, cut off from home during nine months, obliged to be constantly at Court, being at the height of favour with the Sérénissime Infanta (whom God keep in His glory) and with the first ministers of the King, honoured by the approval and esteem of those with whom I had dealings abroad, I took the resolution to do violence to my own feelings and to cut this golden knot of ambition in order to recover my liberty. Considering that it is meet to carry out a retreat of this kind at the flow rather than at the ebb, and to abandon fortune while she favours us rather than wait until she turns her back upon us, I seized the opportunity of a short voyage I was taking secretly, to go and throw myself at Her Highness's feet and beg of her, as my sole reward for so much endeavour, to exempt me from new missions and to be allowed to fulfil my duties without leaving my home. I obtained this favour with more difficulty than any other which she has been pleased to confer upon me, and, even so, certain negotiations and secret affairs of State, with which I can deal without overmuch inconvenience, have been left in my charge. Since that time, I have not dealt with French affairs, and I have never repented of having taken this resolution. At present, as you have heard, I find myself, by the grace of God, beside my wife and my children, at rest and with no other ambition in the world than that of living in peace.'

This second confession seems far more genuine than the first one, though Helen and her children are timidly placed in the background, whereas in reality they were one of the most absorbing interests in the master's life. That he was tired of politics, and that his retirement was not due to pique or thwarted ambition seems clear from the evidence at our disposal. He had reached the highest honours that any man of bourgeois birth could possibly have desired. He had received from the King of England, in December 1630, the diploma of his knighthood, in which Charles declared that he (Rubens) was particularly dear to him, 'not only because of his affection for us and our subjects, but even more because he has rendered himself worthy in the eyes of our Court by his great fidelity to the King his master, by the wisdom and practical knowledge which so eminently enhance the nobility of his mind and the glory of his race'.[1]

As Rubens could not have used his English title and arms

---

[1] Though Rubens undoubtedly received a knighthood from Charles, the authenticity of this diploma has been questioned.

(a canton gules with a lion or) in his own country, he asked Philip to grant him the same favour as that which he had just received from Charles. This request was strongly endorsed by the Infanta, who, in order to prevent objections on the score of the petitioner's profession, argued that, since this distinction would be conferred by reason of the exceptional services rendered by the painter, the granting of it would not constitute a precedent for similar requests from other artists. Besides, had not Charles V made Titian a Knight of St. Jacques?

After the usual delays, the Spanish diploma reached the new knight six months later, and he was able to read with satisfaction a great many gratifying remarks concerning the 'good and agreeable services' which he had rendered the King on various occasions, in the Netherlands, Spain and England, 'having honourably and usefully acquitted himself of his duties, with commendable zeal, skill and competence'.

If he had formerly felt some scruple in devoting himself to the pursuits of art and the study of antiquities, at a time when Europe and Belgium were threatened with a political catastrophe, he could now quiet his mind by thinking that he had sacrificed, during the last seven years, most of his time to political work, spending many months away from his home and his family. Though the Anglo-Spanish peace, which he had done so much to bring about, had not proved as efficient a remedy for the crisis as he had hoped, it was nevertheless a concrete achievement of which any statesman might have been proud. Peter-Paul felt therefore that he had taken his full share of worldly affairs, paid his debt of loyalty to his country and earned the right to resume the work for which he had been born and which he had so long neglected. If, according to his letter to Peiresc, he had to 'do violence to his feelings', it was a sweet violence which drove him to his studio and to Helen's arms.

An incident which occurred on the morrow of Rubens' marriage shows that, even before taking his final decision, the master felt little inclination to leave his home again and to take on new diplomatic duties. After the signature of peace, the Junta had designated Juan de Necolalde, the King's secretary, who had been in Brussels for the last two years, to represent Spain in England. As the Infanta still required the secretary's services at this time, the King advised her to send Rubens instead, because he was 'in very high favour at the English Court and fit to negotiate all kinds of affairs, considering the prudence which he shows'. Two months later, on June 18, 1631, Isabella announced to the King Necolalde's imminent departure for England, adding that, if she had not sent Rubens, it was because 'she had not found him willing to accept this mission unless it were only for a few days'.

* * *

The workshop was as busy as ever, though some of the old pupils had gone and new ones had replaced them.[1] The rate of production does not seem to have been quite so high, perhaps because the master, under the new circumstances, exercised greater control over the important works. This certainly seems to have been the case with the series of decorative pictures illustrating the life of Henry IV, which he was then preparing for the Luxembourg Palace. This was the second part of the commission entrusted to him by Marie

[1] Van Dyck, of course, had left the studio long before and Jan Breughel had died in 1625.

de Medici eight years earlier, which he had not been able to fulfil before owing to the unfinished state of the building. Judging from the two great pictures in Florence, 'Henry IV at the Battle of Ivry' and the 'Entry of Henry IV into Paris',[1] as well as from various sketches still preserved in England, Berlin and Vienna, the Henry IV series, had the master been allowed to finish it, might have been his finest decorative work. This time, at last, the painter had a hero to deal with, and the consciousness of that fact inspired him to greater efforts.[2] The sketches are reminiscent of the 'Decius Mus' series, of the great battle scenes of the first Antwerp period, and of Mantegna's 'Triumph' which the master had had a recent opportunity of admiring again and very likely of 'copying' during his stay in London.[3] We find in them the old energy and imaginative power, but the mellowness of the colouring and a certain classic restraint in the composition would stamp these works as belonging to the last period, even if we did not know the historical circumstances which prevented their completion.

* * *

Richelieu was a great admirer of Rubens' art, but he was no friend to Rubens' policy, and politics were far more important to him than any pictures. Though the painter-diplomat had held a relatively small position on the world's stage, where the Cardinal's red robes loomed very large, these two great men—perhaps the greatest of their time—had been en-

[1] See pl. 20, p. 236.

[2] See letter to Peiresc, May 16, 1625: 'The subject is vast and magnificent enough to fill ten galleries.'

[3] The Rubens 'copy' is now in the National Gallery and the original in Hampton Court.

20. HENRY IV'S ENTRY INTO PARIS [1628-1631]

Uffizi, Florence. *Photo, Alinari*

gaged in a prolonged conflict during the last five years.
Richelieu's main plan was to isolate the Hapsburg powers
from the rest of Europe and to stir up strife between Catholics and Protestants for this purpose, whereas all Rubens'
efforts tended to bring about peace between England and
Spain and between the Southern and Northern Netherlands.
While in London, he had succeeded in parrying the attacks
of his powerful enemy, and in thwarting his intrigues. It was
not to be expected that the Cardinal would ever forgive him.
As early as 1626, he had tried to persuade Marie de Medici to
entrust the commission of the Henry IV series to Joseppin;
Guido Reni was also mentioned. Then came some difficulties about the measurements of the panels, which caused
further delays. It was evident that, if ever the antagonism
which was growing between the Queen-Mother and her old
councillor came to a crisis, the fate of Peter-Paul's commission would hang in the balance.

That time was not far distant. 'The Day of Dupes',
November 10, 1630, brought about a complete break between the Cardinal and Marie. The latter had been practically imprisoned at Compiègne. Gaston d'Orléans, the
King's brother, and the Duke of Lorraine raised troops to
support the Queen-Mother, and applied to the Infanta for
help. Isabella's position was particularly difficult, for Philip
had written to her to do nothing that might jeopardise the
good relations existing between France and Spain. In the absence of d'Aytona, the Spanish ambassador at her Court,
she again asked Rubens to take charge of the negotiations
and to meet de Valençay, who had been sent by the Duke of
Lorraine to the Netherlands.

On July 18th, Marie succeeded in escaping from Compiègne and was forced by circumstances to cross the frontier. D'Aytona went with Rubens to meet her, and, at their suggestion, she took up her quarters in Mons, where some of her French partisans came to join her. This seemed an excellent opportunity for Philip to interfere in French affairs and wreck Richelieu's prestige. D'Aytona wrote to Madrid emphasising the advantages which might be derived from an alliance with the Queen-Mother's party: 'Neither Your Majesty', he declared, 'nor any of your Royal Predecessors have ever had so propitious an opportunity to humble your greatest enemies.' In a long letter to Olivarez, Rubens urged him to support Marie de Medici, as far as was possible without breaking the peace. He remarked that the Dukes of Orleans and Lorraine did not so much require military as financial help. All they asked for was three hundred thousand golden écus, and Rubens prayed Olivarez 'to free generous Spain from that false opprobrium in which she is held by obstinate opinion, as a nation who cannot promptly grasp opportunities but who, after infinite deliberation, sends help too late. *Post bellum auxilium*.'

As the master seems to have foreseen, events fully confirmed the conclusions arrived at by the 'obstinate opinion' of Spain's critics. The Junta deliberated without coming to any resolution; the King wrote to Isabella, enjoining her to make no promises, and to Marie, who had by now reached Brussels, bidding her welcome in the Belgian capital and expressing platonic wishes that Providence might bring her affairs to a happy solution. Paralysed by lack of funds, the Queen Mother wasted a good deal of time in quarrelling with the Duke of Orleans and found some slight comfort in visiting Rubens' studio, where she may have seen the unfinished

Henry IV series, a symbol of her own curtailed political career. After giving her what help he could in disposing of some of her jewels, Rubens (as recorded in the Peiresc letter mentioned above) finally begged the Infanta to be released from all duties connected with French affairs. He realised that, once again, Olivarez' dilatoriness had made him miss a golden opportunity and that Spanish help, if it did come, as indeed it came during the abortive war which followed, would be too late and, instead of ruining Richelieu, would only contribute to increase his power.

*　　*　　*

These alarums and excursions, though somewhat disturbing, had not interfered seriously with the painter's activity, The Henry IV series had come to naught, but there were many other orders on hand and, whenever opportunity arose and patrons were not too pressing, the lovely Helen was always there to be painted.

There is an almost childlike eagerness in the way the master dressed her for her part. Looking through the series of her portraits, it seems as if he had wished to try the effect of every style and fashion, and to record for all time how she looked with her hair done in one way and in another, with a toque and feathers or a broad-brimmed hat, or that quaint cap surmounted with a pom-pom, which was apparently the latest fashion in Antwerp at the time. There is the same variety in the dresses, from the loose négligé worn at home to the stiff satin skirt and corselet and elaborate sleeves of formal occasions. And with each new dress, shown either in full length, or half-length, or merely head-and-shoulders, the lady wears a new expression and the artist works in a different mood. Some of these paintings are highly finished and almost elaborate in their insistence on details of jewellery, frills and laces, while others—and some of the best, such as the sketch in the Louvre—are hasty impressions, rapidly outlined.

The new mistress of the Wapper house appears never to have wearied of this artistic adulation. She undoubtedly possessed the generous and warm-hearted nature peculiar to women of her type and race; she was not likely to trouble about the past or to worry about the future, being content, without enquiring why or wherefore, to accept the wonderful gifts which Providence had sent her. Nicholas appears in some of these family groups, and such scenes as the 'Morning Walk' (Munich), for instance, leave little doubt that Helen succeeded in spreading contentment and giving comfort to the whole household, from the master himself down to the dog and the peacock running and feeding in the grounds, and from her stepsons down to her last-born baby.

Albert was frequently absent at this time. Helen's four children—two girls and two boys—were born between 1632 and 1637; a fifth, Constance Albertine, was born eight months after her father's death. That there was no antagonism between the past and the present is clearly shown by the names given by Helen and Peter-Paul to their third child: Isabelle-Hélène.

Although the year 1630 marks a new progress in the master's career, his artistic methods do not alter appreciably. Nothing, indeed, is so remarkable as the way in which he succeeds in improving his technique without in the least changing his conception of art and life. There are few men of genius in Renaissance or modern times who do not, at certain periods of their career, alter their outlook and allow such changes to influence their works; but Rubens remains throughout as unperturbed in his Catholic faith and his Humanism as in his conception of pictorial beauty. He goes on producing religious, mythological and allegorical pictures in that semi-realistic and semi-classical style which he has made his own since his return to Antwerp in 1608, using all the material accumulated during his travels, all the antiquarian knowledge which he possesses or borrows from his learned friends and all the experience of his personal life.

The quality of his works improves with the course of time, for every experiment bears fruit and every exploration yields results, but the nature of such experiments and explorations remains the same. This is due no doubt to the strength of his personality, though such strength is at first sight difficult to reconcile with the faculty which allows him to suit his work to almost any contingency. The explanation of this apparent contradiction lies perhaps in the master's extraordinary power of transforming, as well as remembering, every new impression he receives, whether from nature or from art. We have already noticed his peculiar method of 'copying' the works of the great masters, of utilising his memories of or his sketches from antique statues, and of introducing his family and friends into his religious and allegorical compositions. This process of using every opportunity and of replenishing the inexhaustible stores of his art goes steadily on until the end of his career. It is the secret of his eternal youth. At no time does Rubens call a halt and show that, having prepared himself thoroughly for his work, he is now ready to devote himself entirely to production. Education and creation walk hand-in-hand throughout his whole life. He remains un-hampered by theories or abstract generalisations. If he seems to lack ideas, it is certainly not through lack of intelligence. The fact is, that he was too much absorbed by his painting to theorise about it; had he done so, he would probably have observed that the business of a painter is to paint, and have turned back to his palette.

★   ★   ★

A typical illustration of this constant influence of Rubens' life on his paintings is to be found in the change of the dominant type of his Madonnas from the first to the second Antwerp period, which occurs from 1628 to 1630. The dates of certain pictures are so difficult to establish and have already been altered so often, that it can only be tentatively suggested that Helen Fourment was responsible for the substitution of the broad-faced and bright-eyed Mother in place of the early type, which had been based on Isabella's oval face, with frequently downcast eyes looking at the Child.

The Helen type appears in the well-known 'St. Ildefonso' triptych now in Vienna. This work was commissioned in 1630 by Isabella, for the Church of St. Jacques sur Caudenberg in Brussels, to be placed on the altar of the Chapel of the St. Ildefonso Fraternity. Archduke Albert had been a great protector of this brotherhood during his lifetime, and the Infanta—who still lived in the worship of her husband's memory—evidently wished to commemorate this fact. The Archduke and Archduchess are seen kneeling at the sides, while in the central panel is depicted the miraculous gift of a chasuble by the Blessed Virgin to the Saint. On the outside, Rubens painted a 'Holy Family under an Apple-Tree', in which the later type of Madonna is still more clearly defined.

It also appears in the 'Holy Family with Saints' (or 'Repose in Egypt') now at Madrid, and in the 'Holy Family with St. Francis', at Windsor.[1]

At no period of the master's life has the idea of love been so prominent. It finds perhaps its most vivid expression in the 'Sacrifice to Venus' (Vienna), evidently inspired by Titian's interpretation of the same subject which had previously been copied by Rubens. This picture is not only a glorification of Venus, Goddess of Love, but also of the Goddess of Fruitfulness, and, while the dancing figures on the left (among whom, again, Helen is easily recognisable) emphasise the sensuousness of passion, the crowds of winged Cupids dancing on the ground or flying in garlands through the trees are a fresh manifestation of the master's child-worship, which has been mentioned above as coinciding with his first marriage. The same feature is noticeable in the 'Repose in Egypt', the 'Garden of Love', the 'Holy Family' (Cologne) and in other works of the second Antwerp period.[2]

Another development which occurs at this time is the growing importance given by Rubens to landscape. The master is no longer content to paint his figures himself and entrust the execution of the natural setting to Wildens or some other collaborator. He has by now become interested in the countryside, and is tempted to explore further a branch

[1]The likeness to Helen is also sometimes to be found in certain Christian Saints. It is very striking, for instance, in the 'St. Cecilia' which was painted about 1639-1640.

[2]The children of the second marriage appear in several portraits of Helen, such as the group in the Louvre and the picture in Munich. There is in Windsor a miniature ordered by Rubens from Fruytiers, in which the four elder children appear.

of his art which he had hitherto comparatively neglected. This new feature appears in the 'Park Scene' (Vienna), which is usually included in the series of landscapes of a later period connected with the Castle of Steen, although the purely mediaeval aspect of the building in the 'Park Scene' scarcely justifies such a belief. This work may be associated with the well-known 'Garden of Love' (or 'Conversation à la Mode') in the Prado, in which Helen holds a central position in the group of lovers. Here, as in the 'Sacrifice to Venus', there is an almost even balance between figures and landscape. The glorification of Love remains the main theme, but this time the protagonists are in modern dress, although a number of naked Cupids work mischief among them. In this series, Rubens may be said to foreshadow Watteau as he foreshadows Constable, Turner and the whole development of modern landscape in the Steen series. Up to his last years, he continues to enlarge his horizon and to strike out new avenues in the distant future. But under all these various forms of art—portraiture, mythology and genre—his love for Helen remains intimately associated with his efforts.

Another important group of works, probably painted between 1630 and 1635, brings us back to classical tradition and to history. It includes two pictures connected with the fight between the 'Romans and Sabines', the 'Rape of the Sabines' (National Gallery) and the 'Massacre of the Innocents' (Munich). The inclusion of the latter picture is quite justifiable, since the subject is treated in exactly the same realistic style, the Jewish mothers wearing dresses identical with those of the Sabine ladies, which are of course in the fashion of the seventeenth century, and the classical and Renaissance architecture being the same throughout.

In these, the last of his historical works, the master seems to have tried to recapture the violent spirit which inspired his first great battle scenes, but, although from the point of view of execution and colouring the 'Massacre' and the great National Gallery picture stand unchallenged, the grandiose setting so elaborately prepared for them deprives them of some of their elemental force. They are perhaps the only works of Rubens' later days in which the master has failed to surpass himself.

*　　*　　*

There is one last incident to record in Rubens' political career. In the letter mentioning his retirement, he referred to the fact that he had been unable to give up certain negotiations which could be pursued without hindrance to his work. The Infanta had not despaired of coming to terms with the United Provinces, and she knew that she could find no better negotiator than Rubens. It is known from a letter written by Gerbier, then English representative in Brussels, that the master went on a secret mission to The Hague in December 1631. Eight months later, after the Prince of Orange had achieved important successes and while his army was encamped before Maestricht, Rubens had further meetings with the Dutch representatives at Liége and, later, with the Prince himself, in his camp, without however being more successful.

Since the death of Albert, the Infanta's sovereignty had virtually ceased and, though she still held her Court at Brussels, she was more than ever subjected to the controlling power of Spain and of Spain's agents in the Netherlands, while the Belgian nobility, which had been much favoured by Albert, had lost practically all power. The critical situa-

tion resulting from the progress of the Dutch armies encouraged the Belgian aristocracy and their leader, the Duc
d'Aerschot, to press their claim and advise the Infanta to
summon the States-General, which had not met for over
thirty years. They further requested permission to send delegates to Holland. Isabella, unable to resist this demand, entrusted Rubens with a secret mission to The Hague, to
ascertain the steps taken by the Belgian delegates and to safeguard her own interests. Peter-Paul, who had heard of the
objection made by the Duc d'Aerschot to his mission, wrote
to the latter when he was passing through Antwerp on his
way to The Hague, in January 1633, in the hope of pacifying
him without, however, revealing the Infanta's intentions.
He drew upon himself a haughty reply, which surpassed in
arrogance and rudeness the worst criticisms of Olivarez and
the Spanish grandees:

'It matters little to me upon what ground you stand and
what account you can render of your actions. All I can tell
you is, that I shall be greatly obliged if you will learn from
henceforth how persons of your station should write to men
of mine.'

During the following months, the irate duke pursued Isabella's confidant with his vindictive hatred, declaring, on his
arrival at The Hague, that he had not taken Rubens with
him because 'painters had nothing to do with this business';
making use of suspicious documents in order to denounce
Rubens' interference to the States-General, and finally in-
venting a story according to which the painter had sent the
Prince of Orange some designs for tapestries 'in which the
King of Spain and his subjects were most hideously represented'. Since, however, this last calumny is reported by

Gerbier, it must be added that the latter is not an unprejudiced witness where Aerschot is concerned. Needless to say, the negotiations undertaken by this rash nobleman never reached any conclusion.

If the master had had any lingering ambition to pursue his diplomatic career, the false position in which he was placed during this conflict with Aerschot would have sufficed to quench it. There is no reason to question his sincerity when he writes that he only undertook these last missions at the express request of the Infanta, towards whom he manifested, all his life, the deepest regard and admiration. When she died, on December 1, 1633, his chief link with public affairs was severed.

His patriotism prompted him nevertheless to offer to act as intermediary between the Cardinal Infante Ferdinand, Philip IV's brother, who had succeeded Isabella in the government of the Southern Netherlands, and the Prince of Orange, with whom he had had previous interviews. By his victory over the Protestant forces in Germany, at Nördlingen on September 7, 1634, Ferdinand had restored the military situation. But, in the following year, after concluding an alliance for the conquest and partition of the Southern Netherlands, the French and the Dutch entered Brabant as far as Louvain, which they besieged. Ferdinand, with the help of Piccolomini, at the head of the Imperial troops, was able to expel the invaders from Belgium and to take the offensive in Gelderland and in the Duchy of Cleves.

These successes were followed, as practically every Spanish success had been before, by fresh attempts to negotiate peace, and, through the agency of the Bishop of Ghent, Antoine Triest, who had some connections on the Dutch side, Rubens was asked to go to Holland on the pretext of inspecting some Italian paintings, and to try and sound the Prince of Orange as to his intentions. But, when Peter-Paul asked for his passports, in October 1635, the French ambassador in Holland declared that his visit would be most disagreeable to Louis XIII and could not fail to arouse suspicion. The States-General did not wish to alienate the sympathies of their allies, and Rubens' request was ignored.

In a letter to Peiresc dated March 16, 1636, there is a last allusion to an abortive negotiation which the master was asked to undertake at the beginning of the next year:

'I stayed a few days in Brussels, against my wish, to deal with certain business. Do not think it is for the mission which you suspect. I admit that, at first, I was asked to deal with that affair, but, as I considered that it was not important enough, and as I had some difficulty in obtaining my passport, I deliberately delayed my departure and, since there were many people only too eager to take my place, I safeguarded my domestic peace and, by the grace of God, remained quietly at home. . . .'

The last remark was not inspired by spite or any feeling of grievance, for, if politically the painter did not enjoy the same influence under Ferdinand as under Isabella, both the King and the Infante plied him with commissions and treated him with the greatest consideration.

On April 15, 1636, Ferdinand had appointed him his official painter and conferred upon him the same pension which he had enjoyed in the lifetime of the Infanta. If, therefore, Rubens had grown so fond of his home and so hostile to the artificialities of Court life, it was because experience had taught him the limits of his power.

He had done his best for the pacification of the Netherlands; he had tried, again and again, to instil wisdom and
foresight into the minds of the Spanish statesmen and to
appeal to the good-will and tolerance of the Dutch. In spite
of his wonderful constitution, he was beginning to feel the
strain of his tireless activity and to realise that he had passed
the age when life opened out its infinite perspectives before
him. He never considered himself to be a courtier or a statesman, and he took such pride in his trade that he would not
have exchanged it for the highest honours in the land. He had
decided, three years previously, to give up his diplomatic
work, and, though he could not resist the temptation to use,
from time to time, the influence he possessed, to further the
interests of his country, he felt that the sands were running
low, that his mind was still teeming with projects, that his
eyes had never been so sure nor his hand so quick, and that
certain pictures remained to be painted before he allowed
death to close those eyes or still that hand.

★　★　★

The master's political testament is written on the triumphal arches, 'theatres' and other pictorial and architectural
designs executed by him for the solemn entry of Ferdinand
into Antwerp in April 1635. Forty years earlier, at the beginning of his career, he had collaborated with Otto Vaenius
in the preparations of the municipality for the entry of Albert
and Isabella; and now, towards the end, he was asked to
assume the direction of this new great scheme of street decoration for the celebration of their successor's victories. The
battle of Nördlingen had given the Cardinal Infante an extraordinary prestige at the time, and the worthy citizens decided
to offer him an 'Ommegang' worthy of his military successes.

Money was collected from all sides, and Rubens discussed plans with Rockox and Gevartius.

The brilliance of the ceremonies surpassed anything ever seen in Antwerp. Ferdinand, with a large suite including the flower of the nobility, entered the town on April 16th, by the Gate of St. George, where he was met by the Burgomaster and representatives of the Guilds, while guns boomed and trumpets sounded. He was greeted by a bevy of pretty girls on a triumphal car designed by Rubens, and one of these, who impersonated Antwerp, presented him with a crown of laurels. He then proceeded towards the Town Hall and Cathedral, admiring a series of theatres and passing through a number of gilded and beflagged triumphal arches adorned with sculptures. First came the Theatre of Welcome, then the Portico of the Emperors, with carved figures of the emperors of his dynasty, then another theatre, devoted to the memory of Isabella, whose image appeared among the clouds like a good spirit presiding over the destinies of the country. Further on came another arch, glorifying Ferdinand's own victories, then a theatre representing the Temple of Janus, with open doors which figures symbolising Peace and Wisdom were endeavouring to close, and then, to the flourish of more trumpets, the sound of more music and the booming of more guns, the massive Arch of the Mint, the wildest expression of Rubens' baroque fantasy.

But all was not flattery in the gorgeous reception. The doors of the Temple of Janus were still standing open, and in the Rue Haute the victorious Prince had seen a theatre in which a weeping Belgium was shown, imploring him to deliver her from her bonds, while, in the central panel (still preserved at Stockholm), the god Mercury was seen flying

21. MERCURY LEAVING ANTWERP [1634-1635]
STREET DECORATION FOR THE ENTRY OF THE CARDINAL
INFANTE FERDINAND

Hermitage, Leningrad

Photo, Braun

from the town, Trade and Commerce lying chained to the ground.[1] Rubens could not have explained more clearly the disastrous effects which the closing of the Scheldt had had on the trade of Antwerp and on the prosperity of the country. It was a clear reminder to Ferdinand that his military glory would be of no avail to Belgium, unless he persuaded his haughty brother to come to terms at last with the United Provinces and to exact from them the freedom of her great port.

Most of the pictures designed by the master for this occasion have disappeared, but the sketches preserved in the Hermitage and in Antwerp give us some idea of the elaborate nature of the architectural, sculptural and pictorial decorations, and of the inexhaustible resources of the designer, who succeeded in improvising them in so short a time.

Rubens was not able to be present at the ceremony. Once again, he was stricken down with the gout and unable to leave his house. But Ferdinand did not fail to visit him, to congratulate him on the results he had achieved and to thank him for the care with which he had carried out the great work. Since we have no details of this conversation, it is impossible to say whether any allusion was made to the Temple of Janus or to Belgium's ardent prayer; it is most likely that the subject was avoided, but at least the master had the moral satisfaction of thinking that he had placed under the eyes of the Spanish prince a true picture of his country's fate.

[1] See pl. 21, p. 250.

CHAPTER IX

THE CASTLE OF STEEN

SINCE 1627, Rubens had owned a country house in the Polders, north of Antwerp, but his diplomatic journeys had left him little leisure, and whenever he was not abroad he was obliged to spend most of his time in town attending to his studio. With his second marriage, the nesting instinct, which had prompted him to settle into the house on the Wapper with Isabella and her children, asserted itself once more and, in 1635, he acquired the domain of Steen, near Malines, and began to spend the summer months there, with Helen and her growing family.

The knighthood Rubens had received from Spain allowed him to hold land of feudal tenure, and the Steen, or Stone House, was really a small castle, with farm attached, surrounded by a moat, the grounds including a garden, an orchard and a pond. From the master's paintings, it would seem that some parts of the building, particularly the battlemented tower, were very old, while the stepped gable and turret indicate that other parts had been added, or rebuilt, in the sixteenth century. The mediaeval tower has disappeared, but otherwise Rubens' Steen can still be seen to-day, and, though the surrounding countryside has lost many of its woods, it has preserved the same characteristics which appear in the master's great landscapes. It is fertile and mainly flat, but here and there a slight undulation of the ground, a last ripple from the hills of Brabant, affords a vantage-point from which the widest horizon is discovered.

Although there is no proof of the fact, it is probable that these prolonged holidays in the country were partly due to the master's failing health. As early as 1625, he had suffered from the gout, and this trouble afflicted him again and again, during his sojourn in Madrid and after his return to Antwerp in 1630. The climate of the latter town not being particularly healthy, especially in those days, Rubens' doctor must have urged him to live in the country for some months every year, and, since he had freed himself from the shackles of the Court, nothing prevented him from following this advice.

His letters remain cheerful to the end, and his keen interest in art and antiquities never relaxes, but he had grown somewhat weary of the society of men and must have welcomed this opportunity of spending at least part of his life in the close intimacy of his family circle.

We may imagine him, at this time, as he saw himself in the great portrait now in Vienna: still strong and proud, his powerful hand, with tapering fingers, resting on the hilt of his sword, and a broad-brimmed hat tilted on the side of his head. But sixty years of one of the most strenuous lives have left their mark on that unbent head. The flesh is no longer so firm on the jaw, and the eyelids droop slightly over the smiling eyes. The lord of Steen is still a man of the world, but he is no longer the brilliant figure who had dazzled four Courts of Europe.

The chief reason, however, for those long summer months spent in and around the Steen, during the last five years before Rubens' death, was not merely one of health or personal convenience. A new and unexpected development had occurred in the master's career which is almost unparalleled in the history of art. At the age of fifty-eight, after having, for so many years, devoted the best of his energy to mythological, religious and allegorical decoration, he had suddenly become the greatest landscape-painter of his time. Something happened during the first weeks at the Steen which will, very likely, never be explained. The master—who had almost entirely neglected landscape during the Italian period, who, in so many pictures, had left the treatment of natural scenery to his collaborators, and who had only recently begun to devote some attention to nature—discovered that, far from being subordinate to the figures introduced into it, landscape could be in itself one of the finest expressions of pictorial art.

This discovery had been made seventy years before by Breughel the Elder (father of Jan Breughel), and we know that Rubens appreciated him and owned several of his works. There is no doubt that the great master of the seventeenth century must have been impressed by the striking originality of his predecessor's landscapes, so different from those of Bril, Jan Breughel and even Wildens, which he had been accustomed to admire. Looking at these old pictures, he must have come to realise that it was at least possible to give a fine interpretation of nature while remaining entirely independent of Italian tradition, and that a realistic rendering of the countryside of Flanders and Brabant, without the introduction of any conventional or academic feature, might lead to great results.

It is, however, impossible to conceive that Rubens could have taken Breughel the Elder as a model. The technique and methods of the two artists are too different to allow of such a supposition. Peter Breughel may seem modern to us, owing to the 'primitive' tendencies so marked in present-day art; but Peter-Paul must have looked upon him almost as a mediaeval painter, a direct successor to Memling and Quentin Massys, who, ignorant of the masterpieces of the Italian School, had jealously preserved the ancient traditions of Flemish art. His whole education and trend of thought prevented him from appreciating the minute methods of the last of the 'Primitives'. It is all the more remarkable that he succeeded in expressing almost the same artistic conceptions through a new and original medium.

The process was no doubt the same as that which Rubens followed almost unconsciously when creating his own religious style. Bearing in mind the great pictures which he had had occasion to admire at home and during his travels abroad, he confronted them with the impressions he gathered from his daily life, and from this comparison between artistic memory and direct and personal observation he evolved a new means of expression. If it were possible to dissociate objective reality from the impression it may produce on the artist's eye and mind, we might try to distinguish in Rubens' pictures the elements which belong to the masters he admired, those which derive from the world in which he lived, and those which bear the imprint of his strong individuality. While such a distinction might successfully be made in the case of his portraits and of all his decorative works, it would not be easily achieved with regard to the group of landscapes of the last period, usually known as the Steen series. A few walks in the neighbourhood of Malines and Elewyt would acquaint us even to-day with some features of the country which the master knew so well, and a closer study of his design and colouring might explain why he delighted in building up these large compositions, widening and illuminating his horizon, throwing into relief the trees of the foreground, and gradually leading the eye from strong shadows to the brightest light, while definitely discarding the conventional formula which opposed a dull foreground to a bluish distance. But there would be some difficulty in finding, among the works of the master's predecessors, any landscape from which he might have drawn his inspiration. The spirit may be akin to that of Breughel and the technique to that of Titian; but the mere mention of these two great names shows the gap which separates them and the impossibility of pursuing such a line of investigation. The originality of Rubens has never been questioned, even by his sterner critics, but in none of his works does he stand so entirely alone as in the Steen series. The poetic realism of these pictures can only be compared with the master's conception of feminine beauty, and this is perhaps the reason why the last ten years of his life, filled with the loveliness of Helen and the splendour of Belgian fields, mark the climax of his career.

But there is a certain intimacy in the apotheosis of the Helen type which restricts its influence. To take an extreme example, the nude portrait known as the 'Pelsken', in which Rubens' wife is shown half draped in a fur coat, though unrivalled as a piece of painting, cannot have the same appeal for the world at large as the great 'Castle of Steen' landscape in the National Gallery, which exerted such a powerful influence on Turner, Constable and Crome when it was exhibited at the British Institution in 1815.[1] It would be rash to say that the 'Pelsken' can only be fully appreciated by a Fleming, but realism, when carried so far in the interpretation of the feminine type, strikes a chord the full harmony of which can only be realised with the help of racial sympathy. This difficulty does not arise where natural scenery is concerned, and it is easy to understand why no paintings by Rubens have acquired a wider range of influence throughout Western Europe than his landscapes. Claude, whose reputation dates from the same years, may have been more admired during the seventeenth and eighteenth centuries; but the Steen series remains as the foundation on which rests the whole magnificent fabric of modern landscape-art.

Most of these pictures were painted with no idea of profit, as a kind of holiday relaxation from the intensive work that was still carried on in the studio during the winter months. No doubt the master had no difficulty in selling some of them, and the number of engravings made from them proves that they soon became popular. But the fashion of the period was for historical and allegorical scenes, and, if Rubens' only wish had been to increase his wealth and reputation, he would have given all his attention to the decorative works which were so urgently demanded of him. The fact that no less than seventeen landscapes were found in his studio after his death is also significant. Apart from the 'Castle of Steen' already referred to, and of the 'Autumn Sunset' also in the National Gallery, this series includes the 'Landscape with a Tower' (Berlin), the 'Tournament by the Moat of a Castle' (Louvre), and a number of summer and autumn scenes, mostly bathed in the early morning or late evening light, which may be

[1]See Sir Charles Holmes' book on the *National Gallery*.

found in the Louvre, the Wallace Collection, at Florence, Munich, Brussels, and in several private collections.

There are two very remarkable pictures which must be included in this group: the 'Flemish Kermesse', in the Louvre,[1] and the 'Dance of Italian Peasants', or 'Rondo',[2] in the Prado. These are almost the only works by Rubens, apart from the 'Garden of Love', which may be classified as genre scenes. The contrast between the 'Kermesse' and the 'Rondo' is an excellent example of the master's understanding of popular life and national character. The 'Kermesse' is a wild and humorous orgy, in which eating, dancing and love-making divide the attention of the crowd. Rubens lets himself go in this unique work, treating his subject in the true vein of Breughel the Elder and of Brouwer, his own contemporary, some of whose works figured in his private gallery and through whom a good deal of the Breughel spirit must have come to him. The foreground is full of burlesque and familiar incidents; pots and pans, barrels and rummaging dogs play an important part. In the 'Rondo', on the contrary, the atmosphere from crude and realistic becomes almost classical. The dancers are poised in elegant and harmonious attitudes, and might as well be satyrs and nymphs as peasants. The lines, instead of breaking into a succession of intricate knots, flow through the picture, and unite the group of dancers into one harmonious whole. The natural elegance of the Mediterranean races has often since been remarked upon by critics and travellers, as opposed to the natural clumsiness of the people of the North, but this contrast has never been so well shown as in these two works of Rubens' last period.

[1]See pl. 22, p. 262.   [2]See pl. 23, p. 267.

They have nevertheless one thing in common: the swift and passionate action of the dancers, in a calm and mellow natural setting. Whether Flemish or Italian, these people belong to the soil and are intensely real. From the point of view of the study of Rubens, the value of these two works cannot be overestimated, for they confirm all we know, from the master's life and correspondence, of his knowledge and understanding of the common people. As an historical document, the 'Kermesse' is far more valuable than Teniers' semi-artificial peasant dances; it is as genuine as a Breughel the Elder or as a Brouwer.

There may be no difficulty in explaining how, besides his decorative works, Rubens could create portraits which stand comparison with the greatest achievements of Van Dyck, but only a miracle of genius can account for the fact that, when a passing fancy prompted him to paint a genre scene, he produced a masterpiece comparable and in some ways superior to the greatest Flemish genre paintings.

That Peter-Paul mixed with the people, and more particularly with Flemish workmen, is evident from the close studies from life of the host of sturdy labourers which he introduced into his decorative pictures from the beginning of the first Antwerp period. Already in the 'Erection of the Cross', physical effort is emphasised with a vigour only to be compared to that which fills some of Tintoretto's paintings. But with Rubens we are brought into closer contact with the struggle of mankind. His soldiers and menials raising the Cross might be a group of workmen setting up a wooden crane in an Antwerp street; their racial type is as strongly marked as their individual characteristics. But, though the master knew the labourers of his day and sympathised with them, it was only during the short respite found by him in the last years of his life that he had an opportunity of showing his interest, not only in their struggles but also in their pleasures, not only in their sufferings (as described, for instance, in the 'Horrors of War'), but also in their boisterous merriment. Rubens painted greater pictures than the 'Kermesse', but none which allows us better to realise the breadth of his genius. He alone could rub shoulders with courtiers and peasants alike in this spirit of debonair understanding, and pass serenely from the description of a coarse incident in some corner of a popular dance to the learned interpretation of some antique coin or engraved stone.

* * *

While in Antwerp the master was kept as busy as ever and, during the last five years of his life, the activity of the workshop never relaxed. New names appear among the collaborators, such as those of Erasmus Quellin, van Thulden, Borrekens, and Jan Cossiers, who helped the master to carry out his commissions. Among the latter, allegorical and historical subjects are not so strongly represented as in the earlier periods, with the notable exception of the 'Horrors of War', in the Pitti, commissioned about 1638 by the Grand-Duke of Tuscany. But there is an important group of sacred works, mainly dealing with the martyrdom of saints, such as the 'Martyrdom of St. Liévin' (Brussels), painted about 1635 for the Jesuit Church of Ghent, that of 'St. Thomas' (Prague), that of 'St. Andrew' (Madrid), painted before 1639 for the St. Andrew's Hospital in that city, and the 'Crucifixion of St. Peter' (Cologne), ordered in 1637 for the Jesuit Church of that town and which had not been delivered at the time of the master's death.

In these great scenes, as also in the 'Way of the Cross'

(Brussels), painted for the Abbey of Afflinghem in 1637 or thereabouts, Rubens seems to return to his earlier style of religious painting, as expressed in the 'Erection of the Cross.' He dwells more than ever on the epic character of the saints' death, and contrasts their patient suffering with the brutal force of their tormentors. We also find in them some of the leading themes mentioned in previous chapters, such as, for instance, the rearing white horse in the 'St. Liévin'. To the end of his life, Rubens' main conception of religious decoration remained essentially the same.

The greater proportion of the pictures produced in the workshop during the last period deal with mythological subjects. The apotheosis of love and womanhood had already prompted Rubens to produce a series of mythological scenes, such as the 'Sacrifice to Venus' (Vienna), the 'Judgment of Paris' (National Gallery), and the 'Bath of Diana' (Munich), which gave him the opportunity of exalting Helen's beauty. But the chief reason for the creation of so large a number of pagan pictures at this time was an important commission given to the painter by Philip IV. The Spanish King seems to have had a premonition that the master's career would soon come to an end. As early as 1628, during Rubens' stay at Madrid, he had given him several orders, and it is known that, from 1630 to 1636, twenty-five pictures left the studio for Madrid. In the latter year, however, the commissions became far more important and pressing.

Philip wished the master to decorate two of his country residences, the Torre de la Parada and Buen Retiro, and sent a series of messages to the Cardinal Infante, asking him to take the matter in hand. The latter did his best, but Rubens would not allow his work to be spoiled in order to satisfy the King's impatience. In one of his letters, the Infante apologises to Philip, explaining that, as the pictures were not yet dry, the artist would not consent to part with them: 'I tried to argue with him as much as possible, but, as he knows more than I do, I had to give in.' There was another argument about the nudity of the three goddesses in the 'Judgment of Paris' (Prado), 'but he says that it is necessary, because it brings out the colours', and Ferdinand adds the following remark, which shows that Rubens' contemporaries were aware of the real motive for his pagan outburst: 'The Venus, in the centre of the group, is an excellent portrait of his wife, who is without doubt the prettiest woman here.' The Cardinal Infante's Spanish origin did not, apparently, prevent him from appreciating Helen's type, indeed he had the reputation of being a connoisseur in such matters.

In March 1638, no less than fifty-six pictures illustrating Ovid's *Metamorphoses* were sent to Madrid. As in the case of the Medici Gallery, and the Whitehall decorations, Rubens himself must have executed all the sketches, a number of which are still preserved at Brussels. It is usually agreed that the master took a prominent share in a large proportion of the thirty-one pictures remaining in Spain (in the Prado). During the following months, fifty-six more pictures were sent from Antwerp to Spain, but most of these, which represented hunting scenes, were painted outside the studio, although under Rubens' supervision. Snyders had a large share in this work, and, in the Infante's letters to Philip, besides constant praise and admiration of the master's feverish activity, there are many complaints of the slowness of Snyders and other collaborators.

22. THE KERMESSE [1635-1638]

Louvre, Paris. *Photo, l'Epi*

In this case, as in that of all Rubens' great decorative works
—apart from the Whitehall ceiling which has suffered so
much from damp and neglect—it is impossible now to see
the pictures in the buildings for which they were painted.
The Jesuit Church in Antwerp was destroyed by fire; the
Medici series was removed from the Luxembourg to the
Louvre where, in spite of the great room reserved to them,
the paintings are no longer in perfect proportion to their
surroundings; while all that remains of the great decorative
scheme for the Torre de la Parada is the series of pictures in
the Prado and the sketches at Brussels. It is impossible to
estimate such losses, for Rubens' genius cannot be judged
from the Medici Gallery alone. Had the Jesuit Church and
the Torre been preserved to us, we might have been able to
form some idea of the master's style at its very best, both in
religious and in mythological painting. The great Jesuit
Church and the Spanish King's country residence would have
been visited by all who wished to appreciate the spirit of the
Counter-Reformation and the later Renaissance, and to
understand how sincere faith and deep devotion could be
combined with a passion for classical beauty and an ardent
curiosity for antiquarian lore. This can only be realised frag-
mentarily to-day, by the patient study of the master's sketches
and correspondence. If it could still be grasped as a whole,
Rubens' greatness would now be as incontestable as that of
Michaelangelo's or Raphael's, after a visit to the Stanze and
the Sistine Chapel.

The ease and rapidity with which the master produced the
pictures destined for the Torre de la Parada is the more remarkable that the work was interrupted again and again by illness.
All through the year 1638, the Infante's letters contain refer-

ence to Rubens' gout, which first 'troubles him' and then 'prevents him from working'. Later, we learn that he has been 'very ill' and even, on December 11th, that he 'has received the last Sacraments'. The next year, however, he recovers, but early in 1640 the warning note re-appears. In April we learn that 'Rubens has been paralysed in the hands for more than a month, without much hope that he will ever again hold his brush'. There was an improvement, however, in May, but at the end of that month we hear from Gerbier, who was still in Brussels, that two physicians had left that town for Antwerp, no doubt at Ferdinand's orders. They arrived too late. Peter-Paul died on the 30th.

★ ★ ★

Very little is known of the master's intimate life at the Steen. He evidently intended to spend his 'holidays' in retirement, and had chosen the house because it stood away from the main road. His desire for peace and privacy increased with his years; he wished to live in comfort, surrounded by his family, devoting all his time to his correspondence and the painting of his landscapes, far from Court and the hurried work of the studio.

Albert, his eldest son, who seems to have been his favourite, had left him in 1634 to travel in Italy. He was in Venice in December of that year and must have returned home some twelve months later. Since as early as 1630 the young man had been appointed secretary to the Privy Council (although he was not supposed to act in this capacity until his father's death or resignation), it may be presumed that he helped the master to fulfil the duties of this post and relieved him of part of his public work. He himself was keenly interested in antiquities, having, at the age of twenty, written a commentary on a collection of Roman coins belonging to the Duc d'Aerschot; and he also took an interest in Rubens' own collections. We know, for instance, that in March 1640 he purchased a Book of Hours and another prayer-book for his father from Moretus' library. This may have been a gift intended to comfort the master during his illness. Rubens' will leaves no doubt as to the warm friendship which existed between father and son.

From the same document we gather that the whole family was closely united. In a codicil added in 1639 to the joint will signed by Peter-Paul and Helen in 1631, it was stipulated that the children of both marriages should have equal shares in the succession. This was confirmed in the last testament made three days before Rubens' death, which left Helen half his property and the share of one child, and divided the remainder equally among his six children. The books, however, were left to Albert and the stones and coins to Albert and Nicholas.

On August 17, 1638, the master wrote from the Steen to his pupil, Lucas Faydherbe, later a well-known sculptor, asking him to bring or send from Antwerp a certain picture of which he was in need. He also enquired about some bottles of Ay wine (champagne) which would no doubt have been welcome at the Steen, since the 'supply' they had brought with them was already exhausted. To this letter was added the following postscript, in which the cares of the artist, the householder and the epicure are quaintly associated:

'Be very careful before leaving to see that everything is well locked up and that no original, either picture or sketch, remains in the studio upstairs. Will you also remind Guillaume, the gardener, that he must send us in good time some Rosile pears and figs, when there are any, or any other dainty from our garden. Come here as early as you can, so that the house may be closed, for as long as you are there you cannot prevent others from getting in. I trust that you have taken care of the gold chain according to my instructions, so that, God willing, we may find it on our return.'

This gold chain was a gift which Charles I had sent in token of satisfaction to Rubens when finally settling accounts for the Whitehall decorations. The English King might have given another commission to the master had death not interfered, for he was at this time thinking of decorating Queen Henrietta Maria's room with groups of cherubs, and Gerbier in his letters urged that Rubens should be entrusted with this work.

The master's very last letter, written from Antwerp on May 9th, is also directed to Faydherbe, and most fittingly reminds us of the gentle humour and kindness with which he treated his subordinates. On the 1st of May, Faydherbe had married Marie Smeyers:

'I heard with great pleasure that, on the first of this month, you planted the may in your beloved's garden. I hope that it will be welcome there and that in good time it will give you fruit. My wife, my two sons and myself heartily wish you and your bride all manner of happiness and a perfect and lasting contentment in the state of marriage. Do not hurry in making the little ivory child,[1] for you have just now on hand some other child-making, which is far more important. In any case your visit will always be most agreeable to us.

'I think that my wife will shortly go to Malines on her

---

[1] Faydherbe was engaged, at the time, in carving the ivory figure of a child for the lid of a drinking-cup, which is now in the Vienna museum.

23. THE RONDO [1636-1640]

way to Steen. She will then have the pleasure of expressing her good wishes by word of mouth. Meanwhile, will you present my cordial greetings to your father-in-law and mother-in-law. Your good behaviour will, I hope, increase from day to day the joy they feel in this alliance. I address the same greetings to your father and mother. The latter must laugh in her sleeve to see your Italian voyage miss fire, and to think that, instead of losing her beloved son, she has gained a daughter who will soon, with God's help, make a grandmother of her.'

These last letters, in which the great artist allows his mind to rest, the courtier lays down his sword, and the Humanist doffs his gown, are almost as valuable in the correspondence as is the 'Kermesse' in the collected works. We perceive at last the homeliness and humour which must have pervaded Rubens' talk from the first, but which can scarcely be detected earlier in his writings. It comes to us like a ripple of brave and hearty laughter—all the more bright and courageous that death was so near—with the scent of ripe pears and figs and the merry glitter of the Ay wine.

* * *

Many praises were bestowed on Rubens by his contemporaries. Peiresc, Dupuy and Gevartius—the latter in an eloquent epitaph—extol in turn his genius, his erudition and his perfect courtesy. Without agreeing with the harsh view of the poet van Fornenbergh, who wrote an ode on the occasion of the master's death in which he denounces such attempts to 'paint the Sun with charcoal', it must be admitted that most of these eulogies are not sufficiently comprehensive.

Rubens' personality should be measured by breadth rather than by height. If the word could be so used, he would not only be one of the 'broadest' artists of the Renaissance, equally successful in every branch and subject of his art, but the 'broadest' man that ever lived. Although in certain features he stands unsurpassed as a painter, some masters have outdistanced him in others, and no doubt there were, even during his lifetime, finer scholars, greater statesmen and possibly men more entirely devoted to their families. But, in some way, he managed to combine the life of the most productive artist of the seventeenth century with that of a scholar and collector who carried on an active correspondence with the finest intellects of his time; of a diplomat, who pursued, successfully and in the most difficult circumstances, delicate negotiations with the three principal Courts of Europe; and of a husband and father who spread contentment and happiness among his two families and contrived to live two great love stories, without damaging his faith or his serene philosophy.

As an artist, Rubens was not only interested in painting but in sculpture and architecture; his designs also exerted a considerable influence on contemporary methods of engraving. He further took a particular delight in book decoration, and his association with the firm of Plantin is as interesting to the bibliophile as to the art lover. He made himself responsible for a large number of frontispieces and illustrations in the books of his brother Philip, the works of Justus Lipsius and others.

As regards size, his art ranges from a small page to the walls and ceilings of the largest churches and palaces. As regards subject, one is tempted to quote Polonius' outburst: 'Tragedy, comedy, history, pastoral, pastoral-comical, historical-pastoral, tragical-historical, tragical-comical-historical-pastoral, scene undividable or poem unlimited; Seneca cannot be too heavy nor Plautus too light.' Seneca, indeed, appears on more than one occasion in Rubens' work and, if Plautus is absent, the fat drunken Silenus of the bacchanals makes a more than adequate substitute. There is tragedy in Christ's Passion, the martyrdom of the saints and the glorious defeat of heroes; there is comedy in the shouts and cymbal-clash of bacchanals and wild popular dances; there is history from Decius Mus to Henry IV and from Judith to Constantine; there is pastoral too, and we might add mythological and allegorical, and mythological-allegorical, and allegorical-historical, in the Medici series, 'Peace and War', and a hundred compositions in which, despite their titles, the subject is open to various interpretations; there is, of course, 'scene undividable' in every isolated picture, and 'poem unlimited' in every series.

The whole rich stream of the Renaissance flows through Rubens' art, as the Scheldt flows through Flanders' plains; and, while Satyrs pursue Nymphs along both banks, under the trees and in the light of the great landscapes, it bears towards the sea a fleet of barges full of praying Virgins, bleeding Martyrs and preaching Saints. And the Satyrs look like the peasants he met in his walks, and the Goddesses like the women he loved or admired, and the Saints and Wise Men like the friends with whom he exchanged learned remarks on antiquarian lore.

His tastes were as catholic as his art. Not only was he ready to admire and even to imitate a number of fellow-artists far inferior to himself, but he wished to possess in his own collection pictures which had very little in common. Besides the great masters of Italy, such as Titian, Tintoretto, and Veronese, Flemish genre painters like Breughel and Brouwer were represented. Though he confessed that he was 'mad on antiquities', he expresses the wish in a letter to Francis Junius, author of *De Pictura Veterum*, that a similar treatise should be written on the Italian painters of the Renaissance, who left 'examples and models that can still be seen by all to-day'. In the same way, his devotion to the classics does not exclude a strong taste for Italian poetry, especially that of Tasso and Ariosto, and a keen interest in French literature. His discrimination is shown in a letter to Dupuy, written in April 1628, in which he questions the value of some severe criticism which had been launched against Balzac, the famous seventeenth-century letter writer:

'It seems to me [he writes] that there is sometimes a great deal of wit in his pleasantries and of irony in his invectives. His thoughts have a pleasant turn and his moral discourses are suitably grave, but all this is spoilt by the bad seasoning of his self-sufficiency (*philantea*).'

The moment we understand the master's artistic method and the way in which he introduces the leaven of realism into the classic tradition he studied in Italy, there can no longer be any question as to the sincerity of his religion. What we know of his private life, his habits and his tastes, entirely confirms this belief. His only fault, if it can be called a fault, was that he belonged to his time, and his time no longer sympathised with mediaeval mysticism and contemplation. In those perturbed days, religion had become a fight and could only be understood when it was expressed in concrete and human values. Although convinced of the moral superiority of Christianity over paganism, Rubens generally preferred classical grace and elegance to Gothic aspirations. His main purpose in his religious pictures, as far as we can penetrate a subject on which he did not seem to care to express himself in words, was to place the resources of the Renaissance and classical tradition at the service of the Church, *ad majorem Dei gloriam*.

But the breadth of Rubens' character is not perhaps its most remarkable feature. Any man so gifted, able to express himself through such widely different mediums, so sensitive to every attraction of exterior life, possessing such an enquiring mind and such an insatiable curiosity regarding the intrigues of politics and the most recent discoveries of science, must have experienced the greatest difficulty in bringing these various thoughts and instincts under control. The Puritan who cuts himself adrift from the world, or the Epicure who renounces all religious aspirations, may conform their conduct to their principles with greater ease, but the Christian Humanist who embraces life passionately and attempts to glorify God and His creation at one and the same time, has a more difficult path to tread. This appears evident when we read the story of the troubled careers of many artists of the sixteenth century, who either became the prey of their passions, or, like Michaelangelo, acquired an embittered and misanthropic attitude of mind.

The secret springs of a man's virtue are destined to remain for ever hidden. Rubens was certainly well equipped for life by his mother's example and the care she took to strengthen his energy, remembering, as she did only too well, the pitiable story of the boy's father, which she so successfully managed to conceal. Another influence which made itself felt during the critical days of Rubens' Italian period, was that of Justus Lipsius, the master of his brother Philip. Lipsius was an enthusiastic admirer of the Stoics; he had edited and commented the works of Tacitus and Seneca; his motto was *Moribus antiquis*, and apparently to him the only ancients worthy of note were the heroes renowned for their honour and honesty. With a somewhat bombastic pride, he confesses, in a letter to Philip Rubens, that he 'bears in his soul the souls of the Catos, the Brutuses and the Senecas', and that he would rather fall asleep in death than in dishonour.

Gevartius, another pupil of Lipsius, devoted his life to the study of Marcus Aurelius, and Rubens felt such confidence in the sincerity of this enthusiasm that he made use of it to comfort his friend for the recent loss of his wife:

'If some comfort is to be sought in philosophy, you possess in yourself an abundant source of it. I refer you to the rich treasure of your Antoninus [Marcus Aurelius] . . . I shall only add this poor kind of consolation, by saying that we live in a time when life is only possible if we discard whatever afflicts us, as does the navigator when, overtaken by a tempest, he prepares himself to swim.'

The best description of Rubens' personality is perhaps the one framed in the words he himself applied to Peiresc: 'a well-balanced soul, tempered in true philosophy'; but the wonder is that a soul of such breadth should be so well-balanced and perfectly tempered. The private man, the statesman, the artist and the scholar appear to have been knit together in him by the unbreakable bond of Christian morality and pagan honour, and this bond, instead of narrowing his outlook, widened and strengthened it.

It is as if the man had felt that discipline increased his powers, as it insured his physical and spiritual health. The same overflowing temperament, which might have proved the undoing of a man of softer fibre, compelled Peter-Paul to place himself under stern restraint, so that, even if at some moment his sense of duty or honour had weakened, his very passion for life would have prompted him to discipline his brilliant faculties, like a good general marshalling his forces on the eve of battle.

Associated with this well-ordered strength, there was another quality in Rubens which is seldom granted to the greatest genius and which, though of a humbler kind, was no less valuable to him. He was essentially practical in the ordinary business of life, and hated wasting time on any enterprise which was not likely to be useful. We have seen too many examples of his disinterestedness to suspect for one instant that such usefulness must necessarily be of a pecuniary nature.

In the letter to Peiresc (dated December 18, 1634) in which he gives an account of his public and private life during the last four years; enlarges upon the merits of an antique silver spoon which was so easy to handle that it could be used by his wife during her confinement; and describes in detail some delicate scales he had seen during his sojourn in Spain—Peter-Paul refers in a postscript to an action he has brought in Paris against an engraver who had infringed upon his copyright by reproducing prints from his works. The man had been condemned in the first instance, but had appealed against the court's decision, and Rubens asks his friend to use his influence to see justice done. He refers to this matter again six months later, suggesting that, if a satisfactory solution were not soon obtained, it would be better to come to some arrangements with the adverse party:

'I am by nature and inclination a man of peace, and the

sworn enemy of disputes, lawsuits and all quarrels, whether public or private. . . . I hate like the pest all chicanery, and all kinds of dissension: I hold that the first wish of every honest man should be to enjoy tranquillity of spirit at home and abroad, to render service when he may, and to do wrong to none. I regret that all kings and princes are not of that opinion.'

Writing again on the 16th of March, 1636, he does not hide his displeasure at the decision taken, which, though it safeguarded his copyright, inflicted no penalty on his opponent. He concludes: 'But let us leave these trifles, which do not deserve such long and tedious discussions', and turns to a commentary on a print from a classical landscape, which Peiresc had sent him for inspection.

He also alludes to delays in the payment of the Whitehall pictures, which had been brought to England in the previous year by one of his pupils; and it appears from the following remarks that the illness which had prevented him from going himself to London on that occasion was of a somewhat diplomatic nature:

'As I have a horror of Court life, I have entrusted to a third party the task of bringing my work to England. It is now in its place, and, according to my friends, His Majesty has declared himself to be entirely satisfied. Nevertheless, I have not yet been paid for it, which might surprise me were I new to public affairs; but long experience having taught me how slow princes usually are in settling business matters, and how much easier it is for them to do evil than good, it has not yet occurred to me that there is any intention of not giving me satisfaction. For the friends I have in that Court fill me with great hopes and go on assuring me that the King will treat me in a manner worthy of him and of myself.[1] I confess, nevertheless, that, according to the well-known proverb, *chi vuol vada, chi non vuol mandi*, I should have done better to negotiate this matter myself. I only mention this to prove to you how much I wish to keep my peace of mind, and how resolved I am to avoid all trouble and intrigue, as far as lies with me.'

If the master was able to 'keep his peace of mind' as far as his private affairs and interests were concerned, he was sincerely distressed by the turn political events were taking in Western Europe. His urgent warnings to Olivarez were soon to be confirmed by the close alliance concluded between France and the United Provinces, and of which the partition of Belgium was the principal condition. After the first successes of the French on the Meuse, the Infante was, however, able to restore the situation. An attack led upon Antwerp by the Prince of Orange was checked in time and, in spite of the defeat inflicted on the Spanish fleet, no decision was obtained by either side up to the time of the master's death. He witnessed, nevertheless, the failure of the policy which he had so actively pursued as confidential agent to the Infanta, and which was the only one that could have saved his country from the deepest humiliation and economic ruin. Thanks to the shortsightedness and dilatoriness of Olivarez, Richelieu's plans had matured, and Belgium was now threatened on both sides by the French and the Dutch.

Rubens' letters to Peiresc contain a running commentary on these events, together with some sad remarks on the evils brought upon their people by ambitious and foolish sover-

[1]As seen above, Peter-Paul's optimism was entirely justified.

eigns. Louis XIII had declared war against the Cardinal-
Infante, on May 19, 1635. Writing on May 31st, the master
deplores the 'break between the two crowns, which has now
reached its climax'. Using almost the same words he was to
use a few months later about the Paris lawsuit referred to
above, he adds: 'It grieves me much, because I am by nature
and inclination a peace-loving man and a sworn enemy to
all disputes, lawsuits and all quarrels, either public or private.'
These lines were written after the French victories which had
brought Belgium within sight of ruin. When, on August
16th, the painter tells his friend of his own party's successes
and of the complete defeat of the French forces, decimated by
desertion and sickness, his peace-loving disposition remains
unaltered:

'Be assured that I speak to you without the least passion,
and that I only tell you the truth. I hope that His Holiness
and the King of England, but above all Providence, will in-
tervene to quench the conflagration, which is already far
advanced and might spread to the whole of Europe. But let
us leave public affairs to those whose concern they are; and,
meanwhile, let us seek some comfort in the study of lighter
things. . . .'

And the master proceeds to examine the contents of a casket
which Peiresc had sent him, and which contains among other
things a glass vase adorned with a figure wearing the Trojan
helmet, 'which might be Paris who, in a lover's attitude, remains pensive, one finger at his lips, and turning over in his
mind some secret enterprise'.

★　★　★

All through his life, Peter-Paul had succeeded in practising
the philosophy he preaches to Gevartius, when advising him

to 'discard whatever afflicts him as does the navigator when, overtaken by a tempest, he prepares himself to swim'. This image illustrates perfectly the attitude of mind with which he faced the blows of fate. He is supposed to have been an exceptionally lucky man, but it is enough to remember the difficulties which hampered his artistic projects, the attacks to which he was exposed during his public career, the premature loss of his brother, his first child and his first wife, and the death of the Infanta, bringing with it an eclipse during which he was obliged to be a powerless witness of the ruin of all his political plans—to realise that such occurrences might have given a normal man some grounds for despondency and that they might have thrown a romantic nature into a bottomless pit of melancholy.

Thanks to his stoical Christianity, Peter-Paul was able to face these events not only with courage and steadfastness but with a curious sense of generous economy. He never wasted his energy in lamenting the irremediable or in attempting to achieve the impossible. This exceptional vigour, both physical and spiritual, which could apply itself to almost any human pursuit, always remained under perfect control and was only used when some concrete result might be expected. Rubens excelled in almost all the arts, but he never practised any art more successfully than the art of living, and his life is perhaps a more perfect masterpiece than any of his pictures. He wished to be happy and, like all great minds, soon realised that his own happiness could only be achieved by trying to extend it to others. But he never indulged in any sentimental self-sacrifice, always keeping a perfect balance between his own desires and the general interests of mankind. Although he was fully conscious of his value, he was so in-

dulgent to others and so ready to admire men of far less distinction than himself, that his self-satisfaction becomes sheer
modesty. He was wrapped up in his artistic pursuits, but
though from time to time the joy he finds in his own work
leads him to praise it, such praise is always short and takes a
very humble place beside his expressions of admiration for
classic sculptures, the masters of the Italian Renaissance and
even the works of some of his contemporaries.

He took great pride in his trade, but when honours came
to him, or when they became necessary for the successful
transaction of his diplomatic negotiations, he accepted them
simply, without vanity or subservience. He took the world
very much as he found it, and had little sympathy for religious or social reformers. This was no doubt partly due to his
practical nature, foreign to ideology, and to his strong tradi-
tionalist education. But though a courtier he was no flatterer,
and, when the fate of his country was at stake, he never hesitated to speak his mind or even to overstep his instructions
without thought of the personal risks he was running. He was
too clear-sighted not to see the abuses and corruption of the
world in which he lived, but, as an artist and an individualist,
he was bound to attach more importance to the personality
of the statesmen than to the constitutional organisation of the
State. He knew that he could make a fine picture of almost
any subject with which he was commissioned to deal, and,
rightly or wrongly, he felt that the happiness of the people
depended more on the quality of their ruler than on that of
the system by which they were ruled.

When he was led by circumstances to try his own hand at
politics, he applied to his diplomatic work the same methods
as those he had so successfully applied to his decorative paint-

ing. He was, first and foremost, a realist, and was more concerned with the difficulties immediately ahead of him than with the intrigues and subtleties so much in favour at the Court of Madrid. But, while setting his hand to the plough in a most business-like way, he lacked neither vision nor imagination, and never started on his course without weighing the advantages or disadvantages that might follow his action.

In his business dealings, he had a very keen sense of what was due to him, refused to haggle over bargains and kept his patrons—even the most powerful of them—to their contracts. But these business methods did not prevent him from showing the greatest generosity to the Church and his fellow-artists and from giving away a picture when occasion arose rather than sell it at an inadequate price. In his relations with his fellow-painters in the workshop, he preserved a keen sense of responsibility. Whenever he had to refuse a commission, he endeavoured to hand it on to some other painter, taking into account the wishes of his client and the special gifts of the artist.

He showed the same foresight with regard to his wife and children, providing for every one of them as the most prudent merchant in Antwerp might have done. To our modern notions, such prudence may appear somewhat incongruous in a temperamental artist who had filled the greatest galleries and churches of his time with his imaginative designs; but it was merely the outcome of the master's steady conception of life, which prevented him from sacrificing his private to his public interests, or his family to his artistic ambition. Here again, Rubens affords an almost unique example of a great artist who is at the same time a good

son, a devoted brother, a loving husband and father, a generous master and a faithful friend. That quality of 'breadth'
which has already been insisted upon with regard to his taste
in art and literature is also revealed in his personal relations
with all those with whom he came into contact. He succeeded in being 'all things to all men' in a remarkable manner,
and the multiplicity of his gifts did not in the least diminish
their individual value.

Peter-Paul belonged essentially to this world, and never
affected to despise its pleasures. His whole artistic work is a
pæan of praise to life, a Te Deum sung by a thousand voices
under the gilded roofs of baroque churches. Every myth,
every sacred story had its place in a great pageant, in which
all classes of seventeenth-century European society were represented. There were great church ceremonies, court receptions, and the wild 'kermesses' of the peasants. There were
angels and cupids, dæmons and satyrs, and all the gods of
Olympus were dragged in the train of Christ. Such art is so
entirely different from that of a Fra Angelico that any comparison between them would be fruitless. They are as wide
apart as Antwerp and Florence, and as the abundant life of
Flanders and the mystic asceticism of Italy.

Rubens was neither monk nor mystic. He has been called a
Cavalier, but from all we know of him he seems far more
like the noblest representative of the bourgeoisie of his time,
at once imaginative and practical, shrewd and generous. He
does not show us how far it is possible for a man to rise by
becoming entirely absorbed in the vision of God, or by
following Christ's example literally in an attempt to attain
heavenly perfection on earth, but he shows us—and the
lesson is no less needful—how far it is possible to bring such

a vision into direct contact with the realities of this world, to
ennoble our passions and to purify our ambitions, so as to
become at least able to deal with the problems which confront us, in a manner worthy of our religious ideals.

If Rubens was no saint, he was certainly one of the best
men who ever lived, and for that very reason one hesitates to
call him a hero, in spite of the nobility of his mind and his
voracious appetite for great deeds. His strength was tempered with too much benevolence and humour to allow of
his indulging in heroics. One of his most lovable traits, which
is revealed again and again in his correspondence, is the way
in which he switches abruptly from serious political or philo-
sophical considerations to some of those 'trifles' of antiquarian lore which were to him of such absorbing interest.
Heroes are wonderful beings in mythology, but they are apt
to do a great deal of mischief when they appear on the historical horizon. They take themselves far too seriously, and
have such faith in their destiny that they refuse to listen to the
warnings of a wise Providence. Among all his successes and
triumphs, Peter-Paul never lost his admirable sense of proportion, which was one of his most precious gifts. He
realised, both in his art and in his politics, exactly how far he
could go, and this is perhaps why he went so far.

His career is the most magnificent challenge to death ever
delivered by any man leading the normal life of a father and
a citizen. When Helen stood at his death-bed, she carried in
her womb his eighth child, the only one he never saw and
never painted, but for whom he had provided in his will;
and above the tomb erected to him in the Church of St.
Jacques stands one of his latest pictures, which he had destined for this particular place, and in which he appears in the

guise of an aged but still vigorous St. George. Though the idea of death seems never to have perturbed his serenity, he perceived in good time that his end was near and made the necessary provisions.

What, with his remarkable modesty, he may not have fore-seen, was the extraordinary and lasting influence which his paintings were to exercise in the future. He left behind him a score of pupils and collaborators, who continued his work and established the reputation of the seventeenth century Flemish school of art. He also left hundreds of pictures which were already scattered all over Europe and which are to be found to-day in every notable art collection. All these children of his are perpetuating his memory, stirring up the enthusi-asm of students, exercising the patience and ingenuity of art critics, cheering the whole world with their colour and movement. Those who live with them will not only better appreciate painting, they will also learn to appreciate life in a wiser and healthier spirit, to drink the cup, whether it be filled with wine, love, art or learning, without false fears or scruples, and, once refreshed, to fill it again and hand it round the table; to do the work they are called to do, without diffi-dence or vanity, and to be satisfied with their reward, even when it does not appear in proportion to the effort made; to dismiss all suspicions and bitterness when faced with obstacles or injustice, and, without further loss of time or energy, to turn their minds to a new field of action; to remain alert and adaptable to the end, always ready to correct their mistakes and to improve upon their finest achievements.

A fortnight after Rubens' death, the Abbé de Saint-Ger-main wrote to Balthasar Moretus: 'He has left us to seek the

24. THE RAINBOW [ABOUT 1636-1640]

Wallace Collection, London

originals of some of the fine paintings he made for us.' There
is a certain wisdom in the thought that men are building up
their future life by the efforts they make in this one, and that
the best and worst of their worldly achievements, in every
branch of human activity, may foreshadow the surroundings
in which they will move after death. If it be so, and if Rubens'
illustrations of his happy human comedy forebode the divine
comedy of his future life, the master has found his reward, and
may still be wandering to-day among such pictures as his
great 'Rainbow Landscape',[1] and hearing the man who leads
the hay-waggon chaffing the girls on the road, and the ducks
quacking in the neighbouring pond, and the cow mooing
in the distance. He sees the rubicund yokel, fork in hand,
walking between the woman in red and the woman in blue,
and he watches the sunlight strike the summit and base of
the great trees on the right, darkened by the shadows of
threatening clouds; and beyond the cornfield on the left he
sees the peasants hastily building up the rick, all aglow with
the blond light of summer. And, as he walks along the deeply
rutted old country road, his sight follows the lines of undulat-
ing fields as far as the horizon, where earth touches heaven.
And he feels that this must be Flanders, and looks very much
like a stretch of land through which he used to wander when
he lived in the Steen. Still, there is a difference. The voices of
men and beasts are not the same, the light on the trees is more
silvery, and that on the rick is of a deeper gold; and above all
the Rainbow, the symbol of peace and good-will, shines
with no earthly radiance. And so Rubens' spirit, walking
under this fantastic triumphal arch, passes into his own landscape.

[1]See pl. 24, p. 282.

LIST OF BOOKS CONSULTED

Literatuur over Rubens. De Gulden Passer, Antwerpen, 1927. (Nr. 3.)

Correspondance de Rubens (Codex Diplomaticus Rubenianus), edited by Charles Ruelens and Max Rooses. 6 vols. De Backer, Antwerp, 1887-1909.

L'Œuvre de Rubens, by Max Rooses.

Rubens, by Max Rooses. 2 vols. Transl. Harold Child. Duckworth & Co., 1904.

Rubens Bulletyn. Antwerp, 1882-1910.

Rubens, his Life, his Work and his Time. Transl. from the French of E. Michel, 1899.

Rubens, by Edward Dillon. Methuen & Co., 1909.

Erinnerungen aus Rubens, by J. Burckhardt, 1918.

P. P. Rubens. Vierte, neubearbeitete Auflage (*Klassiker der Kunst,* V). Deutsche Verlags-Anstalt, Stuttgart.

Jahrbuch der Kunst. Sammlungen des Kaiserhauses. A series of articles by Von Glueck, Haberditzl, Oldenbourg and others, in vols. 27, 30, 33, 34 and 35.

P. P. Rubens, by R. Oldenbourg, 1922.

Rubens, by Louis Hourticq. Librairie d'Art ancien et moderne, Paris, 1924.

The National Gallery, by Sir Charles Holmes. G. Bell & Sons, 1925.

The Picture Gallery of Charles I, by Sir Claude Phillips. 1896.

Journey to Flanders, by Sir Joshua Reynolds (in *Works*, ed. by H. W. Beechey. 2 vols. 1852).

Les Maîtres d'autrefois, by Eug. Fromentin.

Sept Etudes publiées à l'occasion du 4ᵉ centenaire de Christophe Plantin, by M. Sabbe. 1920.

Rubens en zyne Eeuw, by F. Prims, M. Sabbe, V. de Meyere, A. J. J. Delen and Paul Lambotte. L. J. Kryn, Brussels, 1927.

Rubens, Policy and Paint, 1913.

Sir Peter Paul Rubens, by Anthony Bertram. Peter Davies, Ltd., London, 1928.

Histoire de Belgique, by Henri Pirenne. Vol. IV. Brussels, 1919.

Histoire politique et diplomatique de P. P. Rubens, by M. Gachard. Brussels, 1877.

Court and Times of Charles I.

The Court of Philip IV, by Martin Hume. Eveleigh Nash, London, 1907.

La Compagnie de Jésus en Belgique, by A. Poncelet, 1907.

L'Art Religieux à la fin du Moyen-Age, by E. Mâle. Paris, 1908.

The Great Infanta, by L. Klingenstein. London, 1910.

L'Auberge des Princes en Exil: Anecdotes de la Cour de Bruxelles au XVIIIᵉ siècle, by E. Gossart. Brussels, 1905.

INDEX

INDEX

PRINTED IN GREAT BRITAIN BY ROBERT MACLEHOSE AND CO. LTD.
THE UNIVERSITY PRESS, GLASGOW